SOUND IT OUT!

SOUND IT OUT!
PHONICS IN A COMPREHENSIVE READING PROGRAM

JOHN F. SAVAGE
PROFESSOR EMERITUS
BOSTON COLLEGE
LYNCH SCHOOL OF EDUCATION

Boston   Burr Ridge, IL   Dubuque, IA   Madison, WI   New York
San Francisco   St. Louis   Bangkok   Bogotá   Caracas   Kuala Lumpur
Lisbon   London   Madrid   Mexico City   Milan   Montreal   New Delhi
Santiago   Seoul   Singapore   Sydney   Taipei   Toronto

The McGraw·Hill Companies

Higher Education

SOUND IT OUT! PHONICS IN A COMPREHENSIVE READING PROGRAM, SECOND EDITION

5 6 7 8 9 0 DOC/DOC 0 9 8 7 6 5

ISBN 0-07-282320-8

Vice president and editor-in-chief: *Thalia Dorwick*
Editorial assistant: *Christina Lembo*
Senior marketing manager: *Pamela S. Cooper*
Project manager: *Christine Walker*
Production supervisor: *Enboge Chonge*
Media technology producer: *Lance Gerhart*
Design coordinator: *Mary Kazak*
Cover/design: *Eric Kass/Lodge Design*
Cover images: © *John Foxx/Image State;* © *Photodisc*
Art editor: *Jen DeVere*
Compositor: *Carlisle Communications, Ltd.*
Typeface: 10/12 *New Baskerville*
Printer: *R. R. Donnelley/Crawfordsville, IN*

Library of Congress Cataloging-in-Publication Data
Savage, John F., 1938-
 Sound it out! : phonics in a comprehensive reading program / by John F. Savage.– 2nd ed.
  p. cm.
 Includes index.
 ISBN 0-07-282320-8 (alk. paper)
  1. Reading–Phonetic method. 2. English language–Orthography and spelling–Study and teaching (Elementary) I. Title.

LB1573.3.S28 2004
372.46'5 –dc21
                                                    2003046407

www.mhhe.com

ABOUT THE AUTHOR

John F. Savage is Professor Emeritus at the Lynch School of Education at Boston College, where he was Coordinator of the Graduate Reading/Literacy Program for 33 years. He began his career as a classroom teacher when Dick and Jane dominated the reading scene. He taught reading with a phonics/linguistic approach and was an active participant as whole language gained popularity in classroom programs. He has witnessed the ebb and flow of phonics in schools for forty years, and he still maintains an active role in classrooms with teachers and children.

Photographed at the Osterville Free Library by Connie Marr.

Dr. Savage has written five professional books on reading and language arts, including *Teaching Reading and Writing: Combining Skills, Strategies and Literature* (McGraw-Hill 1998) and *For the Love of Literature: Children and Books in the Elementary Years* (McGraw-Hill 2000). He has also authored a children's trade book on dyslexia, scores of professional articles, and other material that ranges from newspaper columns to basal stories.

A popular speaker, John Savage has conducted workshops on reading instruction all over the United States, in Canada, Europe, Asia, and Australia, where he was a Senior Fulbright Scholar.

BRIEF CONTENTS

CONTENTS

▼   ▼   ▼

**Approaches to Teaching Phonics:
Embedded and Direct Instruction 105**

Chapter 5

Phonics and Learning to Spell   137

Chapter 6

Phonics in a Comprehensive Reading Program   163

PREFACE

On January 9, 2002, *The New York Times* reported the following:

Education Bill Urges New Emphasis on Phonics as Method for Teaching Reading

The education bill President Bush signed into law today includes an ambitious federal commitment to teaching reading, which is expected to emphasize phonics over other methods of early reading instruction.

Thus begins a new chapter of increasing emphasis on the role of phonics in the education of children.

For generations, children have heard the advice, "Sound it out!" whenever they've encountered an unfamiliar or difficult word in print. But what does it mean to "sound out" a word? And how can teachers help children develop and apply this strategy consistently and effectively in learning to read and write?

The place of phonics in learning to read has long been one of the most intensely and widely debated issues in education. From the ancient Greeks to the present time, the importance of phonics in learning to read and spell has been a contentious educational topic. Parents, preachers, politicians, policy makers, pundits, and pitchmen continue to tout phonics as the way to address an illiteracy problem that has become a blot on our national conscience. Educators have entered into a "great debate" about the place of phonics in the educational experience of children. Disputes have escalated to a point where they have been characterized as "the reading wars."

In schools, trends have moved several times toward and away from a code-emphasis approach in language arts instruction that relies heavily on phonics—from the alphabetic method of the McGuffey Readers to the look-say method of Dick and Jane; from the whole word approach of conventional basals to the phonics-linguistic emphasis of the 1960s and '70s; from code-emphasis characters like Pam and Pat whose language was controlled by orthographic regularity to whole language programs that emphasized the use of context with authentic reading materials. The emphasis has once again moved toward phonics. The emphasis on children's ability to decode written language and the pressure to make phonics a dominant part of early reading instruction remain exceedingly strong.

As educational policies and practices nudge schools closer to programs that emphasize phonics in beginning reading, it becomes more and more incumbent on teachers to be aware of the place of phonics in the grand scheme of teaching children how to read and write.

Teachers have not only a professional obligation to know *what* digraphs and diphthongs are; they also need to know *why* these elements need to be taught and *how* to teach them effectively. In a very practical manner, this book focuses on the what, the why, and the how of helping children use phonics as part of a comprehensive instructional program that will help them become competent and confident consumers and producers of their written language. That was true when the first edition of this book was published in 2001; it remains no less true today.

Content and Organization

The current edition of *Sound It Out! Phonics in a Comprehensive Reading Program* consists of six chapters. Chapter 1, **The Place of Phonics in Learning to Read and Write,** introduces the topic of phonics, explores historical trends in the ebb and flow of phonics in schools, presents current research related to phonics instruction, and explores some of the arguments for and against a reliance on phonics in teaching children how to read and write.

Chapter 2, **Getting Started: Phonemic Awareness and Alphabet Knowledge,** treats topics that form the foundation of phonics (and later reading) instruction. Educators have come to recognize the vital importance of phonemic awareness to success in beginning reading. Children are introduced to the orthographic system as they become familiar with alphabet symbols. Both are integral parts of emergent literacy and early reading instruction, and they evolve into formal instruction in phonics.

Chapter 3, **Teaching and Learning Discrete Phonics Elements,** concentrates on the what and the how of phonics in the classroom. Specific elements of our orthographic system—consonants, digraphs, blends, vowels, syllables, and the like—are described, along with practical suggestions on how to present these elements to children, with a special emphasis on those who don't learn phonics as easily as others. The chapter also examines the place of phonics rules as part of an instructional program.

Chapter 4, **Approaches to Teaching Phonics: Embedded and Direct Instruction,** examines different ways in which phonics is woven into a language arts program. Some programs integrate phonics into ongoing practices that use children's literature as the main vehicle for instruction. Other programs emphasize direct, explicit instruction in sound-symbol relationships from the beginning. The chapter describes inten-sive, explicit, systematic programs such as Orton-Gillingham and the Wilson Language Program, and examines other means by which phonics is presented to children in school and at home.

Chapter 5, **Phonics and Learning to Spell,** explores and explains the encoding aspects of written language. As much (if not more) phonics can be taught as children learn to spell as when they learn to read. The chapter presents spelling (including the role of invented spelling) as part of process writing as well as direct instruction, examines elements other than phonics knowledge that contribute to spelling competency, and suggests practical techniques that can be used to help children improve their spelling ability.

Chapter 6, **Phonics in a Comprehensive Reading Program,** examines the important role of phonics in relation to other strategies and skills that children use in learning to read and write.

Features of This Second Edition

Practical Teaching Suggestions

As in the first edition of *Sound It Out!,* Teaching Suggestions are included throughout the chapters. Knowing the content of phonics is important; knowing how to design and apply strategies for teaching this content to children is also vital in the practical world of schools. This second edition contains *even more* teaching suggestions, including some to help children develop phonemic awareness, acquire alphabet knowledge, and master discrete phonics elements.

Pretest and Posttest of Phonics Knowledge

The book contains both a pretest and a posttest, which can be used to assess the reader's understanding of phonics before and after reading the book and to compare how that understanding has changed. The posttest is new to this edition.

Appendix

This feature contains position statements from the board of directors of the International Reading Association regarding phonemic awareness and phonics in the teaching of reading.

Updated Research

The text includes current references on phonics as part of reading and writing, including the "latest chapter(s)" in the great debate that is part of the history of phonics.

Expanded Discussion of Students Having Difficulties with Phonics

This second edition includes an expanded discussion of students who need extra attention in learning phonics, including those children whose home language is not English (ELL and ESL children).

National and State Standards

A new section has been added on how phonics relates to national and state standards on literacy instruction.

Expanded Mini-Glossary

The glossary has been expanded to include more definitions of phonics terms.

Supplements

The Phonics Tutorial CD-ROM *Sound It Out! A Self-Instructional Phonics Program* is packaged *free* with each new copy of the text! The CD includes definitions and examples of basic phonics concepts and then follows up each part with a Self-Test section to check for understanding. This organization gives readers the opportunity to practice and solidify their own grasp of phonics skills before presenting these concepts in the classroom.

Acknowledgments

The colleagues with whom I've worked over the years—professional associates and students alike—have helped shape the ideas and information contained in this book, and they have my sincere thanks. Special thanks is due to Pamela O'Day whose indefatigable efforts and research contributed hugely to the first edition of this book, to Mimi Tang who assisted me in preparing the current edition, to Stephany Neely for her help, to Jen Connor for her technical skill, and to Erin Corty for her practical suggestions.

Thanks are due to the reviewers, whose critical comments helped clarify and refine the content in the pages that follow. These individuals include

Diane E. Beals
University of Tulsa
Paula Boxie
Miami University of Ohio
Nancy Boyles
Southern Connecticut State University
Alexander B. Casareno
University of Portland
Martha A. Cocchiarella
Arizona State University
Deborah E. Doty
Northern Kentucky University
Elizabeth Howard
Grand Canyon University
Carol Jenkins
Boston University
Diane L. Lowe
Framingham State College

Linda Jones McCoy
Pittsburg State University
Sallie Averitt Miller
Columbus State University
Karen A. Onofrey
Arizona State University, West
Diana Scott-Simmons
Florida State University
Denise Staudt
University of the Incarnate Word
Jill E. Steeley
Oral Roberts University
Frances A. Steward
Western Illinois University
Lora L. Tyson
North Central College
Michael Uden
Concordia University, Wisconsin

The skilled staff of McGraw-Hill Higher Education—Christina Lembo, editor extraordinaire and Christine Walker, whose attention to details has improved the product enormously—have my deep appreciation as well.

As always, my loving wife Mary Jane continues to support life-long efforts.

To all, I offer my sincere appreciation.

This book is dedicated to Mary Jane

Pretest of Phonics Knowledge

The Pretest of Phonics Knowledge is a very brief self-check designed to assess your knowledge of the basic content on which much classroom phonics instruction is based. When you have finished, check your answers at the end of the test.

1. How many vowel sounds are in our language?
   _____ a. 5, sometimes 6
   _____ b. about 10
   _____ c. approximately 19
   _____ d. over 35
   _____ e. Nobody knows for sure.

2. Which pair(s) of words contain short vowel sounds?
   _____ a. rob and robe
   _____ b. rat and rug
   _____ c. rail and rule
   _____ d. write and right
   _____ e. They all do.

3. Which pair(s) of words contain long vowel sounds?
   _____ a. rob and robe
   _____ b. rat and rug
   _____ c. rail and rule
   _____ d. write and right
   _____ e. They all do.

4. Which pair(s) of words contain vowel diphthongs?
   _____ a. rob and robe
   _____ b. girl and boy
   _____ c. green and field
   _____ d. oil and joy
   _____ e. They all do.

5. Which pair(s) of words contain consonant blends?
   _____ a. slow and fast
   _____ b. good and bad
   _____ c. rain and shine
   _____ d. red and green
   _____ e. cats and dogs

6. Which pair(s) of words contain consonant digraphs?

_____ a. church and state
_____ b. sip and ship
_____ c. when and where
_____ d. here and there
_____ e. fish and chips

7. What's the *onset* in the word **boat?**

_____ a. b
_____ b. bo
_____ c. boa
_____ d. oat
_____ e. It has no onset.

8. What is the *rime* in the word **boat?**

_____ a. b
_____ b. bo
_____ c. boa
_____ d. oat
_____ e. It has no rime.

9. How many phonemes are in the word **laugh?**

_____ a. 2
_____ b. 3
_____ c. 4
_____ d. 5
_____ e. 6

10. How many phonemes are in the word **fox?**

_____ a. 2
_____ b. 3
_____ c. 4
_____ d. 5
_____ e. 6

11. How many syllables in the word **encyclopedia?**

_____ a. 2
_____ b. 4
_____ c. 6
_____ d. 8
_____ e. 10

12. Which pair(s) of words contains open syllables?

_____ a. bear and rabbit
_____ b. leopard and puma
_____ c. koala and kangaroo
_____ d. cat and rat
_____ e. They all do.

For the answers, see page 187.

The Place of Phonics in Learning to Read and Write

Phonics has long been part of literacy instruction and it remains an important part of children's school experiences in the early grades. This chapter

▼ briefly traces the history of phonics in schools

▼ provides an essential definition of phonics

▼ presents major arguments for and against phonics as part of reading and writing instruction

▼ examines phonics in relation to other components that children need in learning to read and write.

The role of phonics in teaching children how to read has remained an educational bone of contention for a long, long time. From Socrates' assertion in ancient Greece that "in learning to read, we were satisfied when we knew the letters of the alphabet," to current state regulations that require schools to include direct systematic, explicit phonics in children's education, experts have argued about the place of phonics in a reading instructional program.

Phonics continues to be the subject of discussion. Few argue that it's a necessary component in learning to read, but many argue about the place of phonics in teaching children to read and write.

Over the years, there has been an ebb and flow regarding the place of phonics in schools. Although phonics has never entirely disappeared from the curriculum, its role in reading and writing instruction has waxed and waned in response to educational research, educational trends, and public opinion. Its popularity has been cyclical in the ongoing attempt to find the most effective means that will enable all children to succeed as readers and writers.

A Brief Look Back

Historically, the assumption that children should learn to read using letters and sounds is fairly well established. Teachers in ancient Greece drilled pupils in the sounds of letters and engaged them in syllable-building and word-building exercises, and the same instructional method was used by the

Greek slave-tutors who taught upper-class children in ancient Rome. The Romans ruled England for 350 years, and children of the aristocracy learned to read both Latin and English. Similar techniques emphasizing letters and sounds were used to teach reading through the Middle Ages. In those days, written text was a rare commodity. Until the invention of the printing press, the few books that did exist were owned by religious institutions and the wealthy aristocracy. Literacy was not part of the day-to-day lives of the common people. Even as printed texts became more readily available, literacy remained the possession of the privileged few, although in more and more villages, ill-prepared teachers working in "petty schools" attempted to teach reading by having children learn their ABC's. Throughout the sixteenth century, reading methodology remained the same as was used by the ancient Greeks and Romans. "First one learned the names of the letters; then one learned letter sounds through work on vowel-consonant, consonant-vowel-combinations, and syllables" (Mathews 1966, 19).

On this side of the Atlantic, similar alphabetic methods were used to teach children how to read. *The New England Primer,* the first reading textbook specifically written for use in the American colonies and used widely from the late seventeenth to the middle eighteenth century, began with letters and syllables. Children learned letters of the alphabet and words that corresponded to these symbols. Pages contained individual letters, followed by a rough woodcut, and a rhyming couplet related to the letter:

A *In Adam's Fall*   **B** *Thy Life to mend*
    We sinned all.   *This Book attend. (the Book being*
                          the Bible)

The content was heavily religious and moralistic, since reading was seen not only as a means of achieving literacy but also as a means of achieving salvation. In some respects, early material for teaching reading dealt with religious themes to which alphabetic symbols were simply attached (Smith 1965).

In the early 1800s, other books designed for reading instruction followed in a similar vein, although strong doses of nationalism were added to the religious content after the American Revolution. Prior to the early 1800s, the sole approach for teaching beginning reading was the ABC or alphabetic method, which involved learning the letters of the alphabet and attaching sounds to these symbols (Venetsky 1987). Noah Webster's popular *New American Spelling Book* (commonly known as "The Blue Back Speller"), the most widely used schoolbook at the time, focused on learning the sounds of letters and syllables in teaching children how to read and spell (and to pronounce words as well, which led to the unique sound system that developed for American English as distinguished from British English).

While the alphabetic method was widely used in teaching English-speaking children how to read, Prussian educators argued that children should be taught whole words as meaningful units before learning the sounds of the letters that made up these words. This new "whole word" method—in which children learned to recognize and pronounce the word as a whole before studying the elements that made up the word—became firmly entrenched in German schools, and a whole set of instructional practices and programs evolved from this view.

Horace Mann, the nineteenth century educational reformer who, as "The Father of American Education," exerted considerable influence on American schools, visited Europe and became enamored with this new "whole word" method. He regarded this approach to teaching reading as far superior to what was going on in U.S. schools. When he returned home, he promoted the idea of learning whole words at a time as a method of teaching reading that challenged the widely used alphabetic method.

Throughout the nineteenth century, a number of textbook series were published for use in schools, with separate books designed for use at different grade levels. The best known and most popular of these reading textbook series was the *McGuffey Eclectic Readers*, which were published between 1836 and 1844 and sold over 120 million copies. The McGuffey Readers, with their strong emphasis on phonetic elements in the early grades, dominated reading instruction for sixty years. The series was titled "Eclectic" and teachers were informed that the materials were "especially adapted to the Phonic Method, the Word Method, or a combination of the two." The text of the early lessons, however,

The dog.	*The cat.*	*The mat.*
The dog ran.	*Is the cat on the mat?*	
	The cat is on the mat.	

clearly indicates the degree of emphasis that the program gave to phonetic regularity in teaching children how to read.

In the late 1800s, there was a renewed interest in phonics. "The word method was in vogue until about 1890, when phonics was brought back with a renewed emphasis, as it once again was thought to have merit" (Emans 1968, 603). Newly published programs featured oral introduction of sounds, phonetic blending, diacritical markings, and lots of decoding practice. After the turn of the century, however, there was a shift from oral reading for interpretation to silent reading for comprehension, with a strong emphasis on whole word approaches. This emphasis was cemented with the arrival of Dick and Jane.

Born in 1927, Dick and Jane, their family and their pets, became famous for their world "where night never comes, knees never scrape, parents never yell, and the fun never stops" (Kismaric and Heiferman 1996). The Scott, Foresman readers in which Dick and Jane first appeared exerted enormous influence on how reading was taught. Children used the "whole word" method with tightly controlled text that helped them learn the words that went along with the pictures, recognizing complete words by sight instead of phonetically sounding them out letter by letter. The commercial success of the Scott, Foresman series led other publishers to create Dick and Jane clones (pairs of children such as Alice and Jerry, Jack and Janet, and their respective supporting casts) in similar programs that continued to maintain the look-say or whole word method of teaching children how to read. Although some teachers used phonics as a supplementary or incidental adjunct to their teaching, the look-say approach dominated instruction well into the 1960s.

The pendulum began to swing back toward an increased interest in phonics in 1955 when Rudolph Flesch wrote a book that became a best seller, *Why Johnny Can't Read*. The reason why Johnny couldn't read, according to Flesch, was that he was taught by a look-say method without enough emphasis on phonics. Flesch rejected "the stuff and guff of Dick and Jane" and called for a return to having children sound out words. His passionate appeals caught the attention of the public, and phonics began an increasingly rapid return to center stage in reading instructional programs.

About a decade later, in 1967, another book that profoundly influenced reading instruction appeared, the first edition of *Learning To Read: The Great Debate* by Jeanne Chall. "The Great Debate" was whether to use code-emphasis approaches that relied heavily on phonics or meaning-emphasis approaches typified by look-say programs that had dominated classroom reading instruction for the previous fifty-plus years. Based on an extensive research review, Chall concluded that code-emphasis approaches produced results that were far superior to the conventional look-say approach. Although her findings were at first questioned and criticized by fellow scholars, the book became a powerful force in establishing phonics as the core method of teaching children how to read.

At the same time, the field of structural linguistics was catching the attention of literacy educators, as the work of scholars like Leonard Bloomfield (1961) and Charles Fries (1962) became widely known. Structural linguistics emphasized the importance of regularity and consistency between the sounds and symbols in written language in teaching children how to read. Basal readers featured titles with word patterns like *A King on a Swing,* and children read stories in their beginning reading materials that featured language like *Dad and Nan ran. Ann and Dan ran* (McCracken and Walcutt, 1963, 6) and *Ben had ten hens in a box. He set the box in a pen and let the hens run* (Otto et al. 1966, 18). Basal programs that emphasized consistency in the sound-symbol code of language became just as popular as those that had been used with the look-say approach of Dick and Jane and their contemporaries in the previous generation of reading books.

In the 1970s, the emphasis in language study moved to psycholinguistics, an interdisciplinary field that examined psychology and language, rather than focusing merely on the structure of the language itself. A groundswell of interest in a holistic approach to reading and writing occurred, and a movement that came to be known as "whole language" evolved. Rather than viewing reading as the acquisition of a set of discrete and isolated skills, whole language advocates like Kenneth Goodman (1988) and Brian Cambourne (1988) promoted the idea of using an integrated approach to reading instruction. Whole language relied heavily on the use of children's literature and other authentic reading material, rather than stories that were cobbled out of structured language controlled on the basis of sound-symbol consistency. In basal reading series, the amount of literature increased dramatically, while the amount of phonics taught declined tremendously (Hoffman et al. 1994).

Phonics was not entirely ignored in whole language classrooms (as some critics contend), but children were taught "only as much phonics as they need" in order to construct meaning in reading and writing (Strickland 1995, 280). Most whole language advocates had no argument with using phonics; in fact, instruction in sound-symbol relationships was integrated in practical ways as part of learning to read and write (Mills, O'Keefe, and Stephens 1992). The whole language philosophy, however, generally placed considerably less emphasis on phonics. Rather than starting with the study of sound-symbol relationships, phonics was most often integrated and embedded into literature-based instruction in whole language classrooms. While not ignored, phonics was generally de-emphasized as a method of teaching children how to read and write.

In 1990, another landmark book about teaching reading appeared on the educational landscape: *Beginning To Read: Thinking and Learning About Print* by Marilyn Jager Adams. As Jeanne Chall had done in the 1960s, Adams synthesized research studies related to reading, and she concluded that a heavy emphasis on phonics produced far superior results in teaching children how to read. While she acknowledged the importance of using material that would promote children's inclination to read, Adams emphasized the central role of mastering the code in thinking and learning about print. The book also helped make educators more acutely aware of the importance of phonemic awareness in the literacy development of children.

In the 1990s, the debate about phonics heated up again. Disturbed by the disappointing results of reading achievement tests, legislatures in California, Texas, Ohio, and other states passed laws mandating a stronger emphasis on phonics instruction for children and for those preparing to teach them. Educational experts testified before Congress that the application of phonics in reading and spelling was "not negotiable" in beginning reading instruction (Lyon 1997). Phonics began to enjoy something of a renaissance in schools.

The debate about phonics attracted popular attention of national publications like *Time, Newsweek,* and *The Wall Street Journal,* as well as local newspapers from coast to coast, which reported the debate under the banner of "phonics versus whole language." Phonics became a popular topic of conversation in teachers' rooms and in living rooms. It became a political issue, a prominent plank in the platform of candidates for local and natural offices. Schools found themselves under increasing pressure to reestablish phonics as a central part of the curriculum in the early elementary years.

Not all the experts agreed with the increased emphasis on phonics in schools in response to the perceived literacy crisis. Reacting to what she has called a "Phonics Phobia," Routman cautioned, "If we define reading as getting meaning from print and not just reading the words, overemphasis on phonics is not necessary, and it is inordinately time-consuming. Something else in the curriculum will have to go. What often gets left out are authentic language activities such as reading for pleasure and discussing literature" (Routman 1996, 93).

In fact, some experts questioned if there was a literacy crisis at all (Berliner and Biddle 1995; Bracey 1977). McQuillan (1998) presented evidence that reading scores of U.S. students had not declined precipitously as the popular press reported, and that our children were not among the worst readers in the world. McQuillan defended holistic approaches to literacy instruction and provided statistical data to support the conclusion that children are reading as well or better today than they did a generation ago. Despite the voices of these experts, the move toward more emphasis on phonics in schools continues as a proposed solution to a perceived crisis in children's reading and writing achievement.

Where are we today? Phonics remains "a very hot topic" in today's educational landscape. According to a survey of leading literacy experts, phonics and phonemic awareness remain among the "hottest topics" in schools, as these dimensions of reading receive increasing attention. (Cassidy and Cassidy 2002/3). High value is placed on phonics. The well-publicized report of the National Reading Panel that underscores the importance of phonics and the educational policy decisions that have resulted from this heightened attention has brought phonics once again to the forefront in teaching children how to read. Phonics is a main thrust in the *Reading First* component of the federal *No Child Left Behind* initiative. While remnants of "the great debate" linger, phonics has become a centerpiece in early reading instruction.

As experts argue, teachers teach. And most teachers focus their attempts to achieve a measure of balance in a comprehensive program that will serve the needs of all the children in their classrooms.

A survey of a large national sample of elementary classroom teachers about their beliefs and practices related to reading indicated that "a majority of teachers embrace a balanced, eclectic approach to elementary reading instruction, blending phonics and holistic principles and practices" (Bauman et al. 1998, 641). Overall, teachers reported that they valued and taught phonics as an integral part of their programs, particularly in the early grades; 99 percent of the K–2 teachers reported that phonics was *Essential/Important* in their classrooms, although they also value literature and language-rich activities in teaching reading. Another national survey (Rankin-Erickson and Presley 2000) found that virtually all teachers teach phonics as a reading skill, although they select elements to be taught on the basis of children's needs rather than as a prescribed sequence. In sum, teachers *are* using phonics to teach reading, but faced with the realities of real-life classroom situations, practitioners embrace a balanced philosophy to implement a comprehensive program of reading instruction.

Educational innovations have been compared to tidal waves. Along come new ideas that give teachers and other educators a tumbling and buffeting that significantly alter their thinking and practice. Publishers follow suit and produce materials that both support and influence what goes on in classrooms. But tidal waves eventually draw back and when they do, they deposit objects near the spot where the wave picked them up in the first place. Views are changed, however, as a result of the experience. Whole language opened teachers' eyes to the importance of using literature as part of children's literacy development. The continuing wave of interest in phonics has refocused teachers' attention on the importance of decoding as part of learning to read. The likely result will be a more comprehensive program that will serve the needs of all children.

What Is Phonics, Anyway?

In a nutshell, phonics can be defined as the conscious, concentrated study of the relationship between sounds and symbols for the purpose of learning to read and spell. It is

- *A conscious, concentrated study.* Phonics involves a body of information that needs to be mastered and applied in acquiring literacy. "Phonics is a study unto itself, valued by linguists, philologists, dictionary writers and cryptologists, as well as reading teachers" (Chall and Popp 1996, 4).
- *Of sound-symbol relationships.* The relationship between letters and sounds is at the core of phonics. Phonics is based on the alphabetic principle that requires a knowledge of letter-sound correspondences in pronouncing and producing written language.
- *For the purpose of learning to read and spell.* Phonics is a tool for helping people become literate. Arguments about phonics often degenerate into nasty accusations involving religious and political motivations for those who favor or oppose it. All the political, religious, social, and related baggage that phonics carries notwithstanding, phonics is all about teaching children how to read and spell. The ultimate end of phonics is reading and writing—to help children read accurately and fluently and to spell correctly and confidently.

In order to understand the importance of phonics as part of learning to read and write, it's important to understand the alphabetic nature of our alphabetic writing system. Orthography—a word that derives from two Greek word parts, *ortho-* meaning correct and *-graph* meaning writing—refers to the conventional writing system of any language. "The alphabetic principle is subtle. Its understanding may be the single most important step toward acquiring the code" (Adams 1990, 63).

English orthography is based on the alphabetic principle; that is, individual spoken sounds (called *phonemes*) are represented in writing by individual written symbols (called *graphemes*). The word *bat,* for example, has three sounds /b/ /a/ /t/ and three symbols **b, a,** and **t** representing these sounds on a one-to-one basis. *Jump* has four sounds /j/ /u/   and /p/ and four symbols **j, u, m,** and **p** also corresponding to the four sounds. The system is not perfect, however. Sounding out the letters in the word *laughed* on a one-to-one sound-symbol basis will not produce the word /laft/.

Phonics is important to decoding and encoding this system of written language. A code is a system that enables one to send and understand messages, a system of symbols that people use to communicate. In order to effectively use a code, a person must be able to translate the system into meaningful messages.

The code of written language consists of the alphabetic symbols that represent spoken sounds. In order to decode written language, people need to attach the appropriate sequence of sounds to the series of symbols they encounter in print. In order to encode written language, people need to select the appropriate written symbols that represent the sounds of the words they want to write. Learning to associate these sound-symbol correspondences in reading and writing is at the heart of phonics instruction in schools.

The Controversy about Phonics

Educators commonly use the expression "The Great Debate" to describe the conflicting opinions about the place of phonics in helping children acquire literacy. Journalists typically label arguments as "The Reading Wars." However one labels it, there has long been an ongoing controversy regarding the place of phonics in learning to read. Often couched in a rather simplistic "whole language versus phonics" dichotomy, the popular press has presented these as "dueling methods of teaching reading" and has characterized the debate over phonics as a bruising battle, bitter and irrational. The professional literature (Adams, Allington et al. 1991; Carbo 1988, 1989; Chall 1998a, 1998b) reflects the passion and acrimony with which this debate has been carried on in polarized polemics by respected literacy educators.

There are indeed basic differences in the opinions of those who favor a greater emphasis on phonics vis-à-vis those who favor less emphasis on decoding as part of learning to read. On the one hand, those who favor a strong early emphasis on direct and systematic phonics instruction see decoding as the primary means that ought to be used in helping children (and others who cannot read or write) become literate individuals. Proponents base their views on two factors:

1. the alphabetic nature of our writing system—a system in which spoken sounds are represented by written symbols—suggests the need for teaching this sound-symbol relationship directly and explicitly to young children, and

2. the substantial body of research evidence supports the effectiveness of phonics in helping children achieve success in learning how to read.

On the other hand, those less convinced of the value of a heavy emphasis on phonics at the beginning stages of learning to read base their point of view on two premises as well:

1. although our writing system is based on the relationship between spoken sounds and written symbols, this system is not regular or predictable enough to rely on in helping young children learn to read, and

2. for mature and capable readers (which all parents and teachers hope their children will become), phonics is less useful than other word recognition strategies; readers learn to recognize words by sight and meaning, not by sounding individual symbols in the words they encounter in print.

The Case for Phonics

Phonics advocates base their position strongly on the alphabetic principle, the principle that letters work together in a systematic way to represent sounds of spoken language. Advocates believe that an understanding that written symbols represent spoken sounds is absolutely necessary for the development of reading. This principle is seen as "the underlying framework that anchors beginning reading instruction" (Coyne, Kame'enui, and Simmons 2001, 63).

When the early Phonecians invented alphabetic writing by adapting the hieroglyphics of their Egyptian neighbors, they used individual written symbols to represent sound elements rather than whole objects and ideas. Individual graphic symbols were used to represent individual spoken sounds, and this became the code of written language.

A code is a system for sending and receiving messages. The ability to understand coded messages depends on a knowledge of what the symbols mean. Decoding is the process of changing communication signals into messages, translating one code of symbols into another one. In English writing, written symbols (letters of the alphabet) represent spoken sounds.

Sound-symbol relationships constitute the code of written English. Just as the user of Morse code uses dots and dashes to send and receive messages, readers *decode* print by attaching the appropriate sound or sound sequence to the corresponding letter or letter sequence. Writers *encode* written messages by selecting the appropriate letter sequence for the sounds of the words they want to represent. At the heart of this decoding/encoding process is phonics, a knowledge of the sounds and symbols that constitute the code of written English and the ability to use this knowledge for rapid and accurate reading and writing.

There is also a strong research base that supports an emphasis on decoding and the use of phonics in teaching young children how to read, and this research has strongly influenced the thinking about phonics in schools over the years.

In 1967, *Learning To Read: The Great Debate* by Jeanne S. Chall reviewed research on reading instruction from 1910 to 1965 (an era in which the whole word method of teaching reading was widely used). Chall reported that an approach to beginning reading that emphasized learning relationships between letters and sounds produced better results than that which used a look-say approach to instruction. "It is the acquisition of the alphabetic code, the alphabetic principle, in the early grades that leads to quicker acquisition of reading skills than an emphasis on responding to the text meaning" (Chall 1996, unpaged). *The Great Debate* was updated twice, first in 1983 with a synthesis of reading research from 1967 to 1983, and again in 1996 with a synthesis of research from 1983 to 1993 (the height of the whole language era). In both revisions, findings confirmed the original conclusion: that although reading for meaning should not be ignored, approaches to early reading instruction that emphasized decoding were more effective in helping children achieve in reading than those that did not provide this strong phonics emphasis.

In 1985, *Becoming a Nation of Readers,* a report on the status of reading instruction in the United States compiled by a Commission on Reading appointed by the National Academy of Education, presented another "careful and thorough synthesis of an extensive body of findings in reading" (Anderson et al. 1985, v).The report reinforced the concept of the importance of phonics in early reading instruction. "Classroom research shows that, on the average, children who are taught phonics get off to a better start in learning to read than children who are not taught phonics" (ibid., 37). Reflecting the prevailing educational climate of the time—in which phonics was a more incidental than direct part of reading instruction in most classrooms—the report raised questions about the long-term effects of phonics on children's reading comprehension and raised a number of issues related to teaching phonics.

In 1990, *Beginning To Read* by Marilyn Jager Adams brought the spotlight squarely on phonics. Like Chall, Adams synthesized research related to reading instruction, but she also included a literature review on psycholinguistic processes in learning how to read. While the book acknowledged the advantages of other approaches to reading and praised whole language for making quality children's literature a more integral part of literacy instruction in the early years, the book heavily emphasized the importance of phonics. A summary of Adams' book prepared by the Center for the Study of Reading at the University of Illinois at Champaign-Urbana (Stahl, Osborn, and Lehr 1990) summarized some of Adams' conclusions:

> Explicit systematic phonics is a singularly successful mode of teaching young or slow learners to read (38)
>
> Knowledge of letters and phonemic awareness have been found to bear a strong and direct relationship to success and ease of reading acquisition (54)
>
> Activities requiring children to attend to the individual letters of words, their sequencing, and their phonological translations should be included in any beginning reading program (73)

Sounding out words is a way of teaching children what they need to know to comprehend text (88)

Phonics is of inescapable importance to both skillful reading and its acquisition (117)

In short, Adams recognized the complex nature of learning how to read and managed to avoid the simplistic notion of "phonics in a vacuum." Her conclusions, however, left little doubt about the necessity for explicit instruction about the code of English orthography as part of early reading instruction. Adams' work remained incredibly influential for charting the course of reading instruction into the 21st century.

Another far-ranging and comprehensive synthesis of research on reading instruction is *Preventing Reading Difficulties in Young Children* (Snow, Burns and Griffin 1998). This work was done by a committee established by the National Academy of Sciences at the request of the U.S. Department of Education and the Department of Health and Human Services. The committee's report focused on a broad range of topics related to teaching reading, including the role of parents, components of classroom instruction, the preparation of reading teachers, and establishing a research agenda into the future, among other issues. The committee acknowledged the complexity of learning how to read and the role of experienced and capable teachers in the reading instructional process, but it also recognized the importance of having young children "learn about the nature of the alphabetic writing system and be exposed to frequent, regular spelling-sound relationships" (3). It identified explicit instruction in speech sounds and spelling as cornerstones of reading programs designed to help all children learn to read.

Additional research support for phonics was contained in the Report of the National Reading Panel. In 1997, Congress requested that the National Institute of Child Health and Human Development (NICHD), in consultation with the Secretary of Education, convene a panel of experts to assess the state of research related to teaching children to read. The panel produced final reports of its work (National Reading Panel 2000, 2000a), which was summarized and widely disseminated in *Put Reading First: The Research Building Blocks for Teaching Children to Read* (Armbruster, Lehr, and Osborn 2001). Related to phonics, the summary reported that systematic and explicit phonics instruction:

- Is more effective than non-systematic or no phonics instruction;
- Improves kindergarten and first-grade children's word recognition and spelling;
- Improves reading comprehension;
- Is effective for children from various social and economic levels;
- Is particularly beneficial for children who are having difficulties in learning to read.

In sum, while acknowledging that phonics is not an entire reading program for beginning reading, the National Reading Panel's interpretation of research left little doubt about the importance of direct, explicit, systematic phonics for children learning to read. Although serious discrepancies between the conclusions of the panel and the way the conclusions were reported were identified (Garan 2002), this research summary gathered interest and clout in the educational community.

The work of the National Reading Panel was quickly criticized and its conclusions questioned by many leading literacy educators—including one who was a member of the Panel itself (Yatvin 2002)—on the basis of the panel's composition, its procedures, its view of reading, its selection of studies, its interpretation of the data, and the way in which results were reported. It was characterized as "an extremely flawed research effort" (Garan 2001), a report that "feigns unanimity" (Cunningham 2001), and whose purposes were "blatantly political and shamelessly financial" (Garan 2002).

These criticisms notwithstanding, reports of the work of the National Reading Panel were widely circulated and have played a huge role in shaping the recommendations of the Federal education plan, *No Child Left Behind*. The contents of the Panel's report have played a large role in setting the agenda for reading instruction in schools.

In sum, proponents of phonics use the alphabetic nature of our orthographic system, along with research on early instruction that points to the advantage of including direct and systematic teaching of sound-symbol relationships as part of the instructional regimen, to support the place of phonics in teaching children how to read and write. Although some of this research has been seriously questioned, the evidence remains convincing to many educators and policy makers.

Doubts about Phonics

Although much research evidence and public sentiment support the increased use of phonics in schools, some critics express deep concern about the overemphasis on decoding in helping children learn to read and write.

One concern relates to the nature of our English orthography. Although our writing system is based on the alphabetic principle, its sound-symbol relationships are complex and far from perfect. The letter combination **ow,** for example, represents a different sound in *now* and in *know,* and still another sound in *knowledge.* How, critics ask, can children be expected to master a system that is so complex and so often "irregular"?

Sometimes, a sound can be spelled in several different ways. Consider the number of ways the "long u" sound (the vowel sound in **blue**) is written in the following sentence:

> *Two musical groups thought they could play the new tune "Blue Fruit" in a leaky canoe. It was a cool maneuver.*

And sometimes the same letter represents several different sounds. Count the number of sounds represented by the letter **o** in the following sentence:

> *Do I notice one old woman, her son, and a wolf?*

Teaching Suggestions ▼

Phonics and State Curriculum Standards for Language Arts

Standards that define learning—i.e., what children should know and be able to do in language arts—are a dominant part of education in today's schools. The purpose of standards is to make sure that all children are afforded opportunities to learn about language and to develop the competencies that will enable them to meet their communications needs.

The two professional organizations whose members are most directly and specifically involved with literacy teaching—the International Reading Association and the National Council of Teachers of English—have defined a set of 12 content standards related to language arts. The standards that IRA and NCTE developed place decoding within a broader literacy context with an emphasis on comprehension:

> *Students apply a wide range of strategies to comprehend, interpret, evaluate, and appreciate texts. They draw on their prior experience, their interactions with other readers and writers, their knowledge of word meaning and of other text, their word identification strategies, and their understanding of textual features (e.g., **sound-letter correspondence,** sentence structure, context, graphics).*

> *(Standards for the English Language Arts,*
> International Reading Association and National Council of
> Teachers of English 1996)

State standards are generally far more specific when it comes to teaching phonics. Virtually every state in the U.S. has standards related to language arts and other subjects in the curriculum, and while these standards differ from state to state, they feature phonics in more direct and specific ways than the national IRA/NCTE standards. Most states require that phonics be explicitly taught to children in the early grades. Massachusetts state standards, for example, stipulate that:

> *Students will understand the nature of written English and the relationship of letters and spelling patterns in written English.*

> *(Massachusetts English Language Arts Curriculum Framework.*
> Massachusetts Department of Education 2001)

A description of this standard includes specific reference to phonemic awareness, letter recognition, the ability to use letter-sound matches to decode words, and knowledge of specific phonics elements (onsets and rimes, digraphs and diphthongs, syllables and spelling, and the like).

California is more specific in standards related to phonics instruction. Part of the reading standard for first grade is

> *(students) select letter patterns and know how to translate them into spoken language by using phonics, syllabication, and word parts.*

> *(English Language Arts Content Standards for California Public Schools.*
> California State Board of Education 1997)

Continued on next page.

The standards detail the components of phonemic awareness, identify phonetic and structural elements to be taught, and contain a heavy emphasis on direct phonics instruction throughout.

State standards serve as guidelines for instruction. They indicate what is expected of teachers in helping children learn to read. Most states administer tests that are aligned with these standards. Many of these measures are "high stakes tests" that students are required to pass in order to graduate from high school. These standards have a mighty influence on what goes on as part of reading instruction in the classroom.

State standards for language arts are not limited to decoding, of course. They cover a range of language learning that includes speaking, listening, many aspects of writing (sentence structure, punctuation, etc.), literature, grammar, vocabulary, viewing and analyzing visual media, and the like. Documents differ from state to state in their degree of specificity. Some state standards documents are so specific that they suggest the order in which sounds should be introduced and how these sounds should be taught; others are far less prescriptive. Nor do all states have identical standards. All, however, include phonics as an essential component in the reading instructional process.

The inconsistencies in sound-symbol relationships in our written language system are highlighted in the parody on the slogan for the well-advertised program "Hooked on Phonics":

Hookt on Fonicks Werked Four Me!

Reading requires more than simply a knowledge of sound-symbol relationships. The number, complexity, and unreliability of many of these sound-symbol relationships and phonics rules of English writing cause some to worry about depending too heavily on phonics as a means of teaching reading. "The reason phonics does not work for children (or for computers) is that the links between the letters and sounds cannot be uniquely specified" (Smith 1985, 47).

Those less committed to phonics also argue that good readers don't look at every letter in every word that they read. Word identification does not require identification of all the letters in the word. Letter-by-letter identification is unnecessary and even impossible as children read. Some critics of phonics contend that reliance on phonics may impede fluent reading because too much attention to orthographic features may cause children to ignore or lose a sense of what they are reading. Reading is a meaning-making process, not primarily a decoding activity, and meaning making rather than phonics should be the primary focus of early instruction.

Critics contend that the sound-symbol relationships in our orthographic system—especially in vowels—are not reliable enough to build an entire instructional program upon them. While they acknowledge the alphabetic

Point-Counterpoint on Phonics* ▼

Aunt Millie	Uncle Max
I'll tell you what's wrong with schools today! They don't teach enough phonics.	Hogwash! Phonics is old fashioned and out of date. Besides, nobody taught me phonics and I can read.
How can you read without phonics? You *have* to sound out words you don't know.	Not really. There are often more words that are exceptions than words that follow the rules. Phonics can be misleading to a kid trying to learn to read.
Yes, but you have to use some phonics in reading new words, don't you?	I agree, but that doesn't mean that teachers should spend all their time teaching phonics. They should have kids read more.
But phonics opens the door so that kids *can* read more!	The kids will be so tired of books with sentences like "Flick the tick off the chick with a thick stick, Nick" that they'll be turned off by the time they get to read anything interesting.
I read a book not long ago about how important phonics is to reading.	And I read one that said that phonics is not as important as everyone once thought it was.
But look at cousin Alphie. He failed first grade but once he got a teacher who taught him phonics, he quickly learned to read.	Yes, and what about cousin Rosie? The family thought that she was stupid because she couldn't learn to read. Once they got her away from that phonics stuff, she really bloomed. No pun intended.
I think you're wrong.	And I think *you're* wrong.

Teaching Reading and Writing: Combining Skills, Strategies, and Literature by John F. Savage. New York: McGraw-Hill, 1998. Reproduced with permission of The McGraw-Hill Companies.

nature of our writing system, they question the advisability of building a whole approach to reading around this principle.

The soundness of the research base supporting phonics has also been questioned. Some argue that much of the research supporting a heavy emphasis on systematic phonics is suspect (Carbo 1988; Cunningham 2001; Smith 1999; Taylor 1999). Critics contend that many of the conclusions of these research studies are not, in fact, supported by the data (Allington and Woodside-Jiron 1999). Critics express concern that studies supporting phonics don't use comprehension or the application of phonics in authentic reading experiences as criteria in judging the effectiveness of phonics. Too few studies, critics maintain, require that children apply phonics knowledge in reading (or writing) actual text. Many studies are done with small numbers of children (often those with reading problems) and the results are generalized to normal children in typical classroom environments. Working with struggling readers who had a strong phonics background, O'Donnell (2001) found that "no evidence that exposure to intensive phonics enabled these students to acquire even basic competence for handling unknown words in actual reading situations" (9). More disturbingly, he observed an aversion to anything having to do with print in his intensive phonics students.

In examining state and federal policies and directives on how reading should be taught, Dressman (1999) characterized these policy statements as "research-laced rather than research-based" (279). He concluded that much of this research has been interpreted "to produce policies and literacy curriculums that are as much the product of their makers' cultural policies and normative assumptions as they are the product of a dispassionate use of the scientific method" (258).

In a nutshell, lots of literacy educators contend that reading efficiency suggests that we rely on strategies other than decoding in helping children learn to read. How do children learn to read words they don't immediately recognize in print without phonics? The alternative is psycholinguistic guess at the word, not a guess as in "shot in the dark" but a guess based on the store of language that the child brings to the entire context of the piece. "The whole point about systematic phonics instruction is that, if given too soon, it confuses, and if given too late, it is unnecessary" (Smith 1999, 155).

And so the debate continues. Advocates on one side build their arguments on the alphabetic principle and cite studies that support direct systematic instruction as the central element in effective beginning reading instruction. Those on the opposing side question the validity of many of these research conclusions and propose an emphasis on more meaning-based methods for teaching children how to read. In the practical day-to-day business of classroom instruction, teachers are faced with the challenge of finding an approach that will serve the needs of the children in their class.

Phonics: A Dispassionate View

When all the rhetoric involved in the great debate is stripped away, teachers are left with the essential question, *what's the place of phonics in learning to read?*

Essentially, phonics can be described as "a necessary but not a sufficient" component of becoming literate. Why necessary? Because written English is based on the alphabetic principle, and in order to decode unfamiliar words, one needs to know how to attach the spoken equivalents to the written symbols in those words. One needs a knowledge of the sound-symbol relationships that are part of phonics in order to read expressions like I ♥ LAKE WOLOMOPOG.

Why not sufficient? Because the goal of reading and writing is the construction of meaning, and phonics alone is not a sufficient tool for arriving at meaning. For example, read the following sentence:

The small child had an infractaneous look on his face.

Then make a facial expression similar to the one that the child had on his face.

For most readers, *infractaneous* is an unfamiliar word. You were probably able to read the sentence but unable to reproduce the look on the child's face because you did not know the meaning of *infractaneous*. You were able to pronounce the word by using your knowledge of phonics to "sound it out" by attaching the symbols to the appropriate sounds. You could probably tell *infractaneous* was an adjective describing the look on the child's face. But you were not able to get the meaning of the word because the sound-symbol relationships alone did not provide any clues to meaning. (The word *infractaneous* is a pseudoword or nonsense word; it can be pronounced, but it has no real meaning in language.)

There is more to reading than merely associating sounds and symbols. Reading is a language activity, and language is about meaning. Pronunciation does not assure comprehension. To sound out words without getting meaning from these words has been called "barking at print."

Children (or adult illiterates) who face the challenge of learning to read and write are not blank slates. They bring a considerable amount of understanding and information to the tasks of constructing meaning in decoding and encoding printed text.

Throughout their preschool years, children have learned to use oral language to meet their considerable communications needs. They have learned the meaning of thousands of words, and they can use these words to make statements and to ask questions. They have developed an intuitive understanding of how language works. They have engaged in thousands of hours of conversations with parents, siblings, friends, and others with whom they have maintained daily contact. They have watched thousands of hours of television, some of it "educational." They have been surrounded by alphabet symbols on food containers, toy boxes, billboards, and other environmental print. If they are lucky, they have had parents, older siblings, and other caregivers who have read to them, shared favorite stories and poems, engaged in conversations and language play, and consciously promoted language development. Even without this background, children still bring a wealth of knowledge about language to the learning-to-read process.

As children start to learn to read and write (and as adults continue to engage in literacy activities), they bring a wealth of experiences along with cueing systems that help them become literate.

Schemata

Children bring rich schemata to the process of learning to read. The term *schemata* (the plural of *schema*) refers to the way in which humans organize and store information. A schema is an organized plan or conceptual system for arranging knowledge. Based on their experiences, children acquire knowledge and build concepts that support their learning to read. Consider, for example, children who read the sentence *As the birthday boy blew out the candles on the cake, his friends sang* _____ _____ . Based on the schemata children have constructed from their experiences with birthday parties, they can easily fill in the words "*Happy Birthday.*" They can anticipate what the words should be based on the alignment between the text and their schemata.

Children use their background knowledge in learning to read. The richer the set of experiences that children bring to the printed page, the better will be their chances of building meaning from print. Children who have visited a farm and whose background includes "farm words" will be quicker to recognize these words as they are learning to read. Children whose experiences have been less conventionally tied to curriculum-related topics will use their backgrounds as well, as long as the reading material is tied to their prior knowledge and schemata. No child begins to learn to read as a *tabula rasa.*

Cueing Systems

In addition to their schemata, children bring three cueing systems to the job of learning to read: a semantic, a syntactic, and a phonographic (or graphophonic) cueing system. Phonics is the essential element in this third (phonographic) system, but children use all three cueing systems as they construct meaning from print.

Semantics is the study of meaning in language. Children's semantic cueing system includes all the words they know. Vocabulary growth is rapid in the early years of a child's life. It is reasonable to assume that children have acquired a listening/speaking vocabulary of 5,000 or more words by the time formal reading instruction begins. As children sound out words in learning to read, they draw on this language background to provide semantic cues that enable them to attach meaning to the words they encounter in print.

Syntax is the basic structure of language, the way in which words are arranged to convey larger meaning. Syntax deals with how sentences are formed and the grammatical rules that govern sentence formation. As part of the language acquisition process, children learn the structure or grammar of their language. When they come to school, children can't tell the difference between an adjective and an aardvark, nor do they know how to figure out if a noun is the subject or the object in a sentence. But barring any serious language impairment, they do know enough about the syntax of their language to arrange words in sentences such as *I want a cookie.* and not *Cookie want I a;* and they know that the sentence *John ate the fish.* has a very different meaning than *The fish ate John.* Later in their educational careers, they may encounter "formal grammar" and grapple with topics like gerunds and participles and how to diagram a sentence. But at the beginning stage, children bring their basic knowledge of grammar to the process of learning to read and apply syntactic cues in getting meaning from print.

Phonographic (or graphophonic), as the name suggests, refers to the sound-symbol system of our language. Here's where phonics becomes essential in learning to read. Most children come to school with the "phono" part of the phonographic cueing system intact. In other words, they can pronounce most, if not all, the phonemes in their sound system. Phonics involves learning the corresponding symbols that represent these sounds so that children can draw upon these sound-symbol cues as they engage in reading meaningful text.

This, then, is the place of phonics in learning to read. Phonics is not an end in itself; it is a means to an end. Even the National Reading Panel—whose work unequivocally supports direct, explicit, systematic phonics instruction—sounds a note of caution about giving a blanket endorsement to all kinds of phonics instruction. "Programs that focus too much on teaching letter-sound relationships and not enough on putting this to use (in reading and writing) are unlikely to be very effective" (National Reading Panel 2000a, 10). Phonics is necessary, but it is not the only thing that children need to become literate. It needs to be an essential part of a comprehensive reading program in the elementary grades.

Conclusion

The headline in the newspaper on the rack at the local convenience store screamed, IS PHONICS A "FAR-RIGHT" CONSPIRACY? The story in the newspaper was written in response to a claim that promoting phonics was a right-wing conservative plot to keep children from thinking for themselves by promoting "docility and obedience on the part of the lower classes in order to maintain a socioeconomic status quo."

Stories like these, which abound in the popular press and on the Internet, make phonics a religious and political issue rather than an educational one. Phonics has appeared prominently in political ads on television and as an issue in local and national political campaigns. Phonics is not about religion or politics, however; it's about teaching children how to read and write.

Literacy is a goal in any civilized society and an increasingly important competency in today's complex world. In any literate society, people constantly seek the best way to teach children how to read and write so that the younger generation can become fully functioning members of that society. In schools, reading and writing constitute two-thirds of the 3 R's.

Literacy is at the heart of the curriculum during the early grades, and it remains important to learning throughout children's school careers. Overall school effectiveness is often judged in terms of how well children perform on reading tests.

Over the years, different approaches and philosophies have come and gone, but phonics has always remained part of the mix. It's interesting to consider the debate about phonics in a historical context. Many of the arguments related to phonics today are the same arguments that have been advanced for hundreds of years. And many of the techniques suggested for today's classrooms are the same ones that were used centuries ago. Given the ebb and flow of educational ideas, it is likely that these arguments will continue into the future.

The secret to successful reading instruction continues to remain with the teacher. "If we have learned anything from this effort, it is that effective teachers are able to craft a special mix of instructional ingredients for every child they work with" (Snow, Burns, and Griffin 1998, 2). And phonics is certainly one of these essential instructional ingredients in comprehensive reading instruction.

References

Adams, M. J. 1990. *Beginning To Read: Thinking and Learning About Print*. Cambridge, MA: The MIT Press.

————, R. L. Allington, et al. 1991. Beginning to read: A critique by literacy professionals and a response by Marilyn Jager Adams. *The Reading Teacher* 44:370–95.

Allington, R. L., and H. Woodside-Jiron. 199. The politics of literacy teaching: How research "shaped" educational policy. *Educational Researcher* 28: 4–13.

Anderson, R. ., E. H. Hiebert, J. A. Scott, and I. A. G. Wilkinson. 1985. *Becoming A Nation of Readers: The Report of the Commission on Reading*. Washington, DC: National Institute of Education, U.S. Department of Education.

Armbruster, B., F. Lehr, and J. Osborn. 2001. *Put Reading First: The Research Building Blocks for Teaching Children to Read*. Jessup, MD: National Institute for Literacy.

Bauman, J. F., J. V. Hoffman, J. Moon, and A. M. Duffy-Hester. 1998. What are the teachers' voices in the phonics/whole language debate? Results from a survey of U. S. elementary classroom teachers. *The Reading Teacher* 51:636–50.

Berliner, B., and D. Biddle. 1995. *The Manufactured Crisis: Myths, Fraud, and the Attack on America's Public Schools*. Reading, MA: Addison-Wesley.

Bloomfield, L., and C. L. Barnhart. 1961. *Let's Read: A Linguistic Approach*. Cambridge, MA: Educators Publishing Service.

Bracey, G. 1997. *Setting the Record Straight: Responses to Misconceptions About Public Education in the United States*. Alexandria, VA: Association for Supervision and Curriculum Development.

Cambourne, B. 1988. *The Whole Story: Natural Learning and the Acquisition in the Classroom*. New York: Ashton-Scholastic.

Carbo, M. 1988. Debunking the great phonics myth. *Phi Delta Kappan* 70:226–40.

————. 1989. An evaluation of Jeanne Chall's response to "Debunking the great phonics myth." *Phi Delta Kappan* 70:152–7.

Cassidy, J., and D. Cassidy. 2002/3. What is hot, what is not for 2003. *Reading Today*. December 2002/January 2003.

Chall, J. 1996. *Learning To Read: The Great Debate*. 3d ed. San Diego: Harcourt Brace.

————. 1998a. Learning to read: The great debate 20 years later—A response to "Debunking the great phonics myth." *Phi Delta Kappan* 70:521–38.

————. 1998b. The uses of educational research: Comments on Carbo. *Phi Delta Kappan* 71:158–60.

————, and H. M. Popp. 1996. *Teaching and Assessing Phonics: Why, What, When, How; A Guide for Teachers*. Cambridge, MA: Educators Publishing Service.

Coyne, M. D., E. J. Kame'enui, and D. C. Simmons. 2001. Prevention and intervention in beginning reading: Two complex systems. *Learning Disabilities Research and Practice* 16:63–73.

Cunningham, J. 2001. Essay Book Reviews: The National Reading Panel Report. *Reading Research Quarterly* 36: 326–355.

Dressman, M. 1999. On the use and misuse of research evidence: Decoding two states' reading initiative. *Reading Research Quarterly* 34: 258–285.

Emans, R. 1968. The history of phonics. *Elementary English* 45:602–8.

Flesch, R. 1955. *Why Johnny Can't Read—And What You Can Do About It*. New York: Harper & Brothers.

Fries, C. C. 1962. *Linguistics and Reading*. New York: Holt.

Garan, E. M. 2001. Beyond the smoke and mirrors: A critique of the National Reading Report on Phonics. *Phi Delta Kappan* 82:500–506.

————. 2002. *Resisting Reading Mandates: How to Triumph with the Truth*. Portsmouth, NH: Heinemann.

Goodman, K. 1988. *What's Whole in Whole Language?* Richmond Hill, Ont: Scholastic-TAB.

Hoffman, J. V., et al. 1994. So what's new in the new basals?: A focus on first grade. *Journal of Reading Behavior* 26:47–73.

Kismaric, C., and M. Heiferman. 1996. *Growing Up with Dick and Jane*. San Francisco: CollinsPublishers.

Lyon, R. 1997. Testimony of G. Reid Lyon, Ph.D. on Children's Literacy. Washington, DC: National

Institute of Child Health and Human Development.

Mathews, M. M. 1966. *Teaching to Read: Historically Considered*. Chicago: University of Chicago Press.

McCracken, G., and C. C. Walcutt. 1963. *Book A: Basic Reading*. Philadelphia: J. B. Lippincott Co.

McQuillan, J. 1998. *The Literacy Crisis: False Claims, Real Solutions*. Portsmouth, NH: Heinemann.

Mills, H., T. O'Keefe, and D. Stephens. 1992. *Looking Closely: Exploring the Role of Phonics in One Whole Language Classroom*. Urbana, IL: National Council of Teachers of English.

National Reading Panel. 2000. *Teaching children to read: An evidence-based assessment of the scientific research literature on reading and its implications for reading instruction*. Washington, DC: National Institute of Child Health and Human Development.

National Reading Panel. 2000a. *Teaching children to read: An evidence-based assessment of the scientific research literature on reading and its implications for reading instruction: Reports of the subgroups*. Washington, DC: National Institute of Child Health and Human Development.

O'Donnell, M. P. 2001. Do Intensive Phonics Programs Help Struggling Readers? *The New England Reading Association Journal* 37:4–10.

Otto, W., et al. 1966. *Catch On: The Merrill Linguistic Reading Program*. Columbus: Merrill.

Rankin-Erickson, J. L., and M. Presley. 2000. A survey of instructional practices of special education teachers nominated as effective teachers of literacy. *Learning Disabilities Research and Practice* 15:206–225.

Routman, R. 1996. *Lit¬eracy at the Crossroads: Critical Talk about Reading, Writing and Other Teaching Dilemmas*. Portsmouth, NH: Heinemann.

Smith, F. 1985. *Reading Without Nonsense*. 2d ed. New York: Teachers College Press.

———. 1988. *Understanding Reading: A Psycholinguistic Analysis of Reading and Learning to Read*. 4th ed. Hillsdale, NJ: Lawrence Erlbaum Associates.

———. 1999. Why systematic phonics and phonemic awareness instruction constitute an educational hazard. *Language Arts* 77: 150–5.

Smith, N. B. 1965. *American Reading Instruction*. Newark, DE: International Reading Association.

Snow, C. E., M. S. Burns, and P. Griffin. 1998. *Preventing Reading Difficulties in Young Children*. Washington, DC: National Academy Press.

Stahl, S. A., J. Osborn, and F. Lehr. 1990. *"Beginning to Read: Thinking and Learning About Print" by Marilyn Jager Adams: A Summary Prepared by Steven A. Stahl, Jean Osborn, and Fran Lehr*. Urbana, IL: Center for the Study of Reading, University of Illinois at Champaign-Urbana.

Strickland, D. 1995. Whole language. In *The Literacy Dictionary*, edited by T. L. Harris and R. E. Hodges. Newark, DE: International Reading Association.

Taylor, D. 1999. Beginning to read and the spin doctors of science: An excerpt. *Language Arts* 76:217–31.

Venetsky, R. L. 1987. A history of the American reading textbook. *The Elementary School Journal* 87:247–65.

Yatvin, J. 2002. Babes in the woods: The wanderings of the National Reading Panel. *Phi Delta Kappan* 83:364–369.

Getting Started: Phonemic Awareness and Alphabet Knowledge

2

Phonics involves study of the relationship between phonemes and graphemes in our language. Most children use the phonemes and encounter the graphemes long before they experience any phonics instruction in the classroom. This chapter

▼ examines phonemic awareness and its importance in beginning reading

▼ examines alphabet training designed to familiarize children with letter names and sounds

▼ suggests techniques to promote these important aspects of early learning for young children.

Children's early development in phonics comes through phonemic awareness and alphabet knowledge, two factors that have proven to be the best predictors of success in learning to read. Phonemic awareness involves the ability to recognize and manipulate the basic sounds that make up spoken words. Alphabet knowledge involves knowing letter names and later, letter sounds, which merges into formal phonics instruction. Children's developing awareness of the sounds and symbols of their language is also manifested through invented spelling (see chapter 5) in their early attempts at independent writing.

Phonemic Awareness

Phonemes are the basic units of speech. They are the minimal, indivisible units that constitute the "atoms" of spoken words. Being cognizant of these basic units in spoken words is what phonemic awareness is all about.

Phonemic awareness is the understanding that spoken words and syllables are made up of sequences of basic discrete speech sounds and the ability to hear, identify, and manipulate these sounds. While it has been defined and described in various ways by different experts (Sulzby and Teale 1991; Stanovich 1994; Williams 1995; California Department of Education 1996; Snow, Burns and Griffin 1998; Yopp and Yopp 2000), phonemic awareness essentially involves knowledge of basic sounds in words and the ability to manipulate these sounds in different ways. Torgesen and Mathes (2000) define it in this way: ". . . sensitivity to, or awareness of, the phonological structure of words in one's language. In short, it involves the ability to notice, think about, or manipulate the individual sounds in words" (2).

Phonemic awareness involves more than the ability to hear or produce phonemes in spoken words; rather, it involves conscious attention to the sounds that make up words, as distinct from the meaning of these words. Phonemic awareness helps children become more aware of how language works. While it is not important in learning how to speak, phonemic awareness is important in learning how to read. "Speakers and listeners don't need conscious awareness of phonemes; beginning readers and spellers do" (Richgels 2001, 274).

Although the terms are often used interchangeably, phonological awareness and phonemic awareness are not the same. The former is a general term that refers to all sound features in spoken language; the latter is focused specifically on phonemes, the basic units of meaningful speech sounds. Nor is phonemic awareness synonymous with phonics. The former involves the recognition of sounds; the latter involves written symbols. Phonics deals with connecting sounds to written symbols in decoding and encoding written language. Children do not need to know the letters of the alphabet in order to engage in phonemic awareness activities, although teachers often integrate both aspects of early reading instruction, since instruction in phonemic awareness is more effective when children are taught to manipulate phonemes while using letters. "Research findings suggest that phoneme awareness training coupled with grapheme-phoneme correspondence instruction affords greater treatment effects in reading than phonemic awareness training alone" (Troia, Roth, and Graham 1998, 8).

Phonemic awareness is a relatively new area of reading research and instruction. For a long time, literacy educators took it for granted that if children were able to produce oral language, they were aware of the sounds in spoken words. Awareness of sounds in words may be automatic for some children, but most need to be helped in acquiring an understanding of how sounds come together to make words.

In spoken language, sounds blend together in what the ancient Greeks called "a river of sound." As children acquire language, they combine series of random sounds until they learn to combine tiny segments of sound into combinations that produce meaning. Children learn, for example, that when they combine /m/ and /a/, the combination names someone precious to them. Combining these sounds typically produces a very positive response or reaction from important adults in the child's environment, and children learn to repeat these meaningful sound combinations. As they continue to learn to talk, children's "river of language" flows without much attention to the separate sound segments that make up words. The sounds they make are acoustically invisible from one another. Children learn to run sounds together without being aware of the individual elements that make up the words they speak.

While children string sequences of sounds together to form words, awareness of the segments that make up these words is not automatic. "In conventional phonics programs, such an awareness (of the phonemic compositions of words) was generally taken for granted, and therein lies the force of the research on phonemic awareness" (Snow, Burns and Griffin 1998, 55).

Phonemic awareness is part of metalinguistic knowledge involved in emergent literacy. Metalinguistic awareness is defined as "a conscious awareness on the part of a language user of language as an object in itself" (Harris and Hodges 1995, 153). It involves the ability to reflect on, and talk about, language concepts. Through early encounters with books, children acquire concepts of print. They develop an understanding of what print is, how it's related to speech, the directionality of written language, the relationship between speech and writing, and other components about how language works. This knowledge is typically developed through shared reading lessons, language experience stories, and other reading-writing activities that are typically part of early childhood learning environments. While much of this metalinguistic knowledge extends beyond phonemic awareness, knowledge of sounds in words is certainly part of metalinguistics.

The Importance of Phonemic Awareness

Why is phonemic awareness important in the process of teaching children to read and write? For starters, it forms the foundation of phonics instruction that helps children acquire skill in rapid and accurate decoding. Without phonemic awareness, phonics instruction doesn't make much sense, since children who lack phonemic awareness have difficulty linking speech sounds to letters. "In speech production there is no clear distinction between phonemes, because one phoneme overlaps another. But phonemic awareness is necessary in learning to decode an alphabetic language, as print decoding depends on mapping phonemes to graphemes" (Juel 1988, 437). Torgesen and Mathes (2000) give these reasons why phonemic awareness is important in learning to read: (1) "It helps children understand the alphabetic principle," how the words that they speak are represented in print; (2) "It helps children notice the regular ways that letters represent sounds in words," to match letters to sounds in decoding words; and (3) "It makes it possible to generate possibilities for words in context that are only partially sounded out;" i.e., it gives children clues in decoding unfamiliar words. (4–5)

Research on phonemic awareness and its importance in beginning reading is very impressive regarding the strong correlation between phonemic awareness and literacy learning (Sulzby and Teale 1991; Adams 1990; National Reading Panel 2000). Research summaries related to phonemic awareness report that phonemic awareness is more highly related to learning to read, a better predictor of reading success, than such factors as general intelligence, reading readiness, and listening comprehension. "A child's level of phonemic awareness on entering school is widely held to be the strongest single determinant of the success that she or he will experience in learning to read—or conversely, the likelihood that she or he will fail" (Adams et al. 1998, 2). The ability to perform phonemic awareness tasks is "the best predictor of ease of early reading acquisition—better than anything else that we know of, including IQ" (Stanovich 1994, 284).

Lack of phonemic awareness is a serious impairment in learning to read. Phonemic awareness is one of the primary factors separating normal and disabled readers. Given the strong relationship between phonemic awareness and reading success, it stands to reason that lack of phonemic awareness is a stumbling block in beginning reading and that phonemic awareness is one of the primary factors separating normal and disabled readers. "Twenty years of research has consistently demonstrated that many beginning readers, and nearly all reading-disabled children, have difficulty on phonological awareness tasks" (Moats 1994, 83). Children who enter first grade with little phonemic awareness are at a greater risk of failure.

A child's level of phonemic awareness entering first grade is more important in predicting reading success than the type of instruction (that is, traditional skills-based or more holistic approaches) that the child receives. Because of the orthographic nature of English, children's ability to recognize and manipulate sounds is essential in any approach or model of reading instruction used in the classroom. Phonemic awareness is important in learning to spell and write as well (Juel 1988; Orton 2000).

Developing Components of Phonemic Awareness

Phonemic awareness is not a unitary, singular entity or ability. It develops gradually over the preschool years, but it's not a skill that children develop spontaneously. It involves a variety of tasks that range from the ability to identify rhyming words to the ability to decompose syllables and reconstruct them to form new words. It involves tasks that are appropriate to preschoolers and those that are developmentally appropriate for the end of first grade.

In the practical world of the early childhood classroom, children can develop phonemic awareness through direct and explicit instructional activities, through incidental or informal occasions that arise many times as part of the normal routine of classroom events, and through literature-based activities. Occasions for all three types of activities occur all the time in the language-rich environment of the early childhood educational setting.

Direct activities involve specific instruction that are used to develop phonemic awareness. Children are instructed to count the number of syllables in the word *computer,* to identify the initial sound of the word *desk,* to tell which word rhymes with *book,* to determine what word is created when the sound /b/ is dropped from *beat,* and to tell what word is made up of the sounds /p/ /e/ and /n/. These direct instructional activities involve the manipulation of sounds in words and focus specifically on components of phonemic awareness that have been shown to be important in learning to read.

Incidental occasions arise all day long for informal instruction and practice in phonemic awareness within the context of language play and other oral language activities. As morning messages are dictated and transcribed, the teacher calls attention to how many syllables are in the word *Monday*. As children line up to go to the playground, the teacher says, "The line leader today will be /j/ /a/ /n/ " (Jan), or "The first children in line will be the two boys whose names rhyme with 'rim' " (Jim and Tim). These are all incidental occasions in which opportunities for phonemic awareness are embedded, as the teacher calls attention to the sound elements in the normal course of the school day.

In planning phonemic awareness activities, Torgesen and Mathes (2000) suggest the following eight guidelines: (1) instruction should begin with easier tasks and move to tasks that are more difficult; (2) instruction in phonemic awareness should be a regular part of the curriculum; (3) teachers should expect that children will respond at widely varying rates to instruction in phonemic awareness; (4) instruction in phonological awareness should involve both *analytic* and *synthetic* activities; (5) because the first goal of instruction in phonological awareness is to help children notice the individual sounds in words, teachers should speak slowly and carefully and should pronounce individual sounds correctly; (6) it is not easy to pronounce individual phonemes correctly without some careful practice; (7) methods to stimulate phonemic awareness in students are limited only by the creativity of teachers; and (8) instruction in phonological awareness should be fun for teachers and students (45–48). In describing what phonemic awareness instruction should look like in the classroom, Yopp and Yopp (2000) suggest that it should be developmentally appropriate, that it should be deliberate and purposeful, and that it be only part of a broader literacy program carried on in a language- and literature-rich environment.

Children's literature can be effectively integrated and balanced with phonemic awareness activities. "Many children's books emphasize speech sounds through rhyme, alliteration, assonance, phoneme substitution, or segmentation and offer play with language as a dominant feature" (Yopp 1995a, 27). Books for young children that focus on language play—books such as Dr. Seuss' popular *Green Eggs and Ham*, Deborah Guarino's *Is Your Mama A Llama*, or classics like *Henny Penny* retold by Paul Galdone and other authors—are ideal vehicles for helping children attend to the sounds of their language as they enjoy stories. These books contain elements of rhyme, alliteration, and sound substitution. Since language play is an explicit feature of the text, these stories require that children pay attention to the sounds of their language. Besides, they're great fun! Prekindergarten, kindergarten, and first grade children delight in listening to stories and in repeating the lines over and over. Lists of books that lend themselves especially well to phonemic awareness have been suggested by Yopp (1995b), Opitz (1998), and Bishop et al. (2000). Opitz also suggests outreach activities to help parents learn to use these books at home.

The components of phonemic awareness include

- rhyming, the ability both to recognize and to produce words that rhyme;
- segmentation, the ability to break words into their component phonological parts;

- isolation, the ability to identify individual sounds within words;
- deletion, the ability to delete phonetic elements from spoken words;
- substitution, the ability to create a new word by replacing one phoneme for another;
- blending, the ability to identify a word on the basis of hearing the discrete phonemes that constitute the word.

Each of these components can be part of incidental and direct instructional activities in a balanced literacy program in the early grades. Instruction in phonemic awareness is most effective when it focuses on one or two components at once rather than on several types at the same time. Also, "instruction should proceed in a logical sequence of activities that require increasingly sophisticated metaphonological skills. . . . For example, it has been demonstrated with relative consistency that certain metaphonological skills seem to be easier than others and thus emerge earlier in a child's development. Specifically, rhyming is less difficult than sound blending, which is easier than sound segmentation, which is simpler than phone deletion" (Troia, Roth, and Graham 1998, 5).

Rhyming

Rhyming, comparing and contrasting sounds, is perhaps the most essential aspect of phonemic awareness. Anyone who has listened to young children on the playground is well aware of children's propensity to build like-sounding versions (often with no meaning) based on playmates' names or other words. While it may be the easiest of all phonemic awareness tasks, rhyming does require a level of abstraction in approaching sounds in words. "In order to tell whether the words *man* and *ran* rhyme, the child must be able to abstract *an* from both words, compare them, and note that they are the same" (Gunning 2000, 3).

Phonemic awareness involves both the recognition and production of rhyming words.

Recognition of rhyming words is a focus that can begin early as children recognize words that rhyme and those that don't. Children continually delight in the element of rhyme as they experience *Mother Goose* and other simple verses in the early years. In fact, children often acquire the concept of rhyme from these poems.

Teaching Suggestions ▼

Recognizing Rhyming Words
Matching   With a stack of pictures, the teacher asks children to indicate rhyming words: "Show me a picture that rhymes with *big*."

Recognizing Rhyming Words, continued

Minimal Pairs

The teacher says pairs of words and asks children to indicate if they rhyme:

bat-cat   cup-book   mouse-house

Children respond with a "Yes" or "No," by holding up Y/N cards, or by giving the Thumbs Up/Thumbs Down signal.

Categorizing Words

The teacher says three words, two of which rhyme, and children indicate which one doesn't belong:

bat-cat-sit   book-ball-look   mouse-door-house

Again, children respond with a "Yes" or "No," by holding up 1/2/3 cards, or with Thumbs Up/Down.

SIT DOWN!

Teachers assign three words, two of which rhyme, to children. Children say their words in order (or the teacher says the child's word while placing her hand on the child's head), and when the non-rhyming word is spoken, the entire class yells "SIT DOWN!"

Rhyming Chairs

As a variation of the old party game Musical Chairs, chairs are placed in a circle. The teacher says a series of words with changing rhyming patterns as children walk about the circled chairs, for example, *pin, bin, thin—book, look, took, shook—rat, bat, cat, that, fat—rope, hope, dope, slope.* Each time the teacher changes the rhyming pattern, children scramble for chairs or change direction.

Rhyming Pictures

Children can draw pictures or find pictures in magazines of objects whose names rhyme—*king, ring, swing*, for example, or *boat, coat, goat*—and match these pictures. Cards can be distributed and children can find their "partner words." (These picture cards can be used repeatedly for other phonemic awareness activities.)

Production of rhyming elements is a second level in rhyming practice. Recognizing that **bat** rhymes with **mat** is one level; producing a word that rhymes with **bat** is another level.

Nursery rhymes are important devices for rhyming practice. In addition to the pure joy involved in sharing nursery rhymes, rudiments of phonemic awareness may be seeded in children's knowing these rhymes. And what preschool or kindergarten program does not include *Mother Goose* as part of children's language experiences?

Teaching Suggestions ▼

Production of Rhyming Words

Toss the Ball

Children sit in a circle with a large rubber ball or a beanbag. One child says a word, such as *game*. He/she rolls the ball or tosses the beanbag to another child, who must then say a word that rhymes—*name, tame, same,* and so on.

Animal Sounds

Children enjoy imitating animal sounds. The teacher (or one of the children) can make up silly riddles involving words that rhyme with animal sounds, for example:

"I'm thinking of a word that rhymes with the sound a cow makes." (*boo, shoe, new*)

"I'm thinking of a word that rhymes with the sound a dog makes." (*now, cow, how*)

Children can supply either real words or nonsense words, as long as they rhyme.

Fill in the Rhyme

The teacher reads the lines of a popular *Mother Goose* rhyme aloud, pausing before the rhyming words:

> *Humpty Dumpty sat on the wall;*
> *Humpty Dumpty had a great* (pause)

or

> *To market, to market, to buy a fat pig,*
> *Home again, home again, jiggedy* (pause)

Children supply the end-line rhyme.

Alternative Rhymes

Teachers read a popular nursery rhyme and invite children to substitute alternative rhyming words at the end of lines:

> *Hickory, dickory, dock,*
> *The mouse ran up the* _____ (rock, sock, block, and so on)

or

> *Jack and Jill*
> *Went up the* _____ (bill, fill, pill, and so on)

The words that children suggest should make sense in context.

Original Verse

It's not a giant step from having children supply rhyming words in *Mother Goose* to having them supply rhyming words for their own simple verses. The teacher can begin by providing a stem on which to build:

> *I looked up into the air*
> *And I could see a* _____.

or

> *I went to the park to play*
> *And there I saw* _____.

Again, children suggest their own end-line rhyming words.

Production of Rhyming Words, continued

Adding Rhythm

While the focus in language activities like these is on rhyme, another important feature of poetry—rhythm—often creeps in. In the first preceding couplet, while some children will add single rhyming words like *chair, bear,* and *hair,* others will add a rhythmic pattern consistent with the first line—*an easy chair, a dancing bear,* or *a star up there.* (Of course, others will suggest a word like *rabbit,* which indicates the need for lots more practice in rhyming words as part of phonemic awareness!)

Who Said That?

The children's trade book *I Can't, Said the Ant* by Polly Cameron (Scholastic, 1961) is an ideal jumping-off point for a rhyming activity. When the teapot breaks, all the other objects in the kitchen comment upon it—*"What's the clatter?" asked the platter. "Teapot fell," said the dinner bell.* After reading this book aloud, the teacher can suggest another setting for the use of rhyming words, using the model language in the book. For example:

Playground   *"Look at me," said the* (tree).
                       "Can you sing?" asked the (swing).

School   *"Can you cook?" asked the* (book).
                       "That dog's a barker," yelled the (marker).

A wealth of other children's trade books can be used for similar phonemic awareness activities.

Mother Goose is part of children's literary legacy and these poems continue to constitute a staple in the literacy diet of most early childhood settings. While they can be used effectively for the development of phonemic awareness, the instructional focus should never overpower the sheer enjoyment of encounters with *Mother Goose,* Jack Prelutsky's work such as *Poems of A. Nonny Mouse* and *The Baby Uggs are Hatching,* and other simple forms of poetry in the early years.

Children's literature provides a treasure trove of material for focusing on both the recognition and the production of rhyme. Children can focus on rhyming words as teachers share books like:

- *Brown Bear, Brown Bear, What Do You See?* by Bill Martin, Jr, illustrated by Eric Carle, a book that is hugely popular with young children. (This author/illustrator team also collaborated on *Polar Bear, Polar Bear, What Do You Hear?*);
- *The Fat Cat Sat on the Mat* by Nurit Karlin, a simple "I Can Read" story loaded with rhyming words;
- *Silly Sally* by Audrey Wood, a story that young children love about a girl who walks backwards on her hands;
- *Louella Mae, She's Run Away* by Karen Beaumont Alarian, illustrated by Rosanne Litzinger, a book in which children need to turn the page to find the rhyming words.

Traditional folk literature is also full of rhymes that are repeated as part of the story

> *Run, run, run as fast as you can,*
> *You can't catch me, I'm the Gingerbread man.*

and

> *Little pig, little pig, let me come in.*
> *Not by the hair of my chinny chin chin.*

And consider the rhyming elements in the names of the friends in the popular *Henny Penny* (Cocky Locky, Ducky Lucky, Goosey Loosey, Turkey Lurkey, Foxy Loxy).

In short, teachers rarely have to look beyond the classroom bookshelf to find material that can be effectively used to help children recognize and produce rhymes as part of instruction in phonemic awareness.

Segmentation

Segmentation involves breaking words into their component phonological parts. It requires an awareness of sound elements and the ability to recognize these sound elements in spoken language. Segmentation includes identifying independent elements in compound words, syllables in longer words, onsets and rimes, and phonemes in monosyllabic words.

Compound words are not difficult to segment, because they consist of two independent parts or free morphemes that children can often identify as meaningful units. (The nature of the relationship between the two parts is interesting; a *snowman* is a man made out of snow, but a *fireman* is not made out of fire. But that's the subject of a discussion other than one on phonemic awareness.) Obviously, it's important for children to understand the concept of a compound word before these are used in phonemic awareness activities.

Teaching Suggestions ▼

Segmenting of Compound Words

Clap Your Hands

The teacher says the first part of a compound word, followed by the second part about a half a second later: *I'm going to say some compound words. Clap one time for each little word you hear in each compound word:*

toothbrush   baseball   bathroom   bedroom

Children clap for each of the independent parts they hear in the word.

Breaking Compound Words Apart

To see how compound words can be broken into two independent units, children can use two pieces of Legos or other interlocking plastic or wooden blocks. Each child is given two interlocking pieces of contrasting colors. Using familiar compound words, the teacher can demonstrate how the blocks break apart as she says the two parts of the word—*sun/set, meat/loaf.* Children break their pieces apart as the teacher says other compound words.

These interlocking blocks can also be used as children break words into syllables and/or identify phonemes in words. Also, children can join the pieces together in activities involving blending word parts.

Words for Practice: Compound Words

Here's a list of compound words that may be useful for practice:

classroom	popcorn	toothbrush	fireworks
snowball	hallway	newspaper	earthquake
outside	football	mailbox	fireplace
airplane	driveway	sailboat	cupcake
flashlight	goldfish	playground	backpack

Segmentation also involves identifying the number of syllables in a word. Syllables are clusters of vowel and consonant sounds in words. Counting syllables has long been part of phonetic training for young children. The ability to break a word into syllables as part of word analysis gives children "bite sized portions" as they try to derive the pronunciation of unfamiliar words in print. Since the concept of syllable may be foreign to young children at first, Cunningham (2000) suggests referring to syllables as "beats"; using words for common classroom objects, *desk* is a "one beat" word, *table* is a "two beat" word, and *projector* is a "three beat" word.

Teaching Suggestions ▼

Segmenting of Syllables

Touch Your Chin

Clapping is the response technique that has long been used in having children identify the number of syllables in words. Holding their hands under their chins is a "quieter" way of helping children respond to the number of syllables in words. Children gently place their fingertips on their chin and count the movements as they pronounce words. (Since all syllables have a vowel sound and since the mouth has to open to let the vowel sound escape, each syllable will produce a chin movement.)

How Many Syllables in Your Name?

Children often enjoy counting syllables in their own names. *John* is a one-syllable name; *Jamal* a two-syllable name; *Marianne* a three-syllable name; *Alejandra* a four-syllable name. In addition to counting syllables in their own names, they can count syllables in the names of characters from stories they have heard—for example, Rudyard Kipling's Rikki, Tikki, Tavi (6), Mem Fox's

Segmenting of Syllables, continued

Wilfred Gordon McDavid Patridge (9) or Arline Mosel's Tikki Tikki Tembo No Sa Rembo Chari Bari Rucki Pip Perry Pembo (21). First and last names of students can be combined for a total "name syllable count." To extend into math, the teacher can make a chart showing the number of children whose names have the same number of syllables.

Number Boards

Each child has a board with the numbers 1 2 3 4. Children place markers on the board to indicate the number of syllables they hear in a word. The markers can be round plastic disks, small oaktag squares, or small toy figures. Using snack foods like raisins, peanuts, M&M candies, or Goldfish crackers makes clean-up a lot easier!

Giant Steps

Children line up and take "giant steps" for each syllable they hear in a word. The children can count the number of steps it takes to cross the room or estimate how many syllable-steps it will take to walk down the corridor. (The word *supercalafragilisticexpialadocious* from the film *Mary Poppins* helps them cover distances very quickly.)

Words for Practice: Multisyllabic Words

Here's a list of multisyllabic words that may be useful for practice:

2-Syllable Words	3-Syllable Words	4-Syllable Words	5-Syllable Words
teacher	potato	television	refrigerator
pencil	principal	alligator	congratulations
table	telephone	information	international
Monday	alphabet	supermarket	cafeteria
sister	syllable	America	elementary
children	Saturday	January	anniversary
purple	animal	interesting	disagreeable
April	electric	disagreement	imagination
fifteen	dinosaur	understanding	indestructible
circle	hospital	calculator	operational

At the phoneme level, segmentation involves identifying the individual speech sounds that make up a word. As the teacher pronounces a word, the children identify discrete phonemes in that word. At the beginning stages, rather than starting with individual phonemes, it is easier for children to segment onsets and rimes—to separate *b* from *-at* in *bat* or *r* from *-im* in *rim*—because children grasp control over larger units of sound before smaller ones. As children progress to segmenting individual phonemes, it is a good idea to use words that have a consistent consonant-vowel-consonant pattern (words like *cat, pet, rim, hot,* and *tug*) in which the vowel sound is short. It is also wise to use sounds represented by single letters rather than digraphs or blends and to start with consonants that can be "stretched out" when you say the word, like *sssssss-un,* or *llllllll-ip.*

Teaching Suggestions ▼

Segmenting Phonemes

Counting Sounds

The teacher pronounces short familiar words *hit, cap, gum*. Children count the number of phonemes in each word and indicate the number by jumping up and down, touching their toes, or hitting a drum or xylophone for each sound that they identify in the word.

High Five

Children stand back-to-back as the teacher pronounces words. Children hold up fingers to indicate the number of phonemes they hear in each word. At a given signal, they turn and compare their responses. If they both indicate the same number of phonemes, they give each other a "high five." If not, the teacher reviews the number of phonemes in each word.

Sound Squares

Children use pictures of common objects mounted on cards, with connected boxes drawn under each picture according to the number of phonemes in the word. As the teacher slowly pronounces the name of the object in the picture, children move plastic disks or other markers from one box to the other according to the phonemes that they hear in the word.

What's in a Name?

Our names are personally precious to us all. Children identify individual phonemes that make up their own names. Since many children will be learning to write their names, this provides a link with learning sound-symbol correspondences.

Segmenting words into individual phonemes is not always easy for children to do, but focusing on individual sounds in words is an essential component of phonemic awareness. Linking symbols to these individual spoken sounds is essential to later decoding.

Isolation

Isolation involves the ability to identify individual sounds at the beginning, middle, and end of words. It requires children not only to identify which sounds make up words but also to identify where these sounds occur.

Activities involving the isolation of individual speech sounds normally start with beginning phonemes, since the initial sound is usually the one most easy to identify. As with segmentation, it's a good idea to start with words that have the consonant-vowel-consonant pattern, since the initial sound can be easily separated from the rest of the word. It's also wise to start with continuant sounds like /m/ /s/ or /f/ because these sounds can be sustained without distorting them. Starting with sounds like /b/ or /t/ necessitates the addition of a vocalic quality ("buh" or "tuh") to keep the sound going.

Teaching Suggestions ▼

Identifying Beginning Sounds

Secret Sounds

The teacher pronounces a series of four or five words with the same initial sound (*ring, right, rug, rabbit*). Children listen for the initial sound and whisper it to a partner.

I Spy

For identifying initial sounds, children typically enjoy the popular game I Spy. As children look around the classroom (the playground, or other environment in which they find themselves), they can identify objects by their initial sounds:

I spy with my little eye something beginning with /p/.
I spy with my little eye something beginning with /s/.

In playing I Spy, phonemic awareness demands that the focus be on the initial sound, not the letter. Letter identification is certainly appropriate when the game is used for alphabet training, but sound identification is the primary focus of phonemic awareness.

Tongue Twisters

Children and adults have long enjoyed tongue twisters such as "Peter Piper picked a peck of pickled peppers . . ." Children can make up their own alliterative sentences based on initial sounds, perhaps based on their own names: *Sam sipped six sasperilla sodas.* Children might dictate and illustrate these sentences, which can be gathered into a class book.

Final sounds are not as easy to identify as beginning sounds, since ending sounds are not as prominent as initial sounds. Children may need practice with lists of words having similar ending sounds.

Teaching Suggestions ▼

Identifying Ending Sounds

Yum, Yum!

The teacher identifies a food she says she loves, prolonging the final sound, for example, *I love pizzaaaaaaaaaa. I love ice creammmmmmmmm.*

Children identify the final sounds. Children can also take turns identifying foods they love (or don't).

Sounds in a Cup

Each child is given two paper cups, one labeled B for "beginning" and one labeled E for "ending." The teacher says a word, identifies a phoneme, and asks if the sound occurs at the beginning or end of the word; for example, *The word is "big." Do you hear the* /b/ *at the beginning or end of the word?* Children place a plastic disk or other marker in the B or E cup to indicate where they hear the sounds. Once again, snack foods like raisins, peanuts, M&M candies, or Goldfish crackers add another element to the activity.

In one-syllable words, the vowel often occurs as the medial sound. Isolating medial sounds can begin with long vowels, since long vowel sounds tend to be more phonologically prominent. The teacher can begin by reading a list of familiar words with the same long vowel sound, for example, *face, race, cage, grapes, save,* and so on, before moving to words with other medial long vowels. Similar procedures can be followed with lists of short vowel words. With phonemic awareness practice, there's no need to worry about the variant spelling of the sounds, since the focus is on the phonemes, not the graphemes that represent these sounds.

Word List for Identifying Vowel Sounds in Words

The following lists may be useful in the practice of isolating vowel sounds in words:

Short	*a*	*e*	*i*	*o*	*u*
	cab	web	bib	job	cub
	mad	bed	hid	fog	mud
	bag	fed	did	hog	bug
	ham	leg	dig	mom	hug
	fan	hen	pig	hop	gum
	nap	men	dim	pop	fun
	gas	met	pin	cot	cup
	hat	wet	tip	not	bus
	tap	bet	sit	fox	nut
	cat	yes	bit	box	cut

Long	*a*	*e*	*i*	*o*	*u*
	face	feed	mice	robe	cube
	made	niece	hide	rode	tube
	bake	Pete	life	joke	cute
	page	team	bike	hole	rule
	rake	keep	dime	home	June
	sale	theme	pipe	rope	tune
	name	thief	wise	nose	duke
	tape	field	bite	note	fuse
	base	priest	dive	cove	rude
	gate	feat	mile	zone	lube

Medial consonants are not nearly as easy to identify. They usually occur in the middle of two-syllable words (and thus are represented in writing by double letters): *ladder, funny, rabbit, mommy, puppy,* and so on. The focus of these words extends beyond the isolation of sounds in single syllables.

Deletion

Deletion of phonemes and larger word parts indicates a child's awareness of sounds and how they are used to build words. It involves mentally removing part of a word to create another word. The ability to delete one of the independent units in a compound word indicates an awareness of larger word parts. Syllable deletion gives children practice with manipulating units larger than single phonemes and reinforces their auditory awareness of the number of syllables in words. Phoneme deletion begins with onsets and rimes and requires the awareness of precisely how phonemes combine to make words.

Teaching Suggestions ▼

Deleting Sounds in Words

Compound Words

The teacher says a compound word (see p. 35 for list of compound words) and asks children to repeat the word without one of its parts:

*Say **classroom** without the **room**. Say **wallpaper** without the **wall**.*

Children can use the shortened word in a sentence.

Syllables

The teacher says, "I'm going to say some words that have more than one syllable (see p. 36 for list of multisyllable words). Listen carefully, because I want you to repeat each word without one of the syllables. Ready?"

*Say **carpet** without the **car**. Say **umbrella** without the **um**.*

Two-syllable words work best for this activity.

Phonemes

The teacher says, "I'm going to say some words. Listen carefully, because I want you to repeat each word without one of its sounds. Ready?"

*Say **bat** without the /b/.   Say **cheese** without the /ch/.*

It's helpful for teachers to select words that, when one phoneme is deleted, result in a word that is meaningful to the child (even though the spelling doesn't always correspond to the sound switch).

Word List for Phoneme Deletion

The following lists may be useful in the practice of phoneme deletion in creating new words.

Beginning Sounds		Ending Sounds	
	cape—ape		road—row
	fake—ache		toad—toe
	dear—ear		beat—bee
	beat—eat		meal—me
	meal—eel		soap—so
	boat—oat		heat—he
	mate—ate		mate—may
	cart—art		cart—car
	band—and		band—ban

The phonemic manipulation involved in deleting single sounds is not always easy for children. It's important for teachers to model the process so that children can understand what's involved.

Substitution

As part of phonemic awareness, substitution involves changing a word by changing the initial, final, or medial sound to create a new word. The process has been called "syllable splitting." It requires the ability to delete a phoneme and put another in its place, for example, changing /b/ to /r/ to change **bat** to **rat,** or substituting /b/ for /t/ to change **cab** to **cat.** Substitution can be done with initial phonemes, final phonemes, and medial phonemes.

Teaching Suggestions ▼

Phoneme Substitution

Word Magicians

The teacher asks the children to become word magicians by changing sounds in words. The teacher explains that a word magician can change a *cat* into a *rat* by changing the initial /k/ to an /r/, and can change a *cat* into a *cab* by changing the final /t/ to a /b/. The teacher can ask children to become word magicians with the following:

Change the /p/ *in* pan *to an* /f/. *Change the* /h/ *in* hand *into an* /s/. (initial phonemes)
Change the /p/ *in* cup *into a* /b/. *Change the* /t/ *in* net *into a* /k/. (final phonemes)
Change the /i/ *in* disk *into an* /e/. *Change the* /a/ *in* map *into an* /o/. (medial phonemes)

A simple hand puppet can be effectively used in this activity.

"Goofy" Words

Within the context of a classroom activity, substitute initial consonants to make up goofy words; for example, "I'm going to read a rook." or "Please close the boor." Children supply the correct word and make up their own sentences using goofy words by substituting initial consonants.

   A delightful children's trade book that can be used in this type of activity is *The Hungry Thing* by Jan Slepian and Ann Seider. "Feed me!" a creature demands and it requests *shamkakes.* The villagers decide he wants pancakes. The story continues with a series of similar requests for *feetloaf, hookies, gollipops,* and the like. In a subsequent book (*The Hungry Thing Returns*) the creature appears with a small hungry thing on its back and requests food like *flamburgers, bellyjeans, blownuts,* and the like, which the villagers manage to decode. Children delight in the absurdity of the story, along with the sounds of the words. (The books also contain language that focuses on rhyme: *"He's underfed/Have some bread"/Said the lady/dressed in red.*)

As with other aspects of phonemic awareness instruction, sound substitution requires lots of teacher modeling and practice to develop children's competency in this dimension of phonemic awareness.

Blending

Blending is an effective phonics strategy. It is the flip side of segmentation; instead of taking words apart, it involves the ability to identify words by blending individual speech sounds to make words. In blending, children manipulate individual sounds and combine them into words. Like other components of phonemic awareness, blending can be taught directly or incorporated incidentally into an instructional program.

Teaching Suggestions ▼

Blending

Onsets and Rimes

Practice in blending activities should begin with onsets and rimes, since onsets and rimes are natural units in words. The teacher can begin by blending onsets and rimes in familiar words—*c-at, m-ouse, b-oy, g-irl*—and children can identify the words. Children can suggest their own words for onset-rime blending practice. Pictures can be used effectively in this activity.

Secret Words

The teacher tells the class that she is going to say sounds in a word and asks the children to whisper the secret word to their neighbor.

/a/ /t/   (at) /t/ /e/ /n/ (ten)   /l/ /a/ /m/ /p/ (lamp)

The "secret words" can relate to school experiences; for example, *Today we're having* /m/ /i/ /l/ /k/ *with our snacks.* or *In science, we're going to learn more about* /r/ /o/ /k/ /s/ (rocks). Remember, sound elements rather than spelling is the focus of these activities.

I Know a Word

The teacher selects a category (clothing or furniture, for example) and says a word from that category in a segmented fashion, for example, /d/ /r/ /e/ /s/ or /d/ /e/ /s/ /k/ and children identify the words. With enough practice, children can become leaders in this activity.

Robot Talk

When they produce spoken sounds, robots often blend discrete syllables into words. At incidental times in the classroom, the teacher can "talk like a robot" with expressions such as "I want /t/ /o/ /m/ to be at the front of the line," or "I notice that it is /t/ /e/ /n/ o'clock."

Practice in blending should begin with onsets and a rimes. While blending onsets and rimes can be relatively easy, most children find that blending separate phonemes into words is not easy and "it should be undertaken with patience and as much practice as necessary" (Chall and Popp 1996, 69). Nevertheless, it is an essential skill as children progress to sounding out unfamiliar words in reading and in deciding which letters to use in spelling.

By their nature, phonemic awareness activities are oral exercises. While the primary emphasis is on auditory elements, alphabet symbols are often integrated into instructional activities, in part because letters of the alphabet contribute to effectiveness in phonemic awareness activities. Working with letter cards and other alphabet manipulatives provides a visual/kinesthetic dimension to reinforce auditory elements that phonemic awareness entails.

The amount of teaching and practice necessary for developing different aspects of phonemic awareness will differ from child to child. While some children will learn fairly easily, others need many more repetitions and lots of practice. For those children, extra practice and instructional adjustments might include:

- Working exclusively with continuant sounds, sounds that can be prolonged, such as /s/ /l/ and /r/ rather than stop sounds such as /b/ /k/ and /t/. Sounds in words like *Sam* can be stretched out or elongated (*sssss-aaaaa-mmmmm*) and can be more easily perceived;
- Lots of practice with words with fewer rather than more phonemes (words such as *at* or *up*) since words with fewer phonemes can be easier to deal with;
- Multisensory support, using manipulatives like chips, blocks, and other objects that will support learning with visual, tactual, and kinesthetic reinforcement.

Not all children respond as well to phonemic awareness training as others. This is especially true for children from linguistically and culturally diverse backgrounds, children who typically bring a different sound system to the process of learning to read in English. "Although more elaborate, intensive, or prolonged instruction in phonological awareness may help these children, a completely different approach or combination of treatment methods may be necessary" (Troia, Roth, and Graham 1998, 8). Early intervention is essential. Instruction often needs to progress more slowly. The use of multisensory supports like chips and blocks become especially important, including the use of letter symbols to support phonemic elements. Repeated practice is often required.

Instructional Programs for Phonemic Awareness

Most instruction in phonemic awareness will be carried on through activities embedded in spontaneous, authentic encounters with oral language and routine classroom activities. However, formal published programs are available for direct instruction in whole class and small group settings. A sampling of these programs includes:

Phonemic Awareness in Young Children: A Classroom Curriculum, a sequenced program of 51 activities contained in a teacher's manual. The program includes activities that focus on listening games, rhyming activities, syllables, identify and manipulating initial and final sounds in words, phoneme identification, and letters.

> *For More Information:* Brookes Publishing Co., P.O. Box 10624, Baltimore, MD 21285.

The Sounds Abound Program, a program that makes extensive use of singing and musical activities. The kit (which includes a video) has activities for rhyming, syllable awareness, phoneme segmentation, phoneme deletion, phoneme substitution, and phonemic blending. Materials and games are also available.

> *For More Information:* LinguiSystems, Inc., 3100 4th Avenue, E. Moline, IL 61244.

Launch into Reading Success Through Phonological Awareness Training, a program intended for use in small groups of at-risk children. Highly scripted, the program contains instructional activities that range from awareness of whole words to linking phonemes and letters.

> *For More Information:* Pro-ED, Inc., 8700 Shoal Creek Blvd., Austin, TX 78757.

Ladders to Literacy, a program with two activity books (one for preschool and one for kindergarten) with a range of activities related to emergent literacy and a strong focus on phonemic awareness.

> *For More Information:* Brookes Publishing Co., P.O. Box 10624, Baltimore, MD 21285.

Some instructional programs in phonemic awareness for young children are presented as computer programs. Some of these include:

Daisy Quest and Daisy's Castle, programs with engaging graphics and digitized speech that provide instruction and practice in rhyming, identifying phonemes, blending, and sounding sounds. Management features enable the teacher to track activities and report the level of performance for each child.

> *For More Information:* Adventure Learning Software, Inc., 965 North Eastview Dr., Alpine, VT 84004.

Earbonics, a two-level program designed to build listening skills and phonemic awareness. With provisions for both home use and school use, the program has a comprehensive range of activities in a game-like format.

> *For More Information:* Cognitive Concepts, Inc., 207 Hamilton St., Evanston, IL 60202

Read, Write, and Type, a program that links reading and writing. It contains activities that are explicitly designed to stimulate phonemic awareness in children by providing lessons on hearing sounds in words and having children type letters, words, and stories related to the sound.

For More Information: The Learning Company, 6160 Summit Dr. N., Minneapolis, MN 55430.

These are just a few of the formal programs available; more and more programs appear in the marketplace all the time. Instruction in phonemic awareness is not, however, a stand-alone proposition. "Phonemic awareness supports reading development only if it is part of a broader program that includes—among other things—development of students' vocabulary, syntax, comprehension, strategic reading abilities, decoding strategies, and writing across all content areas" (Yopp and Yopp 2000, 142)

The current emphasis on phonemic awareness has not been without its critics. Critical analysis of experimental research studies has raised questions about the link between phonemic awareness and reading success (Taylor 1999). Using the results of research in phonemic awareness to guide instructional practice and educational policy has also been questioned (Dressman 1999). Some experts question the value of phonemic awareness activities such as segmenting sounds in words, believing that "you can no more separate the sounds from a word that has been uttered than you can extract the ingredients from a cake that has been baked" (Smith 1999, 153). Some critics wonder if the relationship between phonemic awareness and reading success is a "chicken and egg" situation; in other words, if phonemic awareness is the consequence of becoming literate rather than the cause of reading success.

Despite these concerns and criticisms, phonemic awareness remains an important part of today's early literacy curriculum, a component that is widely considered essential for early success in reading and spelling.

Assessing Phonemic Awareness

Children's awareness of sounds in spoken language and their ability to manipulate these sounds can be assessed both formally and informally. "The assessment of phonemic awareness typically involves tasks that require the student to isolate or segment one or more of the phonemes of a spoken word, to blend or combine a sequence of separate phonemes into a word, or to manipulate the phonemes within a word (e.g., adding, subtracting, or rearranging phonemes of one word to make a different word)" (Snow, Burns, & Griffin 1998, 51).

Informal assessment is especially important. Most of the norm-referenced and criterion-referenced measures that are available have been developed with—and are designed for use with—kindergarten and school-age children. For younger children, the teacher's professional judgment is an essential component of assessment. Informal assessment can be done with many of the activities suggested for each of the components previously identified: rhyming, segmenting, isolating, deleting, substituting, and blending sounds. As teachers engage in formal and informal activities involving phonemic awareness tasks, they begin to recognize which children "get it" and which need help and additional practice. Diagnostic decisions are combined with instructional activities.

Formal tests are also available to determine children's level of phonemic awareness. Some of these tests are comprehensive measures; for example, *Group Achievement and Diagnostic Evaluation—GRADE* (Circle Pines, MN: American Guidance Service) is a standardized, comprehensive battery that includes measures of phonemic awareness components of blending and sound matching, along with phonics, vocabulary, and text comprehension that readers develop as they mature.

Other formal tests assess particular aspects of phonemic awareness. Tests like the *Phonological Awareness Test* (East Moline, IL: LinguiSystems, Inc.) which has an intermediate grade component for older students in grades 3–9, *Test of Phonological Awareness* (Austin, TX: PRO-ED), the *Comprehensive Test of Phonological Processing—CTOPP* (Austin, TX: PRO-ED), and the *Dynamic Indicators of Basic Early Literacy Skills—DIBELS* (Eugene, OR: University of Oregon) are formal measures that can be used to get a more formal assessment of the child's ability to recognize and manipulate sound in words. Different aspects of phonemic awareness are also measured in tests like the *Roswell-Chall Auditory Blending Test* (Cambridge, MA: Educators Publishing Service), the *Test of Awareness of Language Segments* (Frederick, MD: Aspen Publications), and the *Lindamood Auditory Conceptualization Test* (Austin, TX: DLM Teaching Resources). Some resource books on phonics instruction also contain checklists and tools to assess various aspects of phonemic awareness (Blevins 1998; Johns, Lenski, and Elish-Piper 1999).

The administration of formal tests may require considerable preparation and practice on the part of the test-giver, and the format of response may be unfamiliar and/or confusing to children. That's why teacher judgment is important in backing up the results of formal assessment.

A test that is readily accessible and easy to administer is the Yopp-Singer Test of Phonemic Segmentation (Yopp 1995a). This instrument can be administered in five to ten minutes and measures a child's ability to identify the individual sounds in spoken words in order. Only words correctly segmented into each constituent phoneme are counted as correct; in other words, in item number 1, if the child responds /d/ /og/, the response is recorded in the blank, but no partial credit is given. The test can be effectively used as a diagnostic measure. When children's responses show no recognition of phonemes whatsoever or when children merely name all or some of the letters in the words, the teacher has an indication of where she needs to go in helping the child develop phonemic awareness.

Teaching Suggestions ▼

Assessing Phonemic Awareness

Yopp-Singer Test of Phonemic Segmentation

Student's name _____   Date _____

Score (number correct) _____

Directions

Today we're going to play a word game. I'm going to say a word and I want you to break the word apart. You are going to tell me each sound in the word in order. For example, if I say "old," you should say "/o/ /l/ /d/." (*Administrator: Be sure to say the sounds, not the letters, in the word.*) Let's try a few together.

Practice Items

(*Assist the child in segmenting these items as necessary.*) ride, go, man

Test Items

(*Circle those items that the student correctly segments; incorrect responses may be recorded on the blank following the item.*)

1. dog_____	12. lay _____
2. keep _____	13. race _____
3. fine_____	14. zoo _____
4. no _____	15. three _____
5. she _____	16. job _____
6. wave _____	17. in _____
7. grew _____	18. ice _____
8. that_____	19. at _____
9. red _____	20. top _____
10. me _____	21. by _____
11. sat _____	22. do _____

A full description of the test, along with data on its validity and reliability, appears in the September 1995 issue of *The Reading Teacher*.

Given the importance of phonemic awareness as a foundation for early reading success, assessing when children need help and support is an essential component of preschool and early reading activities.

Alphabet Knowledge

A very early step in phonics instruction is helping children learn to recognize the names and forms of letters. As in the case of phonemic awareness, research has clearly established the link between alphabet knowledge and success in beginning reading (Bond and Dykstra 1967; Durrell 1980; Adams 1990). One of the best predictors of beginning reading achievement is a child's knowledge of letter names; knowing the alphabet is closely tied to success in learning to read.

Alphabet knowledge involves more than the ability to rattle off the letters from A to Z. In addition to the ability to recite the alphabet in order, knowing the alphabet involves the ability to recognize the names of individual letters in and out of sequence, to match the upper case form with the lower case form, and, in conjunction with beginning phonics instruction, to recognize the sounds that letters represent.

Most children arrive at school with some knowledge of letter names, at least the names of upper case letters. They may be able to recognize the letters in their own names, and most are familiar with some of the letters that they have encountered in environmental print such as the words on food containers, road signs, and other labels and logos in their environment. Teachers build upon this knowledge in a systematic way to help children recognize and name all the letters of the alphabet with speed and accuracy.

Before they come to school, many children have been introduced to the alphabet through the "Alphabet Song," the familiar song sung to the tune of "Twinkle, Twinkle Little Star." As they sing this song at home and in early childhood instructional settings, children need to understand that each of the letters in the "Alphabet Song" is a separate entity. Some children come to school thinking that "elemenopee" is one of the letters of the alphabet. As children sing this song in early stages of alphabet training, teachers need to point to the individual symbols that each letter name represents.

In reciting (or singing) the alphabet, children learn the names of the letters before learning the form. In other words, we don't show the letter and then name it; rather, we first say the name and then look at the form. "By thoroughly learning the names first, the child has a solid mnemonic peg to which the precept of the letter can be connected as it is built. By thoroughly teaching the names first, the teacher can methodically exploit them toward developing the child's sense of functionally equivalent and distinctive differences between characters" (Adams 1990, 359).

Alphabet cards are especially useful in teaching children letter names and forms. Many teachers start the year with several sets of large alphabet cards, well laminated to withstand lots of use. These cards can be used in a variety of alphabet training activities involving naming, matching, and sequencing letter names and forms. Some teachers also have alphabet strips taped to each child's desk so that children have access to letter forms right under their noses, and they don't have to look up from their desks during activities involving practice with letter names.

Teaching Suggestions ▼

Alphabet Cards

Sequencing Letters

Cards are arranged along the chalk tray in proper alphabetical order. Children "march by," pointing to each letter as they recite the alphabet or as they sing the "Alphabet Song." Then the order of the cards is scrambled and teams of children arrange the letters in proper sequence.

Matching Upper and Lower Case Letters

Alphabet cards can be repeatedly used in a variety of activities for teaching and practice. Children can play card games such as Go Fish! ("*Got any r's? Go fish!*") in matching upper and lower case letters. Cards can be scattered around the room and teams can be timed as they search for matching upper and lower case forms. Children can play concentration, with cards placed face down and matched.

Alphabet Path

Laminated sets of alphabet cards are taped to the floor, and children walk the alphabet path, saying the name of the letters on which they step. Children can also play games like Twister ("*Put your right hand on the A and your left foot on the D.*") Colorful carpets with large letters are a feature of many early childhood classrooms.

Usually, upper case letters constitute the starting point for alphabet training because upper case forms are easier to distinguish visually from one another. When children are solidly familiar with upper case letters, corresponding lower case forms are introduced. For children who come to school with no knowledge of letter names at all, it's not advisable to teach upper and lower case forms together. In helping children learn to recognize lower case letters, teachers need to pay special attention to letters that are similar and often confused by children, for example, the letters **b** and **d** and the letters **p** and **q** (which have a different left-to-right orientation) and the letters **m** and **w** and the letters **n** and **u** (with different top-to-bottom orientations).

Alphabet books, a subgenre of children's literature containing letters of the alphabet in alphabetical order and pictures corresponding to the symbols, can be useful devices for helping children become familiar with letter symbols. Alphabet books should be treated like any other piece of children's literature in the early childhood setting; that is, they should be read and reread, discussed, shared, and enjoyed. In addition to dealing with letter symbols, alphabet books support language development and add a dimension to the literature component of the language arts program.

Not all alphabet books are appropriate to use as teaching tools in alphabet training for young children. Some of these books are more notable for their sophisticated artwork; for example, Graeme Base's *Animalaia* or Roberto de Vicq de Cumptrich's *Bembo's Zoo: An Animal ABC Book* are characterized by stunning and/or unique illustrations that reflect the author's artistic style. Some books are marked by sophisticated content; for example, Jonathan Hunt's *Illuminations* is a lavishly illustrated account of life during the Middle Ages, and Jerry Palotta's many alphabet books (such as *The Icky Bug Alphabet Book*) are full of information that requires a relatively high level of reading ability. The focus of some alphabet books is multicultural; *Jambo Means Hello: Swahili Alphabet Book* by Muriel Feelings focuses on the Swahili language and culture, and *Arrow To the Sun: An Alphabet Book in Spanish and English* by Alma Flor Ada is a bilingual alphabet book that honors Latino farm laborers. While alphabet books like these can be enjoyed and appreciated in their own unique ways, they are not always the most useful tools for helping children learn the names and sounds of letters.

Many alphabet books—those with a clear presentation of letter forms and a clear and accurate connection to the pictures/objects/ideas that represent the sounds of the letters—lend themselves perfectly well to alphabet training for young children. A *tiny* sampling of the hundreds of these books includes:

- *Dr. Seuss's ABC* by Theodore Geisel, an alphabet book that retains its popularity across generations;
- *26 Letters and 99 Cents* by Tana Hoban, a simple concept book that includes numbers and letters;
- *Eating the Alphabet* by Lois Ehlert, with colorful illustrations of food;
- *Annie, Bea, and Chi Chi Dolores; A School Day Alphabet* by Donna Maurer, with clear relationships between letters and words related to children's school experiences;
- *ABC Pop!* by Rachel Isadora, with colorful pop art illustrations linked to letters;
- *A, B, See!* by Tana Hoban, black and white illustrations with upper case letters highlighted within the entire alphabet on each page;
- *ABC Drive! A Car Trip Alphabet* by Naome Howland driving related terms that correspond to upper case letters.

This list could go on and on for pages and pages. Alphabet books have long been a regular part of young children's literacy diet and these books can be useful tools for alphabet training as well. A highly popular alphabet book with young children (and their teachers) is *Chicka Chicka Boom Boom* by Bill Martin, Jr. and John Archembault. This book is a narrative account of letters who climb to the top of a coconut tree before the weight of the alphabet causes the tree to topple. The book is written in a jazzy style that engages children immediately.

Many of these books are presented as CD-ROMs. The CD-ROM version of *Chicka Chicka Boom Boom,* for example, allows children to listen to the story read by Ray Charles and to interact with the text in a number of ways. By pointing and clicking, children can generate playground chants and jump rope rhymes related to individual letters, hear sentences that illustrate the sound of each letter ("R is for *rainbow.*"), and place randomly arranged letters into the proper alphabetical order. Thus, the book becomes not only a delightful piece of children's literature but also an instructional tool in helping children learn the symbols and sounds of their language. Other alphabet books, such as *Dr. Seuss's ABC,* are also available on CD-ROM to provide children with interactive presentations that offer music, animation, and other features for alphabet training.

In addition to alphabet cards and alphabet books, materials designed specifically for teaching children letter names abound. Most phonics workbook programs such as *Modern Curriculum Press Phonics Program* and *Sadlier Phonics* have specific components for teaching the alphabet. Practice books, pocket charts, games, tapes, computer programs, and other devices are available for use in the classroom and at home. Many of materials will be described in chapter 4 (126–131).

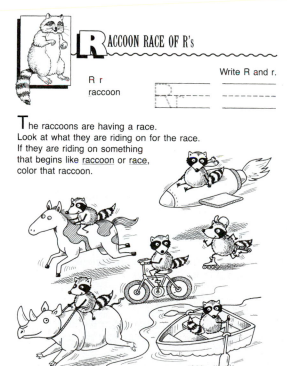

Children first learn letter names and initial letter-sound relationships through pencil-and-paper practice and computerized exercises like these.

Left: from Spotlight on Literacy *Phonics Activity Book, Grade 1. New York: Macmillan/McGraw-Hill, 2000. Reproduced with permission of the McGraw-Hill Companies.*
Right: from "Leap Into Phonics" *CD-ROM. Omaha, NE: Leap Into Learning. Reproduced with permission.*

Teaching Suggestions ▼

Alphabet Books

Select Carefully

Not all alphabet books are equally useful in helping children become familiar with letter symbols. Teachers should be sure that letters are presented in appropriate form (it makes little sense to teach young children to recognize Old English script), that the letters are clearly presented (and not intricately integrated in the illustrations), and that the letter-object relationship is clear (that a *ship* is not presented for the letter **S,** since *ship* begins with a digraph and not with the phoneme /s/). Children can be encouraged to select their own alphabet books and share these books with the group.

Comparing Books

Children can compare alphabet books to see what objects are used to illustrate letter sounds—is **A** always for *apple,* **B** always for *ball,* and **Q** always for *queen*?

Making Alphabet Books

Children can create their own class alphabet books. With pictures clipped from magazines and other sources, children can make alphabet books about their favorite foods, games, locations in the neighborhood, and other topics of interest.

Teaching Suggestions ▼

Alphabet Training

Alphabet Centers

A learning center should be stocked with alphabets of many kinds—letters cut from sandpaper, window screen, felt, wood, foam rubber, Styrofoam, sponge, plastic, and other material to give children a tactile sense as they manipulate letters. Children can trace letters in sand, form letters with clay or dough, use rubber stamps, or engage in other activities in the alphabet center. They can also play with alphabet puzzles, such as connect the dots following alphabet sequence.

Alphabet Hopscotch

Letters are written in chalk on the playground or on the floor of the play area in a hopscotch "frame." As children hop from one square to the other, they say the name of the letter on which they land.

Alphabet BINGO

Bingo cards covered with letters of the alphabet in random arrangement can be distributed. Children can use plastic disks or other markers to cover the letters as they are called.

I SPY

The popular game I Spy can be used to reinforce letter names, and it also involves awareness of initial sounds. Instead of saying the name of the letter, the teacher can hold up a letter card.

Alphabet Training, continued

Red Letter Days

Special days or weeks are set aside to focus on certain letters. Learning the letter **m,** for example, is featured in conjunction with a curriculum unit on the moon. The teacher reads books such as *Thirteen Moons on a Turtle's Back* by Joseph Bruchac and Jonathan London, which has moon legends from different Native American tribes presented as poetry, *Why the Sun and Moon Live in the Sky,* the traditional Nigerian myth retold by Niki Daly, or Seymour Simon's informational book *The Moon.* Michael and Melinda play a special role as class helpers because their names begin with **M. M** is the featured symbol as part of handwriting practice. For homework, children are asked to clip pictures of "**m**-words" from magazines or catalogues. In short, no opportunity is overlooked to help children become familiar with the form and sound of the letter.

Body Letters

Groups of three or four children can use their bodies to form letters on a mat or carpet.

Alphabet Snacks

Alphabet crackers or cereal can be used in different ways. Children can arrange them in order, count and chart the number of times they find a particular letter, use the snacks to spell their names, or otherwise use them for alphabet practice before devouring them.

Children who have trouble remembering letter names will need extra help and reinforcement. Visual memory problems, language-based learning disabilities, cognitive delays, or other problems may make it more difficult for some children to recall the symbols of their written language. These children will require intensive instruction, review, reteaching, and reinforcement in learning the alphabet.

Teaching Suggestions ▼

Review and Reinforcement Activities

Multisensory Practice

In addition to working with letter cards children can gain extra practice materials from the Alphabet Center (see Teaching Suggestions on the previous page). They can manipulate plastic or foam letters while they say the letter names, write or trace the letters in sand or clay, write the letters in large form on a chart while "talking through" the movement of making the letter, and otherwise engage their visual, kinesthetic, and tactual modalities to support visual recognition of letters.

Alphabet Sorts

Children can use letter cards or three-dimensional alphabet symbols to sort letters by different criteria. For example, they can group "straight line" letters (A, N, X, etc.), "curved line" letters (C, O, S, etc.), and "letters with both curves and lines" (B, D, J, etc.). Children can sort letters from the first half and second half of the alphabet, letters that they know and those that they don't (the objective being to make the former category larger than the latter), and by other criteria.

Mnemonic Pictures

Pictures associated with letters may provide memory clues that will help some children recognize letter names. For example, when they connect a picture of a *dog* to D or a *goat* to G, they may easily remember the symbol. Caution needs to be exercised in using pictures as mnemonic reminders for children whose native language is not English, however. We are used to seeing charts like this in classrooms:

| apple | egg | igloo | octopus | umbrella |

For the Spanish-speaking child, a similar chart might look like this:

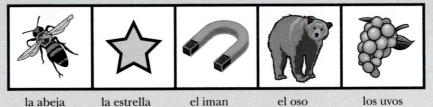

| la abeja (bumblebee) | la estrella (star) | el iman (magnet) | el oso (bear) | los uvos (grapes) |

For the Spanish-speaking child, *cat* is a "**g**-word" (*gatto*) and *dog* is a "**p**-word" (perro).

Writing activities are also useful in helping children master the alphabet. As children dictate stories based on their experiences, compose morning messages, or engage in other authentic writing experiences, the teacher calls attention to letter names and sounds. For example, the morning message that begins *Today is Tuesday* suggests opportunities for special attention to the form and sound of the letter **T.** In a print-rich environment, these opportunities arise all day long. Alphabet training extends to handwriting in copying, tracing, and finally writing letters independently. As children practice forming letters, they can repeat the name of the letter or the sound that the letter represents.

Learning letter sounds is a short step from learning letter names. In fact, as teachers focus on letter names and shapes as part of integrated literacy activities such as writing morning messages or calling attention to print features in shared reading lessons, there is typically a corresponding attention to the sounds that these letters represent. The names of many letters contain clues as to their phonetic equivalents. In phonics activities such as word building or working with onsets and rimes, teachers often deal with the sound that letters represent as they introduce letter names and forms. Children are asked to find "**b**-words" and "**m**-words." They talk about the pictures of objects representing letter sounds as they discuss alphabet books. They make letter charts with pictures and written words illustrating the sounds of the letters. They become aware of the sounds of the letters that make the names of their friends. In short, learning letter sounds is a natural extension of alphabet training that involves learning letter names and forms.

Given individual differences in the typical classroom, there is no absolute timetable for children to learn letter names and sounds. As a general rule, however, preschoolers should be able to recognize many, if not most, upper case letters and at least some lower case forms. Kindergarten is typically a time of intense alphabet training where children learn the names and shapes of letters and begin to make association with the sounds these letters represent, at least in the initial position in words. Early in first grade, children need to have mastered letter names and sounds as they move toward independence in reading and writing.

In any language-rich environment at home or in school, learning alphabet symbols is a natural part of the process of dealing with print, integrated into all aspects of learning to read and write.

Conclusion

Research over the past two decades leaves little doubt about the importance of phonemic awareness and alphabet knowledge in the beginning stages of learning to read and write. Richgels (2001) characterizes the last decade in education as "The Age of Phonemic Awareness." Questions have been raised as to whether phonemic awareness is a prerequisite to, or a consequence of, reading ability; and the causal connection between knowing letter names and early success in learning to read is not entirely clear. Nevertheless, both remain important cornerstones of early literacy instruction and the foundations of learning phonics.

As important as both are, phonemic awareness and alphabet training are not "stand alone" features in the process of learning to read. Instruction in phonemic awareness needs to be combined with lots of other opportunities to interact with a rich variety of oral and written language activities to promote emergent literacy. Learning letter names and sounds is best carried on in integrated activities, with letters presented as part of meaningful words within the context of authentic language-learning activities. But with a solid background in both phonemic awareness and alphabet knowledge, children have an important advantage in achieving early reading success.

References

Adams, M. J. 1990. *Beginning To Read: Thinking and Learning About Print.* Cambridge, MA: MIT Press.

Adams, M. J., B. R. Foorman, I. Lundberg, and T. Beeler. 1998. *Phonemic Awareness in Young Children.* Baltimore: Brookes Publishing Company.

Bishop, A., R. H. Yopp, and H. K. Yopp. 2000. *Reading for Reading: A Handbook for Parents of Preschoolers.* Boston: Allyn and Bacon.

Blevins, W. 1998. *Phonics from A to Z: A Practical Guide.* New York: Scholastic.

Bond, G. L., and R. Dykstra. 1967. The cooperative research program in first-grade reading instruction. *Reading Research Quarterly* 2:5–142. 1997. Reprinted in *Reading Research Quarterly* 32:348–437.

California Department of Education. 1996. *Teaching Reading: A Balanced, Comprehensive Approach to Teaching Reading in Prekindergarten Through Third Grade.* Sacramento: California Department of Education.

Chall, J. S., and H. M. Popp. 1996. *Teaching and Assessing Phonics: Why, What, When, How, A Guide for Teachers.* Cambridge, MA: Educators Publishing Service.

Cunningham, P. A. 2000. *Phonics They Use: Words for Reading and Writing.* 3d ed. New York: Longman.

Dressman, M. 1999. On the use and misuse of research evidence: Decoding two states' reading initiative. *Reading Research Quarterly* 34:258–85.

Durrell, D. D. 1980. Commentary: Letter name values in reading and spelling. *Reading Research Quarterly* 16:159–63.

Gunning, T. G. 2000. *Phonological Awareness and Primary Phonics.* Boston: Allyn and Bacon.

Harris, T. L., and R. E. Hodges, eds. 1995. *The Literacy Dictionary: The Vocabulary of Reading and Writing.* Newark, DE: International Reading Association.

Johns, J. L., S. D. Lenski, and L. Elish-Piper. 1999. *Early Literacy Assessment and Teaching Strategies.* Dubuque, IA: Kendall Hunt Publishing.

Juel, C. 1988. Learning to read and write: A longitudinal study of 54 children from first through fourth grades. *Journal of Educational Psychology* 80:437–47.

Moats, L. C. 1994. The missing foundation in teacher education: Knowledge of the structure of spoken and written language. *Annals of Dyslexia* 44:81–102.

National Reading Panel. 2000. *Teaching Children to Read: An Evidence-Based Assessment of the Scientific Research Literature on Reading and its Implications for Reading Instruction.* Washington, DC: National Institute of Child Health and Human Development.

Opitz, M. F. 1998. Children's books to develop phonemic awareness—For you and parents, too! *The Reading Teacher* 51:526–28.

Orton, J. G. 2000. Phonemic awareness and inventive writing. *The New England Reading Association Journal* 36:17–21.

Richgels, D. J. 2001. Phonemic awareness. *The Reading Teacher* 55:274–78.

Smith, F. 1999. Why systematic phonics and phonemic awareness instruction constitute an educational hazard. *Language Arts* 77:150–55.

Snow, C. E., M. S. Burns, and P. Griffin. 1998. *Preventing Reading Difficulties in Young Children.* Washington, DC: National Academy Press.

Stanovich, K. E. 1994. Romance and reality. *The Reading Teacher* 47:280–91.

Sulzby, E., and W. Teale. 1991. Emergent literacy. In *Handbook of Reading Research.* Vol. 2. Edited by R. Barr et al. New York: Longman.

Taylor, D. 1999. Beginning to read and the spin doctors of science: An excerpt. *Language Arts* 76:217–31.

Torgesen, J. K., and P. G. Mathes. 2000. *A Basic Guide to Understanding, Assessing, and Teaching Phonological Awareness.* Austin: Pro-Ed.

Troia, G. A., F. P. Roth, and S. Graham. 1998. An educator's guide to phonological awareness: Assessment measures and intervention activities for children. *Focus on Exceptional Children* 31:1–12

Williams, J. 1995. Phonemic awareness. In *The Literacy Dictionary: The Vocabulary of Reading and Writing.* Edited by T. L. Harris and R. E. Hodges. Newark, DE: International Reading Association.

Yopp, H. K. 1995a. A test for assessing phonemic awareness in young children. *The Reading Teacher* 49:20–9.

———. 1995b. Read-aloud books for developing phonemic awareness: An annotated bibliography. *The Reading Teacher* 48:538–42.

Yopp, H. K., and R. H. Yopp. 2000. Supporting phonemic awareness development in the classroom. *The Reading Teacher* 54:130–43.

Children's Trade Books Cited in This Chapter

Ada, A. F. 1997. *Gathering the Sun: An Alphabet Book in Spanish and English.* Illustrated by Simon Silva. New York: Lothrup.

Alarian, K. B. 1997. *Louella Mae, She's Run Away.* Illustrated by R. Litzinger. New York: Henry Holt.

Base, Graeme. 1986. *Animalia.* New York: Abrahams.

Bruchac, J., and J. London. 1997. *Thirteen Moons on a Turtle's Back.* New York: Putnam.

Cameron, P. 1961. *"I Can't" Said the Ant.* New York: Scholastic.

Daly, N. 1995. *Why the Sun and Moon Live in the Sky.* New York: HarperCollins.

De Vicq de Cumptrich, R. 2000. *Bembo's Zoo: An Animal ABC Book.* New York: Henry Holt.

Ehlert, L. 1989. *Eating the Alphabet.* San Diego: Harcourt Brace.

Feelings, M. 1976. *Jambo Means Hello: Swahili Alphabet Book.* Illustrated by T. Feelings. New York: Dial.

Fox, M. 1989. *Wilfred Gordon McDavid Patridge.* Illustrated by J. Vivas. Reading, MA: Scott Foresman.

Galdone, P. 1984. *Henny Penny.* Boston: Houghton Mifflin.

Geisel, T. (Dr. Seuss). 1963. *Dr. Seuss's ABC.* New York: Random House.

———. 1960. *Green Eggs and Ham.* New York: Random House.

Guarino, D. 1991. *Is Your Mama a Llama?* New York: Scholastic.

Hoban, T. 1987. *26 Letters and 99 Cents.* New York: Greenwillow.

———. 1982. *A, B. See!* New York: Greenwillow.

Howland, N. 1994. *ABC Drive! A Car Trip Alphabet.* New York: Clarion.

Hunt, J. 1989. *Illuminations.* New York: Bradbury.

Isadora, R. 1999. *ABC Pop!* New York: Viking.

Karlin, N. 1997. *The Fat Cat Sat on the Mat.* New York: HarperCollins.

Kipling, R. 1997. *Rikki, Tikki, Tavi.* Illustrated by J. Pinkney. New York: Morrow.

Martin, W., Jr. *Brown Bear, Brown Bear, What Do You See?* 1994. Illustrated by E. Carle. New York: Henry Holt.

———. 1991. *Polar Bear, Polar Bear, What Do You Hear?* Illustrated by E. Carle. New York: Henry Holt.

Martin, W., Jr., and J. Archembault. 1989. *Chicka Chicka Boom Boom.* Illustrated by L. Ehlert. New York: Simon and Schuster.

Maurer, D. 1993. *Annie, Bea, and Chi Chi Dolores: A School Day Alphabet.* Illustrated by D. Cazet. New York: Orchard.

Mosel, A. 1968. *Tiki Tiki Tembo.* New York: Henry Holt.

Palotta, J. 1986. *The Icky Bug Alphabet Book.* Illustrated by R. Masiello. Watertown, MA: Charlesbridge.

Prelutski, J. 1982. *The Baby Uggs Are Hatching.* New York: Greenwillow.

———. 1989. *Poems of A Nonny Mouse.* New York: Greenwillow.

Simon, S. 1984. *The Moon.* New York: Simon and Schuster.

Slepian, J., and Seidler, A. 1967. *The Hungry Thing.* New York: Scholastic.

———. 1990. *The Hungry Thing Returns.* New York: Scholastic.

———. 1993. *The Hungry Thing Goes to a Restaurant.* New York: Scholastic.

Wood, A. 1992. *Silly Sally.* San Diego: Harcourt Brace.

Teaching and Learning Discrete Phonics Elements

3

Knowledge of content and teaching technique are important for teachers in any subject area. The content of phonics is an essential component of the knowledge base of teachers. But knowledge of phonics alone is not enough; teachers need to be aware of how to help children put this knowledge to work in order to become effective readers and writers. This chapter

▼ focuses on major components of the sound-symbol relationships of English orthography, discrete elements that constitute the content of phonics instruction

▼ suggests ideas for helping children learn phonics elements so that they can apply this information in decoding and encoding words as part of language arts experiences.

A teacher's ability to teach any subject will be influenced by the teacher's knowledge of that subject, and phonics is no exception. Tests of teachers' knowledge of phonics, with items like the pre- and posttests in this book, indicate that this background is sorely lacking, that teachers' knowledge of phonics is surprisingly weak (Moats 1994). Given the importance of phonics and the emphasis on systematic and explicit instruction in teaching reading in today's schools, it's important that teachers be familiar with the nature and details of our writing system that constitute the content of phonics.

44 Sounds and 26 Letters

English orthography is based upon the alphabetic principle. Spoken sounds (called *phonemes*) are represented by written symbols (called *graphemes*). Phonics involves learning the relationships between these sounds and symbols; it also involves learning to use this information in decoding unfamiliar words as part of reading and in exercising appropriate orthographic options in spelling words as part of writing.

All languages have two broad categories of sounds: consonants and vowels. Very early in their school lives, children learn that "The vowels are **a, e,**

i, o, u, and sometimes **y** (and sometimes **w** in some programs), and that the consonants are all the other letters." English orthography, however, is considerably more complicated than that. Indeed, there are five (sometimes six) vowel letters, but these letters are used in various combinations to represent a multiplicity of different sounds.

The overall sound system of American English contains approximately forty-four phonemes or basic units of sound. "Approximately" is used because not all experts agree on the exact number of phonemes we use (see Eldredge 1999; Baer 1999; Wilson and Hall 1997; Ladefoged 1982; and others). Besides, not all speakers of every dialect of American English use each of these phonemes in their daily oral communication. Variations in the way people pronounce words is a fascinating part of language and life. To some speakers, the words *caught* and *fought* rhyme; to others, they don't rhyme at all as *caught* is pronounced as *cot*. When one examines the overall speech patterns of American English, however, forty-four is the number consistently used to indicate the number of phonemes in our language.

These forty-four sounds are represented in writing by twenty-six symbols or letters of the alphabet. The relationship between these sounds and symbols is certainly not perfect. A perfect alphabetic system would have one symbol for each sound, and there would be a consistent one-to-one relationship between both. That is, each time a sound was used in speech it would be written in one and only one way; and each time a symbol was written, it would represent the same sound all the time. Some English words do have a consistent sound-symbol relationship, but many do not.

When children come to school for the first time, barring severe language handicaps, they can produce most if not all of the phonemes of their sound system. As part of the language acquisition process, they learn to combine phonemes into words to fulfill their basic communication needs. They may talk about "Balentine's Day" or the "gaspetti" they had for lunch, but despite occasional mispronunciations here and there, children can effectively produce all the phonemes in their dialect. When they learn to read and write, they learn to attach letters to the sounds that they speak.

The mismatch between the forty-four sounds and the twenty-six letters used to represent these sounds is the chief factor that causes the inconsistencies that children (and many adults) encounter in trying to master reading and spelling. Of our forty-four sounds, twenty-five are consonants and nineteen are vowels. Of our twenty-six letters, twenty-one are consonants and only five are vowels.

What's the result of the numerical mismatch in the sound-symbol relationships between vowels and consonants? Try spelling the word that names the small stringed, guitar-like instrument that musicians strum on the beaches of Hawaii. (Don't just say the letters aloud; write the word on a piece of paper. Spelling is, remember, a written language activity.)

If we gathered an inventory of all the words written in response to this request, we would likely have a list similar to the following:

ukalele	ukealaylee	eucalaley	ukelele
ukillaylee	euckolalee	yucalaylay	ukulalee
yukalele	ukilalee	ukallali	ukalaily
ukulele	yukalaili	ukeleyllee	eukalehlee
eukallelay	eukaleli		

This list by no means exhausts all possible spellings of this word! The proper or standard spelling of the word found in the dictionary is *ukulele*. The point, however, is not what the correct spelling is but rather what happens when you try to spell the word.

When you examine the words in the list, you notice considerable consistency in letters that are used to represent the consonant sounds but great variations in letters and letter combinations representing the vowel sounds. All the words in the list have letters representing the /k/ sound in the second position, symbols representing /l/ in the middle of the word, and the letter **l** (or double l) as the second-to-last element. Letters like **b, g, t, q,** or other letters representing other sounds are not included at all. There is consistency in the letters used to represent the consonant sounds where each consonant sound appears in the word.

Now consider the phoneme-grapheme relationships in the vowels. A wide variation of letters and letter combinations representing the vowel sounds are used. That's because the ratio between the number of vowel sounds in the language and the letters available to represent these sounds allows many options for representing these sounds in written form. With only five graphemes to represent nineteen phonemes, there are many more options for representing vowels in different ways in writing (and therefore many more opportunities to spell the word incorrectly).

With this type of mismatch between letters and sounds in vowels and consonants, it's not difficult to understand why children often find vowels the most difficult part of learning phonics and why when we make a mistake in spelling a word, the mistake most often involves the vowel elements in the word.

In written language, consonants carry significant phonetic information. You can often figure out words by leaving out vowel letters, for example, d*ff*d*l (daffodil), c*mp*t*r (computer), r**d*ng c*mpr*h*ns*n (reading comprehension). "The vowel nucleus of the syllable conveys most of the acoustic energy in the stream of speech and envelops the adjacent sounds" (Troia et al. 1998, 5). The importance of vowels rests in their function in producing sounds in the stream of spoken language.

Speech sounds are produced as air passes from the lungs through the larynx, causing the vocal cords to vibrate (like the string of a musical instrument). Then we manipulate our organs of speech to modify the sounds. For example, we place our two lips together and stop the stream of air in producing the initial sound of **bat;** we redirect the stream of air through the nasal cavity in producing the initial sound of **mat;** we force the air through our upper teeth and lower lip in producing the initial sound of **fat;** and so on.

This physical action of producing speech accounts for the essential difference between consonants and vowels. Consonants are produced by interfering with the stream of air as it passes through the vocal tract. Vowels escape when there is no significant interruption in the stream of air; the mouth opens to let the sound escape in an uninterrupted fashion. Vowel sounds are determined by the position of the tongue rather than by other organs of speech.

Studying how sounds are produced is the stuff of articulatory phonetics and an important part of the knowledge base for speech therapists and language specialists. Being aware of the physical side of speech also helps make teachers aware of the way in which children produce sounds and suggests some of the reasons why certain symbols are attached to certain sounds. It accounts in large measure for sound variations that mark different dialects. Some intensive phonics programs build directly on physical aspects of speech production. For example, the Lindamood Bell program (see chapter 4) calls the phonemes /p/ and /b/ "lip popping sounds" because of the way in which they are articulated. Physiological features explain the major difference between the two basic categories of sounds in English, consonants and vowels. In short, understanding how we produce vocal sounds has much to do with how we teach children to attach symbols to these sounds in learning to read and spell.

Teaching Discrete Phonics Elements

As young children learn the sound-symbol relationships of their language on the way to becoming literate, there will be times when it becomes appropriate for the teacher to provide direct instruction on discrete phonics elements that children encounter in reading and writing. Discrete phonics elements are those aspects of phonics that children need to decode and encode written language. They consist of

> *consonants*—letter-sound correspondences that include *single consonants*, such as **l** - /l/ and **p** - /p/ that occur at the beginning and end of words like *lap* and *pal*, respectively
>
> *consonant digraphs*, sounds represented by the letter combinations at the beginning of words like **ship, chip, thin,** and **whip** and at the end of *click* and *sing*
>
> *consonant blends*, the initial sound combination at the beginning of words like **stop, tree, black,** and **flag** and at the end of *send* and *left*
>
> *silent letters*, words that include letters with no corresponding sound, such as the **k** in *knee* and the **b** in *lamb.*
>
> *vowels*—letter-sound correspondences that include *short vowels*, vowel sounds that occur in words like *cat* /ă/ *hen* /ĕ/ *pig* /ĭ/ *dog* /ŏ/ and *bug* /ŭ/

long vowels—vowel sounds that occur in words like *ate /ā/ eat /ē/ ice /ī/ oat /ō/* and *use /ū/*

other vowels—such as medial vowel sounds as the /ä/ in *father,* double vowels that make variant sounds as the **oo** in *boot* and *book,* vowel diphthongs as in *boil* and *boy,* r-controlled vowels as in *star* and *bird,* and schwa /ə/ which is the unaccented vowel sound as in the initial phoneme in *about.*

syllables—combinations of phonemes that make up larger sound units in words (*syl.la.ble*) in which consonants cluster around vowels.

These are the elements that constitute content of the phonics curriculum, the "stuff" of phonics teaching in any instructional program.

Consonants and vowels occur in combination in *onsets* and *rimes* in syllables. The onset is the part of the syllable that precedes the vowel, for example, **str***um.* The rime (notice the different spelling than the conventional *rhyme*) is the vowel and all the consonants that follow it, for example, *str**um.** Rimes are also called *phonograms* or *patterns.* They constitute the basis of "word families" in phonics instruction.

Because discrete phonics elements occur in close combination with one another in words, phonics instruction deals extensively with onsets and rimes. "Instruction that includes the use of onsets and rimes is supported by research indicating that readers look for letter patterns rather than individual letters as they decode words" (Allen 1998, 255). As children work with word families, they prepare themselves for independent decoding, since so many word families that occur as one-syllable words (*cat, bat, fat*) also occur in multisyllable words (***cat***egory, *acro**bat**, **fat**igue*) that children decode by analogy.

In English orthography, common word patterns are easily observable. Common patterns include

Consonant-Vowel-Consonant—**CVC**—in which the vowel is usually short. Variations of this pattern include words that have no initial consonant **(C)VC** (*at* or *up,* for example), words in which the first element is a consonant digraph or blend **CCVC** (*ship* or *brat,* for example), and words where the final consonant is a digraph or blend **CVCC** (*dish* or *milk,* for example).

Consonant-Vowel-Vowel-Consonant—**CVVC**—in which double vowels occur. The double vowel combination may represent a single sound, usually a long vowel (*boat* or *meat,* for example) or two closely associated sounds (*boil* or *shout,* for example). Variations of this pattern include words that have no initial consonant **(C)VVC** (*eat,* for example), words in which the first element is a consonant digraph or blend **CCVVC** (*chain* or *creak,* for example), and words where the final consonant is a digraph or blend **CVVCC** (*teeth* or *boast,* for example).

Consonant-Vowel-Consonant-e—**CVCe**—the very common pattern of "silent **e**" words. As in other patterns, the onset might be a digraph (*choke*) or a blend (*stroke*).

Consonant-Vowel—**CV.** This pattern occurs rarely in single words (*we* or *sky,* for example), but it is common in "open syllables" that are part of longer words (the first syllable in words like *major, became, tiger, hotel,* and *music,* for example).

These are the patterns that teachers use in helping children master the discrete elements in the sound-symbol system in their language for the purpose of learning to read and spell.

For teaching all discrete phonics elements, certain teaching strategies have proven especially effective. These teaching strategies include

- word building, in which children use their knowledge of sound-symbol relationships as they combine letters to create words with cards, tiles, and in writing;
- word families, in which children work with onsets and rimes to create lists of words that are phonetically related. Johnson (1999) provides suggestions for using word families in a developmental fashion with young children: (1) focus on one word family at a time, starting with short **a** rimes because words with this pattern are so common in the reading material of young children; (2) introduce two or more families with the same short vowel, such as *-at* as in *mat* or *-an* as in *man;* (3) compare word families with different short vowels, for example, *bat, bit, bet,* and *but;* (4) introduce blends and digraphs during the study of mixed vowel word families; and (5) extend to patterns with long vowel sounds;
- word sorts, which involve separating or categorizing words according to orthographic similarities and differences, "provide opportunities for students to make logical decisions about word elements, including sound, pattern, meaning, and use (and which) help students identify and understand invariance or constancy in the orthography" (Bear et al. 2000, 59);
- word walls, areas of the classroom where words are written for public display, which have proven to be especially popular and effective devices to support spelling, writing, and phonics activities (Cunningham 2000);
- word games, including variations of BINGO, card games, board games, and other motivational devices designed to help children learn, practice, and apply their knowledge of discrete phonics elements. Games are popular with children outside of school, and playing these games as part of phonics is no less enjoyable in the classroom.

All of these strategies will be applied as appropriate in the succeeding sections of this chapter.

Children acquire the ability to apply these strategies in the classroom through direct instruction, incidental instruction, paper-and-pencil practice, and computerized activities.

Direct instruction, as the name indicates, involves presenting phonics components in a direct, straightforward manner. Based on its review of research, the National Reading Panel has concluded that direct, systematic, explicit phonics instruction is particularly effective in promoting children's reading growth (National Reading Panel 2000).

There are plenty of opportunities for informal phonics instruction in the classroom as well. These are occasions when the teacher helps the child use phonics in authentic reading and writing activities.

Worksheets that engage children in paper and pencil exercises are extensively used as an ingredient of direct teaching. While workbook programs should not dominate phonics instruction, well-designed worksheets provide children with opportunities to practice and apply phonics strategies and can be the source of diagnostic information that can help teachers plan instruction (Allington 2002). "Workbooks are great for independent practice when concepts have been well taught. They are not categorically despicable, just often misused as a substitute for teaching" (Moats 1998, 48).

Computer programs can also be helpful in giving pupils opportunities to interactively learn and apply phonics elements.

Samples of worksheets and screen shots are included in this chapter, not as an endorsement of these devices but as examples of what is available for classroom use. Some of these programs are described more fully in the next chapter.

Consonants

Consonant phonemes are made when there is maximum closure or interference with the column of air as it passes through the vocal tract. We completely block the column of air and then release it (as with the /b/ in *bat*), force it through a small opening (as with the /s/ in *sat*), redirect the column of air through the nasal cavity (as with the /m/ in *mat*), let the stream flow around an obstruction (as with the /l/ in *lap*), or otherwise interfere with the column of air as it passes from the larynx to the "outside world."

Consonants can occur at the beginning or end of syllables. The inventory of consonant phonemes that are part of the overall sound system of American English, along with the common spelling of each sound as it appears in the initial and final position in words, are presented in figure 3.1.

Two consonant phonemes never occur in an initial position in English words, /ng/ as in *sing* and /zh/ as in *beige*, although the former sound is commonly used in the initial position in words in Asian languages. The three phonemes /h/, /w/, and /y/ are not listed in final position in words because they are *glides*, a class of sounds that will be described later in this chapter.

Eighteen of the conventional letters of the alphabet are used to represent corresponding phonemes. Seven phonemes are represented by double

Symbol*	Initial Position	Final Position
/p/	pan	nap
/b/	boy	nab
/t/	tin	hit
/d/	dot	red
/k/	kit	tack
/g/	get	tag
/f/	fan	stiff
/v/	van	love
/th/	thin	breath
/TH/	then	clothe
/l/	lip	curl
/r/	ran	fur
/m/	man	rim
/n/	nap	tin
/ng/	—	sing
/h/	hit	—
/w/	win	—
/y/	yellow	—
/s/	sit	this
/z/	zipper	doze
/sh/	ship	dish
/zh/	—	beige
/ch/	chill	catch
/j/	jail	ledge
/hw/	white	—

Figure 3.1 *Consonant phonemes in the overall sound system of American English.*

Different phonetic symbols are often used by different authors to transcribe phonemes. Whatever symbol system is used, phonemes are always indicated by / /.

letters, most of which represent consonant digraphs such as /ch/ as in *chick* and /sh/ as in *ship*. Three of the conventional graphemes are not included as symbols in transcribing speech sounds:

> the letter **c** because it represents the phonemes /s/ as in *city* or /k/ as in *cat;*
> the letter **q** because it represents the phoneme combination /k/ /w/ as in *quick*
> the letter **x** because it represents the phoneme combination /k/ /s/ in *box* or the phoneme /z/ as in *xylophone.*

Consonants occur as single elements at the beginning (*bit*) and at the end (*rub*) of words. Their sound-symbol relationships are much more consistent than those of vowels. Consonant letters generally represent only one sound, and as a rule, they present no major problems for children learning to decode.

Teaching single consonants at the beginning and end of words is a natural extension of instruction and practice in phonemic awareness and alphabet training. As children are focusing on phonemes in words and are being introduced to letter names, attention to sound-symbol correspondences is unavoidable.

Teaching Suggestions ▼

Working with Beginning Consonants

What's in a Name?

The names of all the children are written on cards and sorted according to first letter/sound. The teacher should be aware of names that begin with digraphs (like *Charleen*), blends (like *Brendan*), vowels (like *Aileen*) and different sound-symbol relationships (like *Julio*). Names with the same letter/sound can be written on the board, for example, *Tabatha, Timothy, Tamara*. Children can brainstorm other names that begin with T-/t/ and other T-words they can think of.

Sound Sentences

The teacher dictates alliterative sentences, such as:

Bashful baboons bounce brightly.

Dreadful dragons dress differently.

Or the teacher dictates sentences with words beginning with a particular sound, such as:

Sam the squirrel is eating salad, sandwiches, spaghetti, and soda.

Marvin the mouse is eating muffins, macaroni, mustard, and milk.

As the teacher reads or dictates these sentences, the children hold up cards to indicate the target sound and/or make up their own "sound sentences."

Class Alphabet Books

When children make class alphabet books as part of learning letter names, there is a direct focus on initial consonant sounds. Children can also build picture collections using pictures clipped from magazines and catalogues. Red letter days, beginning writing activities, and other activities suggested earlier for alphabet training lend themselves naturally to instruction in initial consonant sounds.

Word Building

The teacher uses a set of alphabet cards, one card per letter, with the capital letter on one side and the lower case form on the other. Five or six cards are placed in an envelope, with one or two vowels and the rest consonants. As the teacher says a word, children use the cards to build the word. For example, by manipulating these six cards,

b	t	r

n	a	i

children can build words like

bat	rat	rain	ran	at
tin	an	bit	bran	train

While begun as a whole class activity, children can engage in word-building exercises in small groups or in pairs, copying the words that they build with their letter cards. Letter cards can be arranged on a table, on the chalk tray, or in a pocket chart. Capital letters are used when a word might be a proper noun—*Pat* as a person's name, for example—or if sets of cards are used in sentence-building activities. Word building can also be extended through adaptations of the popular games Scrabble and Boggle, games that have tiles and cubes that children can use to build more and more words as their knowledge of phonics increases.

Word Families

Working with common rimes or word families, children add different initial consonants to build lists of new words:

-at	-en	-ig	-og	-ug
cat	hen	pig	dog	bug
bat	Ben	big	bog	hug
fat	den	dig	fog	jug
hat	men	rig	hog	rug
rat	pen	wig	log	tug

This activity also applies to learning short vowel sounds.

Using Context

Since children use both decoding and context as strategies in figuring out unknown words, some exercises in beginning consonant sounds can be placed in the context of whole sentences:

My family just bought a new _ar.
Foxes live in _ens.
The _ug covers the floor.

Sentences like these require children to focus on meaning as well as decoding elements.

In English orthography, the consonant letters **c** and **g** represent two distinct sounds at the beginning of words or syllables. The letter **c** represents the "hard" sound of /k/ when it is followed by the vowels **a, o,** and **u** in words like *cap, cop,* and *cup* and the "soft" sound of /s/ when followed by **e, i,** or **y** in words like *cent, city,* and *cyst.* Similarly, the letter **g** represents the "hard" sound /g/ when followed by **a, o,** and **u** in words like *gap, got,* and *gut,* and the "soft" sound /j/ when followed by **e,** and **y** in words like *gent,* and *gyro.* When followed by the vowel **i,** the sound of **g** can be "hard" as in *girl* or "soft" as in *giraffe* (which emphasizes the importance of combining context with phonics in decoding written language). Both letters represent their respective "hard" sounds as part of blends in words like *cry, clean, grade,* and *glide.*

Teaching Suggestions ▼

Working with the Two Sounds of C and G

Cards

Each child has a pair of cards with the letters **H** and **S** to indicate hard and soft. As the teacher reads a list of words beginning with **c** and **g**, children hold up the card to indicate if the sound is hard or soft. Words for dictation:

> **Hard c**—*cone, came, camp, cold, call, carry, etc.*
> **Soft c**—*celery, cigar, cereal, cent, ceiling, cinder, etc.*
> **Hard g**—*go, garden, game, gift, good, etc.*
> **Soft g**—*George, giraffe, gentle, general, gym, etc.*

Word Sort

Children can sort words according to their initial sounds in exercises such as

C as /k/	C as /s/	G as /g/	G as /j/

Words for the sort: *cab   gum   gym   catch   giant   bicycle   cot
center   cut   gave   gerbil   caught   gift   game   city*

Consonants also occur at the end of words. Identifying and substituting final consonants is typically more difficult than working with initial consonants because beginning sounds are more prominent. Besides, final consonant sounds are not always represented by single consonant letters. Changing *rat* to *rack,* for example, requires the use of a digraph, and changing *cut* to *cuff* requires doubling the letter at the end of the word. Nevertheless, phonemic awareness exercises requiring isolation and substitution can be extended to working with final consonant letters.

Teaching Suggestions ▼

Working with Final Consonants

Final Consonant Substitution

As children are working with word families, they can substitute final letter/sounds to make new words:

cat	bet	pig	top	bug
can	beg	pin	Tom	bud
cap	bed	pit	tot	bus

Substituting blends and digraphs expands possibilities for creating new words that make sense with final consonant sounds.

Using Context

As in the case of beginning consonants, some exercises in final consonant sounds can be placed in the context of whole sentences:

There is a ma_ of the United States on the classroom wall.
We ra_ all the way home.
I like to chew gu_.

Once again, exercises like these give children practice in using context clues in conjunction with decoding strategies.

Consonant Dominoes

Pairs of words are written on cards such as

ten	rug

nap	book

gum	rat

Children match the ending sound of the second word with the beginning sound of the first word on another card:

ten	rug

gum	rain

nap	book

kite	rim

In addition to single letter-sound correspondences, two of the most frequently used phonetic elements in our overall sound system are consonant digraphs and blends. Digraphs are two consecutive consonant letters that represent a single phoneme; blends are two or three consonant letters that represent closely associated but separate sounds. The difference between consonant digraphs and blends can be illustrated by pronouncing the following sets of words with the *sl* blend and the *sh* digraph:

sip	lip	slip
sip	hip	ship

The initial /s/ and /l/ are clearly pronounced in *sip* and *lip,* and each retains its unique sound when blended into /sl/. There is no such sound separation in the digraph /sh/, however. While the /s/ phoneme and the /h/

phoneme retain their distinctive sounds at the beginning of *sip* and *hip* respectively, the two letters represent a single /sh/ phoneme at the beginning of *ship.*

Consonant Digraphs

Consonant digraphs are two consecutive consonant letters that represent a single phoneme. The most common consonant digraphs in English are

/ch/ at the beginning of words like *child* and *chime* and at the end of words like *much* and *itch;*

/sh/ at the beginning of words like *ship* and *shout* and at the end of words like *dish* and *crush;*

/TH/ and /th/, the former of which occurs at the beginning of words like *then* and *this* and at the end of *bathe* and *clothe;* the latter of which occurs at the beginning of words like *thin* and *thick* and at the end of *bath* and *breath;* /TH/ is a voiced sound, while /th/ is voiceless.

/hw/ at the beginning of words like *which* and *white* but does not occur as a final phoneme in the English sound system;

/ng/ which only occurs as the final sound in words like *song* and *thing.*

Two other consonant letter combinations that are considered digraphs are **ph** and **gh,** but these represent sounds that are most often represented by the single grapheme **f** at the beginning of words like *phone* and *phonics* and at the end of words like *rough* and *laugh.* As in the case of all phonetic elements, the sound-symbol relationships of digraphs is not perfect. The digraph **ch,** for example, which typically represents the /ch/ phoneme in **chip,** represents /k/ in **chorus** and /sh/ in **chef.** Similarly, the /sh/ phoneme is represented by the single letter **s** in *sugar.*

Teaching Suggestions ▼

Consonant Digraphs

Identifying Digraphs

Lists of words with a particular consonant digraph are written on the board:

shop	chin	what	thin
shout	cheek	where	think
ship	chop	white	thumb
she	chain	wheel	thing
shin	chick	whale	thank

Children can brainstorm other words that begin with these sounds. Having these words come from children's reading or interests will make the activity more meaningful.

Word Families

Working with common phonograms or rimes, children can substitute digraphs to make new words, just as they changed initial consonant letters to make new words:

-ip	*ship*	*chip*	*whip*
-in	*shin*	*chin*	*thin*

Adding blends to the beginning of these rimes extends the range of word choices.

Nonsense Words

The teacher writes a list of words with consonant digraphs and common phonograms on the board; for example:

chack   *whade*   *thame*   *shamp*

Children erase the initial digraph and substitute another digraph that will make the word real.

chack — shack   *whade — shade*   *thame — shame*   *shamp — champ*

Blends can also be added to make the pseudowords into real words. The activity can also be used in helping children learn long and short vowels.

Again, Context

Exercises involving beginning and ending consonant digraphs should involve context so that children can integrate strategies in decoding and context in figuring out unknown words in print:

> *We write on the board with __alk.*
> *My dog is not fat; he's __in.*
> *The clouds are a puffy __ite color.*
> *We're having pizza for lun__.*
> *I wi__ I could visit the moon.*

Got Any /sh/ Words?

The popular card game Go Fish can be used for practice. Using a stack of cards with words containing digraphs, groups of children can ask each other for cards containing consonant digraph words.

Consonant Blends

Consonant blends or clusters are two or three consonant letters that represent closely associated but separate sounds. Blends constitute common phonetic elements in English words.

Three common categories of blends are

- those that involve the letter **l** (*black*, *clap*, *flock*, *slow*, and *please*)
- those that involve the letter **r** (*bright*, *crow*, *drop*, *frame*, *group*, *proud*, and *train*)
- those that involve the letter **s** (*scar*, *skin*, *slim*, *small*, *snore*, *spell*, *star*, and *swim*)

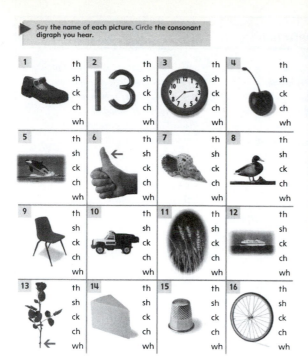

Say the name of each picture. Circle the consonant digraph you hear.

1 th sh ck ch wh	**2** th sh ck ch wh	**3** th sh ck ch wh	**4** th sh ck ch wh
5 th sh ck ch wh	**6** th sh ck ch wh	**7** th sh ck ch wh	**8** th sh ck ch wh
9 th sh ck ch wh	**10** th sh ck ch wh	**11** th sh ck ch wh	**12** th sh ck ch wh
13 th sh ck ch wh	**14** th sh ck ch wh	**15** th sh ck ch wh	**16** th sh ck ch wh

Children apply knowledge of consonant digraphs and blends by identifying and creating these elements in words.

Blends also occur in three-letter combinations such as *street, spring,* and *splash.* As with other consonant elements, blends occur at the beginning and ending of words.

It's very likely that words containing initial consonant blends will occur on other word lists that children develop as part of phonics instruction, words like *brown* on a list of **b**-words and *dress* on a list of **d**-words, for example. Many of the activities for teaching blends will be similar to those involved in teaching initial and final consonants.

Teaching Suggestions ▼

Consonant Blends

Creating Words with Blends

Beginning with words familiar to children, the teacher can add letters to create blends:

car—scar   *rat—brat*   *rip—drip*   *room—broom*   *lamp—clamp*

Children can brainstorm to expand the list of words beginning with these blends. According to Eldredge (1999), the blends that most often occur at the beginning of American English words are

st—*stop, start, sting, stack*   bl—*black, blush, bleed, blink*
pr—*pray, price, prince, prize*   sl—*sly, slow, sleep, sled*

tr—*try, tree, truck, track*
gr—*grin, gray, green, grape*
pl—*plan, plum, place, plane*
cl—*clean, class, clock, close*
cr—*cry, crash, crank, creek*
str—*string, strap, straw, strong*
br—*broom, brown, bring, brook*
dr—*dry, drag, drive, dress*
fl—*flap, flop, flag, flat*
fr—*free, frog, freeze, Friday*

sw—*swim, swing, swamp, switch*
sm—*small, smart, smell, smile*
sc—*scare, scale, scrub, scoop*
sk—*sky, skid, skate, skunk*
gl—*glad, glare, glue, glove*
tw—*twin, twine, twist, twig*
scr—*scrap, scrape, screen, scrub*
spr—*spring, spread, spray,*
sn—*snap, snow, snack, snail*
spl—*splash, splint, splinter*

Word Families

Initial consonant blends can be used as onsets in small group or large group activities in building word families:

an—*plan, clan, scan, bran, Fran*
ing—*sting, swing, string, bring, spring*

Using the preceding list of blends and the list of phonograms presented later (see p. 84), children can create hundreds of new words as part of phonics practice.

Final Blends

Consonant blends also occur in final position in words. According to Eldredge (1999), consonant blends that occur most frequently at the end of American English words are

nt—*bent, rent, aunt, runt*
nd—*and, send, band, behind*
ct—*act, duct, tract, reflect*
nce—*dance, fence*
nk—*ink, sank, rink, sunk*
mp—*ramp, imp, lamp, limp*
nge—*range, fringe*

ft—*lift, left, raft, craft*
sk— *desk, disk, task, tusk*
pt—*apt, kept, slept*
nse—*dense, rinse*
sp—*clasp, lisp*
lt—*felt, lilt, tilt, built*

Context

Children can become aware of consonant blends in final position through exercises that combine decoding and context with sentences such as

I pour water down the kitchen si__.
In Aladdin, *the genie lit the la__.*
I do my schoolwork at my de__.

Sometimes, blends and digraphs can occur in sequence in the same syllable, as digraphs become part of blends. In a word like *throw,* for example, the digraph **th** is blended with the letter **r.** Blends that include digraphs occur at the beginning of words like

shr—*shrub, shred, shrewd, shrank*   **thr**—*throw, thrill, throat, thread*
squ—*square, squint, squash, squeeze*

and at the end of words like

nch—*inch, lunch, ranch, pinch*

Children can practice decoding words while identifying the digraphs that are part of the blends in these words.

Teaching Suggestions ▼

Working with Blends and Digraphs Together

Swapping Blends and Digraphs

Using common word families or rimes, children can substitute different blends and digraphs to create new words. For example:

chest — crest	*shell — smell*	*sheet — street*
sheep — sleep	*whim — slim*	*chill — drill*

Real or Not?

Elements of vocabulary development can be added by making a list of words containing blends and digraphs, some of which are real words and some of which are not:

scare	*blare*	*snare*
slare	*spare*	*square*
stare	*plare*	*trare*
glare	*brare*	*plare*

Decoding pseudowords can be effective in acquiring and applying phonics skills. Besides, as children discuss which words are real and which are not, they acquire the meaning of words they may not have heard before.

Silent Letters

Silent consonant letters are often a source of curiosity for children. The expression "silent letter" is really a misnomer. Since letters represent rather than produce sounds, a letter can hardly be "silent." Nevertheless, the expression is commonly used to refer to letters that don't represent any phonetic element in words.

Common categories of silent consonant letters in English words include the following:

t combined with other letters such as **tch** (*catch* and *watch*), **stle** (*thistle* and *whistle*), and **sten** (*fasten* and *listen*)
d combined with **ge** in words like *badge, edge, judge*
w combined with **r** in *wrap, wrist, write*
k combined with **n** in words like *knee, know, knot*

g combined with **n** at the beginning of words like *gnome* and *gnat* and at the end of words like *sign* and *align*

b at the end of words like *lamb, thumb, climb*

p combined with **s** in words like *psycho* and *psalm*

l inside words like *talk* and *calf*.

Teaching Suggestions ▼

Silent Letters

Discovery

Write a list of words with common silent consonant combinations on the chalkboard or on a chart: for example, *know, knee, knight, knife, knock, knew, kneel.* Pronounce the words as you point to them and see if children can discover the "rule" in these words. Children can also be on the lookout for their own words with silent letters, and can make a list or a mini word wall with such words.

Compare and Contrast

Pairs of words such as the following (called *homophones*) can be written on the board:

wrap—rap	*red—read*	*wring—ring*
know—no	*knight—night*	*knew—new*

Children can compare the orthographic features and the meaning of these words, which extends into vocabulary development and spelling.

Diacritical Marking

As children encounter words with silent letters, they can mark the consonant letters that are not pronounced.

Silent consonants can be accounted for through evolution and borrowing. As our language evolved from the Old English of Beowulf through the Middle English of Chaucer to the Modern English we use today, the pronunciation of certain words shifted while the spelling of these words remained the same. Our early English-speaking ancestors pronounced the initial /k/ in *knee* and the final /b/ in *thumb*. And as our linguistic ancestors borrowed words from other languages—*psychology* from Greek, for example, or *depot* from French—the spelling and pronunciation was carried over as well.

As part of their everyday reading and writing, children will likely encounter words with silent consonant letters. Learning not to pronounce them in reading, and being sure to include them in writing, is part of dealing effectively with our orthographic system.

With early activities designed to teach children consonant sound-symbol relationships, it's impossible not to focus on vowel sounds as well. Creative teachers will find many opportunities for direct and incidental instruction that focuses children's attention on consonant sound-symbol relationships during the day in a language-rich classroom environment.

Vowels

The vowel system of American English is considerably more complicated than the system for consonants. Vowel sounds are produced when there is no interference with the column of air within the vocal tract. The air escapes freely from the lungs to the "outside world" without being impeded, redirected, or blocked in any way. Vowel sounds are determined by the position of the tongue within the oral cavity.

Each syllable contains a vowel and the vowel is the nucleus or most prominent part of the syllable, the element around which other sounds cluster. Instead of having children clap to count syllables, some teachers have children hold their hands under their chins because for every syllable, the mouth opens to let the vowel sound escape in an uninterrupted fashion.

The inventory of vowel phonemes in the overall sound system of American English contains nineteen phonemes, which includes short vowels, long vowels, medial vowels (which are single vowel phonemes that are neither short nor long), diphthongs, double **o,** other vowels, and finally, schwa. These are presented in figure 3.2.

Short Vowels		Long Vowels		Other Vowels	
/ă/	an	/ā/	age	/â/	dare
/ĕ/	end	/ē/	equal	/û/	her, bird
/ĭ/	in	/ī/	ice	/ä/	father
/ŏ/	odd	/ō/	old	/ô/	off
/ŭ/	cup	/ū/	use		
Diphthongs		**Double o**		**Schwa**	
/oi/	oil	/o͞o/	tool	/ə/	about
/ou/	out	/o͝o/	good		

Figure 3.2 *Vowel phonemes in the overall sound system of American English.*

Once again, it's important to remember that different sources of information will identify different vowel phonemes as part of the sound system of American English and that not all vowels exist as part of every dialect in the language. As in the case of transcribing consonants, different symbols are often used to represent vowel sounds, but the phonemes are always enclosed by double lines / /.

In teaching vowels, some teachers prefer to introduce long vowels first, since the letter name itself can be heard as the vowel is pronounced; for example, one can hear the letter name **a** in *rain* and the letter name **i** in *ride.*

Because of the many different ways in which long vowel sounds are represented in writing, however, most programs begin with short vowels, which are generally more consistent in their sound-symbol relationships.

Short Vowels

Short vowels are known as simple syllable nuclei. The sound is articulated with the tongue in a stable position in the mouth. (The tongue, of course, is rarely completely stable, as it is constantly moving toward or away from the position of the sounds that precede and follow the vowel sound.) In transcription, short sounds are marked by the breve / ˘ / diacritical mark above the letter.

Usually, short sounds are represented in writing by a single vowel grapheme in a consonant-vowel-consonant (CVC) syllable pattern or variation on that pattern, like CCVC or CVCC:

/ă/   *cab, bad, tag, ham, clam, drank, stand*
/ĕ/   *bed, leg, net, den, sped, step, blend*
/ĭ/   *hid, big, him, pin, lip, hit, quit, crisp*
/ŏ/   *job, fog, mom, top, hot, box, drop, blond*
/ŭ/   *rub, mud, bug, gum, fun, cup, plum, clump*

Sometimes, short vowels can be represented by other grapheme combinations, however—*pla*i*d, f*ea*ther, b*ui*ld, br*oa*d, d*oe*s.*

As with initial consonants, children often begin to learn about short vowels by creating word families with onsets and rimes. Onsets and rimes are coherent units that are relatively easy to break apart and put back together again. Decoding words by pattern is easier for young readers than trying to sound out words letter-by-letter.

Teaching Suggestions ▼

Short Vowels

Minimal Pairs

As an extension of phonemic awareness, children's attention can be focused on the different short vowel sounds and the letters representing these sounds. Write pairs of words on the board with minimum short vowel contrasts:

bad—bed   bet—bit   big—bog   dog—dug

Children can identify the phonemic differences in these words and note the letters that represent these sounds.

Word Families

From alphabet training and practice with initial consonants, children should be familiar with some simple CVC words from which word families can be built:

cat   *hen*   *pig*   *dog*   *bug*

Adding different initial consonant letters can produce word families like

bat	*Ben*	*big*	*bog*	*hug*
fat	*den*	*dig*	*fog*	*jug*
hat	*men*	*rig*	*hog*	*rug*
rat	*pen*	*wig*	*log*	*tug*

Children can add to these short vowel word lists as they encounter words with similar patterns in their reading and writing.

Short Vowel Substitution

Children can create lists of new words by changing the vowel in CVC words:

bad/bed/bid   *bat/bit/bet/but*   *red/rid/rod*   *pat/pet/pit/pot*

Teams of children can compete to see how many new words they can create in this fashion. The activity can be easily expanded with initial and final consonant substitution as well.

The CVC patterns with short vowels that children learn to decode as part of basic onset-rime combinations often occur in longer, multisyllabic words. As children learn to decode *ten*, for example, they encounter this pattern again in words like *tendency, attention,* and *pretense.*

Context

As in the case of learning other discrete phonics elements, decoding and context strategies can be combined with sentences such as

I ride to school in a v_n.
My little sister can count to t_n.
"Please s_t down," the teacher said.
I like to h_p, sk_p, and j_mp.
The r_g is on the floor.

BINGO

The game BINGO (or if someone objects, WORDO) can be used effectively for practice in short vowel sounds. Teachers prepare cards like the one on the right.

Children place markers in the appropriate spaces as the teacher calls words with the corresponding short vowel sound. This game can be adopted for practice with long vowels, diphthongs, consonants, and other discrete phonics elements.

WORDO				
a	e	i	o	u
		FREE		

The cub is black.

The sun is red.

The gum is green.

The tub is yellow.

The nut is brown.

The bug is orange.

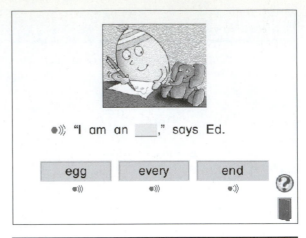

●))) "I am an ____," says Ed.

| egg | every | end |

Short vowel exercises typically focus on words with a (C)VC pattern; children supply the missing words in isolation or in context.

Left: from **Primary Phonics Workbook 1.** *Cambridge, MA: Educators Publishing Service, 1999. Reproduced with permission.*
Right: from "Sounds Great! AEIOU CD." New York: Wright Group/McGraw-Hill, 2000. Reproduced with permission of the McGraw-Hill Companies.

Y and W as Vowels. Children learn early in their school lives that the vowels are **a, e, i, o,** and **u,** and sometimes **y** (and sometimes **w).** When are **y** and **w** vowels? In order to understand **y** and **w** as vowels, it's important to understand the small and unique category of English phonemes called *glides.*

Glides, as the name suggests, are sounds made when the tongue glides from one position to another within the oral cavity as the sounds are being made. These phonemes were identified as /h/, /y/, and /w/ in the inventory of English consonants (see p. 68). When these sounds occur before a vowel sound in words like

    hit   yell   well

they behave exactly like consonants; that is, they are made with interference of air in the vocal tract and have specific points and manners of articulation. When they occur in postvocalic position (after a vowel), however, they have the effect of prolonging the vowel sound as in

    boyyyyyyyyyyyyy or cowwwwwwwww

Glides are involved in long vowel sounds and in diphthongs as part of our speech system.

The letter **y** has long been considered a vowel, since it is the only letter used to represent the vowel sound in words like *cyst* and *by* and in syllables like -*ly*. In the middle of single syllable words, **y** represents the short i sound (*gym, myth*); at the end of syllables or single syllable words, **y** represents the long i sound (*try, typhoon*); at the end of multisyllable words, **y** represents the sound of long e (*sorry, carry*). The glide **y** is also involved in articulating long (or "glided") vowel sounds. **Y** also has a vowel-like quality when it is part of a diphthong, as in *boy* or *toy*.

Unlike **y,** the letter **w** was never used as the only letter representing a vowel sound in a syllable. Like **y,** however, when it immediately follows a vowel, it connects with the vowel to produce a glided vowel sound; that is, it connects to the vowel sound to escape with no interference as it passes through the human vocal tract. As a glide, **w** doesn't represent any distinct vowel phoneme on its own but is always linked with another vowel. That's why some programs add "and sometimes **w**" when naming vowel letters.

Long Vowels

Long vowels are complex syllable nuclei. These sounds are created by combining simple syllable nuclei with glides and therefore are sometimes called "glided sounds." In other words, the tongue starts in a stable position and moves in the direction of the glide as the sound is being articulated. In transcription, long vowel sounds are marked by a macron /¯/ diacritical mark above the letter.

Sometimes, long vowels are represented by a single letter—*<u>a</u>corn, <u>e</u>qual, <u>i</u>odine, <u>o</u>ld, <u>u</u>nion*. More often, these sounds are represented by vowel letter combinations—*<u>ai</u>m, <u>ea</u>t, t<u>ie</u>, t<u>oe</u>, fr<u>ui</u>t*. No matter how they are spelled, long vowels are the sounds that "say their own names."

Teaching Suggestions ▼

Long Vowels

Comparing Short and Long Sounds

The teacher presents contrasting pairs of words like

mad—made	*ran—rain*	*cub—cube*
hid—hide	*cod—code*	*pad—paid*
bat—bait	*pan—pane*	*not—note*

Children separate the words according to the sounds they hear. Contrasting vowel sounds in word pairs like these is an extension of phonemic awareness instruction.

Word Families

Word families can be created as easily with long vowels as with short vowels. With rimes like

ate	*eat*	*ice*	*oat*	*une*

children can build word families by adding initial consonant letters and blends:

date	*beat*	*mice*	*boat*	*dune*
gate	*heat*	*nice*	*coat*	*June*
late	*neat*	*rice*	*goat*	*tune*
mate	*seat*	*lice*	*float*	*prune*

In working with word families in which the vowel sound is long, it's easy to see the variability in the spelling of long vowel sounds. In building a word family for the *ate* phonogram, for example, children will suggest the initial letters **b** (for *bate*, which is spelled *bait*) and **w** for *wate* (which is spelled *wait* or *weight*). This launches teachers and children into a lesson on homophones, which extends phonics into word meaning and spelling.

Edward Fry* (1998) has identified 38 phonograms that can be found in over 650 different one-syllable words. These common phonograms include both short and long vowels:

- ay—*say, pay, day*
- ill—*hill, Bill, spill*
- ip—*ship, dip, tip*
- at—*cat, bat, fat*
- am—*ham, jam, dam*
- ag—*bag, rag, tag*
- ack—*back, sack, black*
- ank—*bank, sank, tank*
- ick—*sick, chick, quick*
- ell—*bell, sell, tell*
- ot—*pot, not, hot*
- ing—*ring, sing, thing*
- ap—*cap, map, clap*
- unk—*sunk, junk, skunk*
- ail—*pail, jail, nail*
- ain—*rain, pain, chain*
- eed—*feed, seed, weed*
- y—*my, by, try*
- out—*pout, trout, shout*
- ug—*rug, bug, hug*
- op—*mop, cop, pop*
- in—*pin, tin, chin*
- an—*pan, man, ran*
- est—*best, nest, pest*
- ink—*pink, sink, drink*
- ow—*low, show, slow*
- ew—*new, few, chew*
- ore—*more, sore, store*
- ed—*bed, red, fed*
- ab—*cab, dab, crab*
- ob—*cob, job, knob*
- ock—*sock, rock, block*
- ake—*cake, lake, brake*
- ine—*line, nine, shine*
- ight—*knight, light, right*
- im—*him, rim, swim*
- uck—*duck, luck, truck*
- um—*gum, bum, drum*

See how many other words you can build from these common rimes.

Long Vowel Word Wall

Long vowel words that children encounter as part of their classroom language experiences can be posted on word walls. These can be arranged in displays such as

List from Fry, Edward B. (1988, April). Teaching reading: The most common phonograms. *The Reading Teacher, 51*(7), 620–622. Reprinted with the permission of Edward B. Fry and the International Reading Association. All rights reserved.

Long Vowels, continued

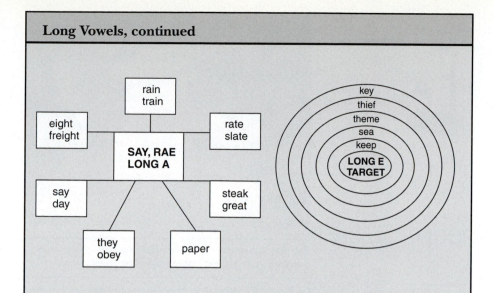

Children can suggest other displays for other discrete phonics elements.

Games

Games such as WORDO, concentration, Go Fish!, and other popular games can be adopted for use with practicing and reinforcing long vowel sounds.

Poetry

Poetry can be an effective means of focusing children's attention on long vowels (and short vowels as well). Poets whose work involves a heavy emphasis on end-line rhyme (poets like Jack Prelutsky and Shel Silverstein, among others) provide vehicles for examining sound (and spelling) features as children enjoy their poems. Books of poems have been specifically compiled for teaching phonics, along with teaching suggestions for using these poems, for example: *Phonics Through Poetry: Teaching Phonemic Awareness Using Poetry* by Babs Bell Hajdusiewicz (Good Year Books, 1998) and *Phonics Poetry: Teaching Word Families* by Timothy V. Rasinski and Belinad S. Zimmerman (Allyn and Bacon, 2001).

Other Vowel Sounds

The vowel sound system of English is complex and contains phonemes other than short and long vowels. They include medial vowels, double vowels that are single phonemes, double vowels that make blended sounds, r-controlled vowels, and schwa.

pine

Exercises on long vowels typically include much practice on letter combinations or patterns that represent these sounds.

Medial vowels occur in words such as *father, wall,* and *water.* The vowel sound is neither short nor long, but may be described as "somewhere in between." Some very fine distinctions exist among these medial vowel phonemes, and not all experts classify them in the same fashion. Some people pronounce the /ä/ in *father* and the /ô/ in *off* differently; to other speakers, these are the same sounds. Instead of trying to explain to children the intricacies of how these sounds work, Blevins (1998) suggests teaching these sounds by spelling patterns.

Teaching Suggestions ▼

Medial Vowels

Spelling Patterns

Rimes or phonograms containing medial vowels can be written on the chalkboard and children can develop lists of words based on these patterns:

-alk *talk, walk, stalk*   -all *ball, call, fall*

Medial Vowels, continued

As in all cases, children should be alert to variations in the pattern, as in *shall*.

Word Sort

Children can categorize words according to their vowel sounds in word sorts. Children can be given a list of "**a**-words"

fame	*ball*	*sail*	*bay*
part	*cab*	*fat*	*rate*
call	*cape*	*fad*	*came*

and asked to sort these words according to the following categories:

Long Sound	**Short Sound**	**"Other" Sound**
fate	*fat*	*father*

Children then place the word in the appropriate list.

"See if It Works."

As children encounter unfamiliar words with medial vowel sounds, they can be encouraged to try the medial sound if the appropriate long or short sound does not make sense in the context of the sentence.

Double vowel letters exist in combination, sometimes making a single vowel sound and sometimes making blended vowel sounds.

Vowel digraphs are two vowel letters that combine to make a single sound. For example, the letter combination **oo** creates two separate phonemes:

/o͝o/ *as in good, book, and cookie*
/o͞o/ *as in too, food, and school.*

Other digraphs are the **ai** in *rain* that makes the /ā/ sound, the **oa** in *boat* that makes the /ō/ sound, and the **ew** in *grew* that makes the /ū/ sound (here is where **w** is considered a vowel). The double **o**'s in *food* and *good* combine to make phonemes that are unique in the overall sound system of American English.

Vowel diphthongs are two vowel letters that represent a "blended" vowel sound as the **oi** in *boil* or the **ou** in *shout*. Just as one can tell the difference between consonant blends and digraphs by listening carefully to the sound divisions (or lack thereof), one can tell the difference between vowel digraphs and diphthongs by listening carefully to the distinction in vowel phonemes. In the word *boat*, there is no separation of sounds in the vowel digraph; all one hears is the /ō/ sound. In the word *boil*, one can hear a blending of the two elements in the vowel diphthong /oi/.

Sound to Symbol

▶ Circle each word that has the vowel digraph **oo** or **ea**. Then write the words in the correct columns.

> **RULE**
>
> In a **vowel digraph**, two letters together stand for one vowel sound. It can be short or long, or have a special sound of its own. The vowel digraph **oo** stands for the vowel sound you hear in *book* and *pool*. The vowel digraph **ea** can stand for the short **e** sound you hear in *bread*.

1. Mike and Joe looked at the clock and saw that it was noon.

2. They stood up and left the classroom.

3. The weather was cool, so they grabbed their jackets.

4. They were ready to play a good game of football.

5. Mike threw the heavy ball, and it sailed over Joe's head.

6. The ball took a sudden turn toward the school wall.

7. Mike watched with dread as it went toward a window.

8. At the last minute, Joe scooped up the ball.

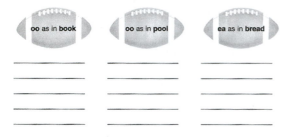

oo as in **book**   oo as in **pool**   ea as in **bread**

_____   _____   _____
_____   _____   _____
_____   _____   _____
_____   _____   _____

TALK What would the boys have done if they had broken a window?

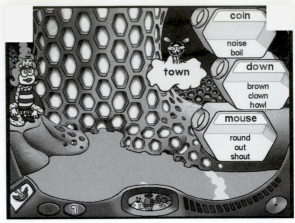

Vowel digraphs and diphthongs are typically taught through patterns in words.

Left: from Modern Curriculum Press Phonics Phonics Level C by Elwell, Murray, and Kucia © 2003 by Pearson Education, Inc., publishing as Modern Curriculum Press, an imprint of Pearson Education Learning Group, an imprint of Pearson Education Learning Group. Used by permission.
Right: from McGraw-Hill Readings: Phonics. "Adventures with Buggles CD-ROM Package, Grade 2–3." New York: Macmillan/McGraw-Hill, 2001. Reproduced with permission of the McGraw-Hill Companies.

Teaching Suggestions ▼

Double Vowels

Word Sorts

Double vowels, particularly those vowel combinations that represent more than one sound, can be taught through word sorts:

oo represents the vowel sound in *boot* and in *book*

ou represents the vowel sound in *soup* and in *sound*

ow represents the vowel sound in *cow* and in *crow*

ie represents the vowel sound in *die* and in *chief*

To alert children to these variants, teachers can make letter cards with different vowel combinations and words on them, and children can sort words that correspond to the vowel sounds they hear as the teacher reads lists of words. For example:

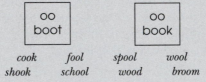

oo	oo
boot	book

| cook | fool | spool | wool |
| shook | school | wood | broom |

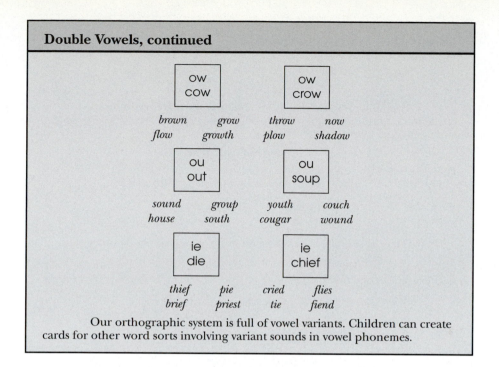

Double Vowels, continued

ow	ow
cow	crow

| brown | grow | throw | now |
| flow | growth | plow | shadow |

ou	ou
out	soup

| sound | group | youth | couch |
| house | south | cougar | wound |

ie	ie
die	chief

| thief | pie | cried | flies |
| brief | priest | tie | fiend |

Our orthographic system is full of vowel variants. Children can create cards for other word sorts involving variant sounds in vowel phonemes.

R-controlled vowels are a special category. Vowels followed by the letter **r** have a unique sound that is neither long nor short:

> **ar** as in *star* and *hard*
> **er** as in *germ* and *fern*
> **ir** as in *bird* and *first*
> **or** as in *fort* and *cork*
> **ur** as in *hurt* and *nurse*

"This phonic fact—as it relates to learning to read—is probably not extremely important; however, calling children's attention to the role of the letter **r** is a justifiable procedure. Since children use and understand hundreds of words that include a vowel followed by *r,* this is not a particularly difficult fact to teach" (Heilman 2002, 106). Words with **er, ir,** and **ur** can cause spelling problems because they all have the same vocalic sound.

Teaching Suggestions ▼

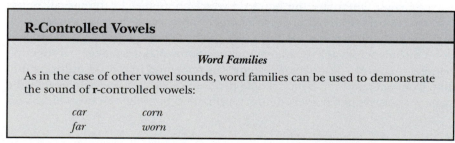

R-Controlled Vowels

Word Families

As in the case of other vowel sounds, word families can be used to demonstrate the sound of **r**-controlled vowels:

| car | corn |
| far | worn |

R-Controlled Vowels, continued

bar	*morn*
tar	*torn*

Beginning with these patterns, other **r**-controlled words can be created with word-building activities, with words such as *farm, dark, barn, horse,* and the like.

Comparing and Contrasting

Pairs of words with and without **r**-controlled vowels can be listed and children can be asked to compare the pronunciation of each of the words:

shark—shack	*skirt—skate*	*surf—safe*
girl—gill	*short—shirt*	*corn—cane*

The effect of the **r** on the sound of the vowel should be noted.

Context

Context can be used to support decoding of words containing **r**-controlled vowels:

When the sun goes down, it becomes _____ . (dark)

I saw a _____ flying in the sky. (bird)

If you light a match, it will _____ . (burn)

When my brother sleeps, he _____ . (snores)

The people in the cafeteria _____ lunch every day. (serve)

Schwa is a unique vowel sound. It is articulated with the tongue in a neutral position in the mid-central part of the mouth. The sound is represented in transcription by the symbol /ə/, an upside-down **e**. As a phoneme, schwa only occurs in unaccented syllables, and it is variously represented by all five vowel letters—*about, children, pencil, button, circus.*

Since the schwa phoneme occurs only in unstressed syllables, its sound remains constant no matter which letter is used to represent it. That's why it's not a major instructional focus in many beginning phonics programs; in fact, many programs omit it entirely. Teaching the schwa sound has little impact on children's initial ability to decode words. When children begin to learn to use a dictionary that includes the /ə/ symbol, however, they need to understand the nature of the sound.

These, then, are the nineteen vowel phonemes in the overall sound system of American English. Once again, different sources of information will include slight changes in the inventory presented on page 77. Some sources don't include schwa as a separate phoneme. Some dialects make no distinction between /ä/ and /ô/; the vowel sounds in *father* and in *tall* are indistinguishable from one another. Some people pronounce *cot* and *caught* in exactly the same way; others make a very definite distinction between the two words. Variations exist based on the system of analysis used, dialect differences, individual speech patterns, and other factors.

Overall, vowels constitute the most complex part of our sound system because of the variability in the way in which these nineteen sounds are represented by only five vowel letters. Vowels can provide daunting challenges for teachers teaching and children learning phonics. It's important to remember, however, that most children enter the classroom having all the vowel sounds in their vocal repertoire. The teacher's job is to help them discover the various ways that these sounds are represented in print.

Vowel sounds are fluid and flexible. The tongue is a very mobile speech organ, and so sounds are made differently from one individual to the next and from one speech area to the next. Vowels make the major difference in dialects. The expression "*The time is . . .*

> *. . . hahf pahst ten"*
> *. . . haf past ten"*
> *. . . hayft payst ten"*

depends on whether one is speaking in (an exaggerated) Northern, Midland, or Southern dialect. Whether one is standing on Beacon Hill in Boston, in the Delaware Gap, or on the Gulf Coast in Texas, consonants are made with precise consistency. The vowel sounds make the difference between one dialect and the other.

Syllables

Syllables are units of pronunciation in words consisting of a vowel or a combination of a vowel and consonant(s). All words are made up of syllables; some words are monosyllabic (such as *each*) while others are polysyllabic (such as *computer*). These pronounceable units are helpful as children attempt to decode new words in reading and as they combine letters for correct spelling in writing.

What do children need to know about syllables as part of phonics instruction? They need to learn that

- a syllable always contains a vowel and the vowel is the nucleus or most prominent part of the syllable; the syllable may consist of a vowel alone (as in **a**-*corn*) or it may consist of a vowel and surrounding consonants (as in *a-***corn**);
- there is a syllable for every vowel sound in a word but not for every vowel letter; *leisure,* for example, contains four vowel symbols but only two vowel sounds; the number of vowel sounds one hears in a word equals the number of syllables in the word;
- sometimes a syllable can be a single phoneme represented by a single letter, as the letter **a** in the word *around;* sometimes a syllable can be a sequence of several phonemes represented by a string of letters, as in the word *stretch;*
- prefixes and suffixes are usually separate syllables.

Syllables can be *open* or *closed*. Open syllables end in a long vowel sound (as in *pa-per*). Closed syllables end in consonant sounds (as in *pa-per*). A syllable can end with a consonant letter, but if it ends with a vowel sound (as in *al-though*), it's an open syllable, no matter how that sound is spelled.

Syllables can be accented or unaccented. A monosyllabic word is always accented. In multisyllabic words, accent patterns vary. In the context of spoken language, accent shifts can determine the meaning of a word. Compare the pronunciations (and meanings) of *conduct* in the following two sentences:

Ivan will cŏn-dúct the orchestra.
Ivan's cón-dŭct was appalling.

Other examples of words that have different pronunciations and meanings depending on syllable shifts include *content, permit, refuse,* and *present*.

Teaching Suggestions ▼

Syllables

Counting Syllables

Syllable recognition and manipulation is part of phonemic awareness (see p. 37–38). Children can continue to clap, hold their hands under their chin, tap the table, place markers on number cards, or use musical instruments and other response techniques as a means of indicating the number of syllables in words.

Stepping Down

The teacher can write familiar multisyllable words on the board by syllables:

cal	in	un
cal cu	in for	un der
cal cu la	in for ma	un der stand
cal cu la tor	in for ma tion	un der stand ing

Children can "walk down" the steps by pronouncing the syllables in order. The activity provides a good opportunity for children to examine vowel-consonant combinations in syllables within the context of real words.

Many of the Teaching Suggestions for segmenting syllables as part of phonemic awareness can be used, with the words in written form.

Having children complete exercises in which they have to mark syllable patterns in words is a questionable practice. The purpose of phonics is to help children learn to read and spell. If a child can recognize the stress pattern in a word, then the child can already recognize the word, so it makes little sense to require the child to engage in busywork exercises on material that he/she already knows.

Rules for dividing words into syllables—*when two consonants stand between two vowels, the syllable division usually occurs between the two consonants; when three consonants stand between two vowels, the syllable division occurs between the blend and the other consonant; etc.*—have been taught as part of phonics instruction. However, this emphasis on rules has diminished. "Syllabication rules are rarely taught these days because teachers realized, and research demonstrates, that there is little relationship between knowing the rules and successful reading" (Cunningham 1998, 190).

Phonics Generalizations

While discrete phonics elements are controlled by rules that children have been required to memorize over the years, the usefulness of the rules or generalizations governing sound-symbol relationships continues to be discussed and questioned. (The term *generalization* is often used instead of *rule* because the latter implies a certain sense of scientific absolutism that certainly does not exist in sound-symbol relationships of English orthography.) On the way to learning to read, children learned maxims such as, "When two vowels go walking, the first one does the talking," and "Magic **e** makes the previous vowel long."

The point of phonics rules or generalizations is twofold. First, they attempt to describe precisely details of the sound-symbol relationships of our language. Second, they are intended to support children in figuring out unfamiliar words they have trouble decoding while reading. Although these generalizations may be easy for children to remember, they are often so unreliable that they are hardly useful enough to justify learning them.

In a classic study, Theodore Clymer (1996) examined the utility of the most widely taught phonics generalizations. Clymer applied generalizations to a list of 2,600 words generally found in early reading books for children in an attempt to determine the utility of each rule. An examination of the results of Clymer's analysis (see figure 3.3) shows that while some generalizations apply all the time—for example, *When a word begins with **kn** the **k** is silent*—some apply in less than half the words a child typically encounters in early reading material—for example, *When there are two vowels side by side, the long sound of the first is heard and the second is usually silent.* "The results of Clymer's study proved disturbing to him and to others because they ran counter to what many instructors had been teaching for many years" (Baer 1999, 49).

A spate of follow-up studies focused on the generalizations that Clymer had examined using longer word lists, words at different grade levels, words from different curriculum areas, and other criteria. The results were largely the same; that is, that many of the phonics rules that children learn are limited in their application in helping children sound out unfamiliar words. However, in reexamining Clymer's original analysis with a specific focus on rules governing

Figure 3.3 *Utility of phonics generalization.*

The chart below summarizes the results of Clymer's analysis of phonics rules as they apply to words that children often encounter in beginning reading materials.

Generalization	No. of Words Conforming	No. of Exceptions	Percent of Utility
1. When there are two vowels side by side, the long sound of the first is heard and the second is usually silent.	309 (bead)**	377 (chief)	45
2. When a vowel is in the middle of a one-syllable word, the vowel is short.	408	249	62
Middle letter	191 (dress)	84 (scold)	69
One of the middle two letters in a word of four letters	191 (rest)	135 (told)	59
One vowel <u>within</u> a word of more than four letters	26 (splash)	30 (fight)	46
3. If the only vowel letter is at the end of a word, the letter usually stands for a long sound.	23 (he)	8 (to)	74
4. When there are two vowels, one of which is a final <u>e</u>, the first vowel is long and the <u>e</u> is silent.	180 (bone)	108 (wire)	63
*5. The <u>r</u> gives the preceding vowel a sound that is neither long nor short.	184 (horn)	134 (wire)	78
6. The first vowel is usually long and the second silent in digraphs <u>ai</u>, <u>ea</u>, <u>oa</u>, and <u>ui</u>.	179	92	66
<u>ai</u>	43 (nail)	24 (said)	64
<u>ea</u>	101 (bead)	51 (head)	66
<u>oa</u>	34 (boat)	1 (cupboard)	97
<u>ui</u>	1 (suit)	16 (build)	6
7. In the phonogram <u>ie</u>, the <u>i</u> is silent and the <u>e</u> has a long sound.	8 (field)	39 (friend)	17
*8. Words having double <u>e</u> usually have the long <u>e</u> sound.	85 (seem)	2 (been)	98
9. When words end with silent <u>e</u>, the preceding <u>a</u> or <u>i</u> is long.	164 (cake)	108 (have)	60
*10. In <u>ay</u> the <u>y</u> is silent and gives <u>a</u> its long sound.	36 (play)	10 (always)	78
11. When the letter <u>i</u> is followed by the letters <u>gh</u>, the <u>i</u> usually stands for its long sound and the <u>gh</u> is silent.	22 (high)	9 (neighbor)	71
12. When <u>a</u> follows <u>w</u> in a word, it usually has the sound <u>a</u> as in <u>was</u>.	15 (watch)	32 (swam)	32
13. When <u>e</u> is followed by <u>w</u>, the vowel sound is the same as represented by <u>oo</u>.	9 (blew)	17 (sew)	35
14. The two letters <u>ow</u> make the long <u>o</u> sound.	50 (own)	35 (swam)	59
15. <u>W</u> is sometimes a vowel and follows the vowel digraph rule.	50 (crow)	75 (threw)	40
*16. When <u>y</u> is the final letter in a word, it usually has a vowel sound.	169 (dry)	32 (tray)	84
17. When <u>y</u> is used as a vowel in words, it sometimes has the sound of long <u>i</u>.	29 (fly)	170 (funny)	15
18. The letter <u>a</u> has the same sound (o) when followed by <u>l</u>, <u>w</u>, and <u>u</u>.	61 (all)	65 (canal)	48
19. When <u>a</u> is followed by <u>r</u> and final <u>e</u>, we expect to hear the sound heard in <u>care</u>.	9 (dare)	1 (are)	90
*20. When <u>c</u> and <u>h</u> are next to each other, they make only one sound.	103 (peach)	0	100
*21. <u>Ch</u> is usually pronounced as it is in <u>kitchen</u>, <u>catch</u>, and <u>chair</u>, not like <u>sh</u>.	99 (catch)	5 (machine)	95

*22.	When c is followed by e or i, the sound of s is likely to be heard.	66 (cent)	3 (ocean)	96
*23.	When the letter c is followed by o or a, the sound of k is likely to be heard.	143 (camp)	0	100
24.	The letter g often has a sound similar to that of j in jump when it precedes the letter i or e.	49 (engine)	28 (give)	64
*25.	When ght is seen in a word, gh is silent.	30 (fight)	0	100
26.	When a word begins with kn, the k is silent.	10 (knife)	0	100
27.	When a word begins with wr, the w is silent.	8 (write)	0	100
*28.	When two of the same consonants are side by side, only one is heard.	334 (carry)	3 (suggest)	99
*29.	When a word ends in ck, it has the same last sound as in hook.	46 (brick)	0	100
*30.	In most two-syllable words, the first syllable is accented.	828 (famous)	143 (polite)	85
*31.	If a, in, re, ex, de, or be is the first syllable in a word, it is usually unaccented.	86 (belong)	13 (insect)	87
*32.	In most two-syllable words that end in a consonant followed by a y, the first syllable is accented and the last is unaccented.	101 (baby)	4 (supply)	96
33.	One vowel letter in an accented syllable has its short sound.	547 (city)	356 (lady)	61
34.	When y or ey is seen in the last syllable that is not accented, the long sound of e is heard.	0	157 (baby)	0
35.	When ture is the final syllable in a word, it is unaccented.	4 (picture)	0	100
36.	When tion is the final syllable in a word, it is unaccented.	5 (station)	0	100
37.	In many two- and three-syllable words, the final e lengthens the vowel in the last syllable.	52 (invite)	62 (gasoline)	46
38.	If the first vowel sound in a word is followed by two consonants, the first syllable usually ends with the first of the two consonants.	404 (bullet)	159 (singer)	72
39.	If the first vowel sound in a word is followed by a single consonant, that consonant usually begins the second syllable.	190 (over)	237 (oven)	44
*40.	If the last syllable of a word ends in le, the consonant preceding the le usually begins the last syllable.	62 (tumble)	2 (buckle)	97
*41.	When the first vowel element in a word is followed by th, ch, or sh, these symbols are not broken when the word is divided into syllables and may go with either the first or second syllable.	30 (dishes)	0	100
42.	In a word of more than one syllable, the letter v usually goes with the preceding vowel to form a syllable.	53 (cover)	20 (clover)	73
43.	When a word has only one vowel letter, the vowel sound is likely to be short.	433 (hid)	322 (kind)	57
*44.	When there is one e in a word that ends in a consonant, the e usually has a short sound.	85 (leg)	27 (blew)	76
*45.	When the last syllable is the sound r, it is unaccented.	188 (butter)	9 (appear)	95

*Generalizations marked with an asterisk were found "useful" according to the criteria.

**Words in parenthesis are examples—either of words that conform or of exceptions, depending on the column.

From Clymer, T. (1996, November). The utility of phonic generalization in the primary grades. *The Reading Teacher, 50*(3), 182–187. Originally published in *The Reading Teacher, 16,* 1963. Reprinted with permission of Theodore Clymer and the International Reading Association. All rights reserved.

vowel combinations, Johnson (2001) concluded that "when broad generalizations with low percentages of utility are broken down into specific vowel combinations, there are, in many cases, high degrees of utility" (139).

The problem with phonics generalizations is that the orthographic system of English is complex, "a mind-boggling web of correspondences" (Moustafa 1997, 10). No simple set of rules can account for the complicated system of sound-symbol relationships in our language. Through careful linguistic analysis, rules governing orthographic relationships can be reliably formulated, but most are too complicated to be of any practical use in helping children learn to read.

Working with Children Who May Have Trouble Learning Phonics

That "all children are different" is an educational truism. Meeting the wide range of abilities in any classroom is perhaps the teacher's greatest challenge. Some children acquire phonics knowledge with ease; others don't. For children with reading difficulties or disabilities—due to a combination of reasons that might include physical factors, cognitive limitations, language-related disabilities or dyslexia, or a complex of other causes—teachers need to make adjustments and accommodations in teaching phonics.

Children Who Have Trouble Learning Phonics in a Conventional Way

Children who have trouble learning phonics in a conventional way require extra time and attention from the teacher. These are the pupils who need the most intensive, systematic, and sustained instruction. Early intervention for these children is important because children whose reading problems are not addressed at the outset continue to read poorly throughout the school years and beyond (McCardle et al. 2001). For children who struggle with learning phonics, the instructional 3 R's include *review, reteach,* and *reinforce.*

Review involves lots of drill and practice with word wheels, flip charts, games, and other devices that will help children work with sound elements that they are expected to learn. Review includes "booster sessions" to help children remember elements that have been previously taught. Review focuses on material presented previously and involves systematic instruction that characterizes good phonics teaching.

Reteaching often involves moving at a slower pace. In working with onsets and rimes, for example, when most children are ready to move from one vowel sound to another (to move from *-am, -at,* and *-ash* to *-im, -it,* and *-ish*), the struggling learner may have to practice with additional short **a** phonograms (such as *-ap, -ag, -ad,* etc.) until the concept is firmly established.

Reteaching may also involve presenting material by multisensory means. Instead of relying solely on auditory processing, children work with visual skills (by color coding certain sound-symbol relationships), tactual devices

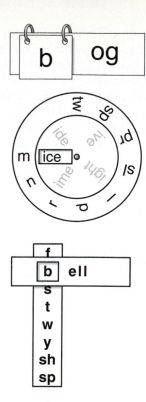

Manipulatives like these can be used for review and practice with children who need extra help in learning discrete phonics elements.

(by focusing on the sense of touch by presenting phonics elements in sandpaper, window screen, or other material that the child can feel as well as see), and kinesthetic movements (by having children move their hands as they blend sound elements in words). The senses are the pathways to the brain, and the more senses teachers can use in helping children learn phonics, the better will be the chances that their children will learn.

Children who struggle with phonics are often prime candidates for the structured language programs described in the next chapter (see pp. 118–123). These programs typically involve an explicit and systematic approach to instruction that involves multisensory learning. The problem is that most of these programs require teachers with fairly extensive professional preparation for using the program, which regular classroom teachers often lack. Besides, in order to offer a particular program to children, the school needs to buy into the philosophy and approach that the program uses (which more and more schools are doing).

To reinforce and apply phonics knowledge, children need lots of practice with decodable text, books that contain stories with vocabulary that is tightly controlled based on a sound-symbol regularity. These books provide a vehicle by which children learn phonics elements and practice decoding within the context of a story.

Scaffolded instruction provides support. "Students with intense learning needs require substantial support to gain cognitive access to the complexities of our alphabetic writing system" (Coyne et al. 2001, 67). The teacher provides scaffolded instruction by modeling strategies used in decoding. For example, the teacher points to letters in a word while saying the sounds and then points to the letters while the child says the sound. Then children learn independently to blend the sounds to read the word. The aim of scaffolding is to support children as they learn to apply decoding strategies as they encounter new words as they read.

Teaching children who don't learn as easily as their classmates has always been a challenge. There are no easy answers. Students who are at risk require more time and attention for review and repeated practice. They need careful guidance in developing strategies for decoding words. They may need the help of a resource person like a learning specialist or a classroom assistant to support the work of the classroom teacher. They may need extra materials especially adjusted to meet their needs. They certainly need a supportive environment in which they are convinced that they can succeed. At a macro level, meeting the needs of all children involves a school-wide commitment to achieving reading goals, early identification and monitoring of children with learning difficulty, and a commitment to instructional intervention. All of this takes effort, but more often than not, the results are worth the effort.

Children Whose First Language Is Not English (ELL)

What about phonics instruction for children who are not native English speakers or who come from homes where English is not the dominant language spoken? A number of expressions have been used to designate or describe these children: bilingual learners, students with English as a Second Language (ESL), children with Limited English Proficiency (LEP), Language Minority Students (LMS). The expression English Language Learners (ELL) is used here because it is a comprehensive term that includes the range of children (and adults) from those who speak no English and are illiterate in their native language to those who can read and write in their dominant language but are learning to become literate in English.

The number of ELL children in schools is growing at an amazing rate. Over 10 million children (about one-quarter of the school population) live in homes where a language other than English is spoken. It's not unusual to find as many as twenty different languages spoken in a single school or to find a majority of children in a particular school speaking a "minority" language, and it's a good bet that sometime in their careers, today's teachers will have ELL children in their classrooms.

Educational policy regarding English Language Learners has become a political football, and various models are used to provide for the educational needs of ELL children, from total immersion to transition programs. Meanwhile, as the political debate continues, teachers are expected to help English Language Learners become proficient readers and writers, and learning phonics is part of that process.

Some English Language Learners can already read and write in their dominant language and their aim is to become biliterate as well as bilingual. Others, while they speak their home language perfectly well, have not yet learned to deal with their dominant language in its written form. Arguments have been made for teaching children to read in their native language before trying to teach them to read in English. Code-switching—alternating two existing codes in a completely appropriate fashion—frequently occurs; that is, children who have a knowledge of sound-symbol relationships in a text can transfer this knowledge from one language to another. For example, the phonemic awareness ability of Spanish-speaking children predicted decoding skills in learning to read English as well (Durgunoglu et al. 1993). Children who can read in their dominant language typically learn to read English more quickly.

The starting point for phonics instruction for English Language Learners is learning the symbols of the alphabet. While languages like Spanish share a common Roman alphabet with English, immigrants from Eastern European or Asian nations are familiar with a different set of written symbols that represent the sounds of their language, and many may be encountering the Roman symbols of the English alphabet for the first time. For these students, learning letter names becomes a prerequisite for learning phonics, as it is for native English speakers learning how to read and write.

Phonemic awareness in English presents problems for many English Language Learners. Since sound systems are different, ELL children may confuse sounds in isolation, which suggests the need for a meaningful contextualized instructional environment. In planning phonics instruction for English Language Learning children, it's important to remember the three cueing systems—*semantic, syntactic,* and *graphophonic*—that support success in learning to read (briefly described at the end of chapter 1, pp. 20–21).

Phonological systems between languages are also different, often markedly so. For ELL children, it's important for teachers to be aware of phonological "conflict points" between the child's dominant language and English. Some children confuse the phonemes /sh/ and /ch/ because of their language background (so that *sheep* becomes *cheep,* for example), or they may confuse the sounds /th/ and /z/ because the former phoneme is not part of the sound system of their native language. (In much the same way, speakers of particular dialects of English confuse the vowel sounds in *pen* and *pin*.) In dealing with sounds (and later sound-symbol relationships), ELL children can be encouraged to reproduce English phonemes as closely as possible to the corresponding sounds in their own language.

Children's own language can sometimes be a resource to be used in helping children learn sound-symbol relationships in English. If the teacher is using the picture of a dog to teach the initial sound /d/, the Spanish-speaking child will recognize the picture as *perro*, which opens possibilities for teaching the **p**-/p/ sound symbol relationship along with the **d**-/d/ relationship. As the teacher writes the morning message—*Hoy es martes, 26 de marzo.* (Today is Tuesday, March 26.)—children's attention can be drawn to the initial **m** in *martes* and *marzo*. Phonics instruction in English is thus linked to phonics instruction in the child's dominant language.

For ELL children, phonics lessons can be embedded in shared reading experiences. For example, as the teacher shares a big book in Spanish like *Al Supermarcado* (the translation of Ann Miranda's *To Market, To Market*), the zany story of a woman's repeated visits to a supermarket to buy animals who eventually take over her house, children can concentrate on phonics elements in the names of the animals—the initial sounds of *la gallana* (hen) and *el ganso* (goose); the short vowel sounds in *el ganso* (goose) and *la vaca* (cow); and the final sounds of *el ganso* (goose) and *el cerdo* (pig). Focusing on common phonics elements helps the child make connections between the two languages.

One way to build on the cultural capital of an ELL child's language and experience is to use children's trade books that reflect the child's culture, books like Gary Soto's *Too Many Tamales* about a Christmas celebration in a Latino household or Michele Stuart's *Angel Child, Dragon Child,* the story of a Vietnamese girl who must adjust to her new life in America. Sometimes these books integrate non-English text into the story. In Arthur Dorro's *Abeula,* the simple story of a girl and her grandmother who take an imaginary aerial journey, the dialogue includes passages like, " 'El parque es lindo,' says Abeula. 'I know what this means. I think the park is beautiful too.' " Not only does this give status to the child's home language in the English Language Learner's eyes, it provides opportunities to focus on the decoding of these words.

Bilingual books with English text on one page and text in another language on the facing page are also valuable resources for English Language Learners. Books such as *Media Pollito/Half-Chicken* by Alma Flor Ada, a pourquoi tale from Cuba, and *Tortillas Para Mama and Other Spanish Nursery Rhymes,* a collection of poems by Margot Griego, allow children to explore orthographic connections in the two languages while enjoying delightful stories at the same time.

Finally, it's important to approach the task of teaching reading to English Language Learners with the attitude that these children/adults are not language-deficient; they are language-different. Students' language and culture should be viewed as sources of strength, not weakness. In most cultures, speaking more than one language is a sign of prestige. Appreciating the cultural and linguistic heritage that English Language Learners bring to the task of learning to read is an important perspective in approaching phonics instruction.

Fluency and the Suprasegmental Phoneme System

Fluency, the ability to read a text accurately, quickly, and with expression, is an important instructional aspect in the teaching of reading. It has been a focus of research for the National Reading Panel (2000) and is measured as part of the National Assessment of Educational Progress (NAEP), "the nation's report card." Fluency bridges the gap between word recognition and comprehension and can be developed through such classroom activities as repeated reading, choral reading, readers' theatre, and other activities in the literacy-rich classroom environment.

Fluency is the mark of the mature reader. When children are struggling to decode the next word in a line of print, they typically read word-by-word. When they can decode easily, their reading becomes smooth and full of expression. Fluency is developed through classroom activities that involve repeated reading, modeling, echo reading, choral reading, readers' theatre, and other oral reading activities that provide a bridge between word recognition and comprehension.

What does fluency have to do with phonics? Apart from automatically connecting symbols and sounds in recognizing and pronouncing words, fluency requires careful attention to punctuation, and punctuation marks relate directly to another part of the sound system of English, the *suprasegmental phoneme system*.

Although the expression "segmental phoneme" has not been used specifically so far in this chapter, the chapter has dealt with segmental phonemes, segments or "slices" of sound within the stream of speech. There is another set of phonemes that operates as an overlay on speech sounds, a suprasegmental phoneme system that gives total meaning to language. This system accounts for intonation in spoken language (and expression in oral reading).

The suprasegmental phoneme system contains three elements: pitch, stress, and juncture. *Pitch* is the level to which the voice rises and falls in the process of oral communication.

In English, there are four levels of pitch:

/1/ the level to which the voice normally falls at the end of a declarative sentence;

/2/ the normal level of the voice as we speak;

/3/ the level to which the voice rises at the end of most questions; and

/4/ the high level to which the voice rises to indicate shock or surprise.

Falling pitch, combined with terminal juncture, indicates the end of spoken sentences. In addition to adding meaning to language, pitch can provide additional clues about a speaker—whether the speaker is male or female, angry or calm, happy or sad.

Stress is the relative force of articulation or emphasis that we place on words and syllables in the stream of speech. Stressed syllables are produced with a greater amount of energy than unstressed syllables. Just as there are four levels of pitch, there are four degrees of stress in spoken English:

/´/ primary stress, the degree of stress found in monosyllabic words in isolation;

/^/ secondary stress, the degree of stress typically applied to the word *blue* in *I saw a blue bird;*
/ˋ/ tertiary stress, normally used in the first syllable of compound words like *blackbird;* and
/ˇ/ weak or minimal stress, characterized by the unstressed syllable in two-syllable words like *teacher* or *pupil.*

Stress patterns in the normal stream of speech become fairly complicated, and they shift depending on the meaning and context of an utterance. In most classrooms, phonics instruction deals with only two degrees of stress, stressed syllables and unstressed syllables in individual words.

Juncture is the transition between segmental phonemes. Juncture allows us to distinguish between pairs of expressions such as *night rate* and *nitrate, I scream* and *ice cream, my son John* and *mice on John,* pairs of expressions in which the segmental phonemes are identical. The different types of juncture are

closed juncture, the normal transition between individual phonemes in spoken words that is generally unmarked;
internal open juncture /+/, which marks the transition between pairs of words like *an aim* and *a name;* and
terminal juncture, the pause that occurs at the end of spoken sentences, either falling terminal juncture /↓/, which occurs at the end of statements or rising terminal juncture /↑/, which occurs at the end of most questions.

All three parts of the suprasegmental phoneme system work closely together to add a layer of meaning in language. Together, they mark the boundaries between speech utterances. These phonemes are represented in writing by punctuation marks and other typographic devices, although the correspondence between suprasegmental phonemes and punctuation marks is no more perfect than the relationship between segmental phonemes and letters of the alphabet.

"It's not what he said but how he said it." The suprasegmental phoneme system allows us to add different layers or shades of meaning to the expressions we speak. These features of language allow us, for example, to distinguish between "You're going OUT tonight?" (I thought you were going to stay in for a change) vis-à-vis "You're going out TONIGHT?" (I thought tomorrow night was the night we were supposed to go out.) Pitch, stress, and juncture can completely reverse the meaning of utterances using the same words. Consider the contrasting meanings of the following two sentences (standard punctuation is used here to indicate how the sentences should be spoken):

For your birthday, I'll send candy and nuts to you, sweetheart.
For your birthday, I'll send candy—and nuts to you, sweetheart!

The first message is a loving one, the second, less so. And consider this pair of sentences:

> *A woman without her man is lost.*
> *A woman—without her, man is lost.*

In the first sentence, it is the woman who is lost without the man. In the second, it is the man who is lost without the woman, a complete 180-degree reversal of meaning from the first.

Teaching Suggestions ▼

Fluency

Repeated Reading

Repeated reading—monitored and guided by the teacher—improves reading fluency, word recognition, comprehension, and overall reading achievement. Children read a familiar text three or four times with feedback from the teacher until fluency is achieved.

Oral Reading

Activities that involve oral reading—such as choral reading, readers' theatre, paired reading, and the like—involve the interpretation of written language through expression. The role of punctuation marks can be tied directly to suprasegmental elements.

One-Liners*

The teacher selects lines spoken by the characters in a popular children's book; for example, here's a brief sample selected from *The BFG* by Roald Dahl:

> *Don't be sad.*
> *Do you like vegetables?*
> *You mustn't feel bad about it.*
> *Giants are everywhere around.*
> *Aren't you really a little mixed up?*
> *Let's go back inside.*
> *I cannot help thinking about your poor mother and father.*

Using pitch, stress, and juncture, pairs of children read the lines with differing interpretations:

> *Don't be sad.* Read pleadingly. Read as a command
> *Let's go back inside.* Read eagerly. Read reluctantly.
> *I cannot help thinking about your poor mother and father.* Read casually. Read sadly.

Using single lines like these allows children to focus on the interpretation of print using the suprasegmental phoneme system of their language.

Teaching Reading and Writing: Combining Skills, Strategies and Literature by John F. Savage. New York: McGraw-Hill, 1998. Reproduced with permission of The McGraw-Hill Companies.

Once again, children learn to use suprasegmental phonemes automatically and unconsciously as they acquire language. These phonemes affect meaning as part of the overall sound system of any dialect of American English. In addition to the suprasegmental phonemes that native speakers use, body language has much to do with conveying meaning in speech. Our smiles, frowns, facial expressions, hand movements, and other paralinguistic features send signals about what we mean when we speak. These features are missing in print, so it is up to readers to interpret this dimension of language as they read.

Conclusion

This, then, is a summary of the orthographic system of the English language. We have an alphabetic writing system, a system in which individual speech sounds (phonemes) are represented by individual written symbols (graphemes) that constitute the letters of the alphabet. The phoneme-grapheme relationship of our writing system is far from perfect, but knowledge of it is necessary for learning to read and write.

The English orthographic system is incredibly complex. Children come to school with intuitive knowledge of their sound system. In achieving literacy, they need to be aware of the letters that represent these sounds as they try to decode unfamiliar words they encounter in print and as they attempt to exercise the appropriate orthographic options in spelling words they want to use in their writing.

Learning to read involves more than learning the details of our orthographic system, but learning discrete phonics elements is part of the process of learning to read and write. "Good phonics instruction might contain a moderate amount of word practice in isolation, enough to get children to recognize words automatically but not enough to drive them to boredom" (Stahl, Duffy-Hester, and Stahl 1998, 342).

Instruction in discrete phonics elements aims at *automaticity*. As the word suggests, automaticity involves the fast, effortless, accurate recognition of words. Automaticity comes from systematic and explicit instruction and from reading practice, and it is essential to reading fluency. It can be practiced by reading lists of decodable words on a chart or a word wall as a means of reinforcing and applying knowledge of discrete phonics elements.

Obviously, thousands of skilled and dedicated practitioners have taught millions of children how to read without in-depth knowledge of the fine details of English orthography. The more familiar a teacher is with information about the nature and structure of English writing, however, the more equipped the teacher will be to go about the business of teaching phonics as part of the larger enterprise of reading and writing instruction. "It seems probable that a better understanding of the American English or orthographic system would lead us toward a better teaching of literacy" (Cummings 1988, cited in Templeton & Morris 1999, 110). Teachers who understand how our orthographic system works will be able to account for the vagrancies of sound-symbol relationships that children encounter on the way to becoming literate. They will have a better handle on invented spelling (a topic that will be addressed on pp. 142–149) and what's involved in moving children from invented spelling to standard orthography. They will be able to interpret more effectively some of the special phonics programs often used with at-risk readers and will be able to better support these children in their classroom encounters with print.

In short, details of English orthography are part of the knowledge base for teachers in today's educational world.

References

Allen, L. 1998. An integrated strategies approach: Making word identification instruction work for beginning readers. *The Reading Teacher* 52:254–68.

Allington, R. L. 2002. What I've learned about effective reading instruction from a decade of studying exemplary classroom teachers. *Phi Delta Kappan* 83:740–7.

Baer, G. T. 1999. *Self-Paced Phonics: A Text for Educators.* 2d ed. Columbus: Merrill.

Bear, D. R., M. Ivernizzi, S. Templeton, and F. Johnson. 2000. *Words Their Way: Word Study for Phonics, Vocabulary, and Spelling Instruction.* 2d. ed. Columbus: Merrill.

Blevins, W. 1998. *Phonics from A to Z: A Practical Guide.* New York: Scholastic.

Clymer, T. 1996. Reprint. The utility of phonics generalizations in the primary grades. Original edition, 1963. *The Reading Teacher* 16:252–8. *The Reading Teacher* 50:182–7.

Coyne, M. D., E. J. Kame'enui, and D. C. Simmons. 2001. Prevention and intervention in beginning reading: Two complex systems. *Learning Disabilities Research and Practice* 16:63–73.

Cummings, D. W. 1988. *American English spelling.* Baltimore: John Hopkins University Press.

Cunningham, P. M. 1998. The multisyllabic word dilemma: Helping students build meaning, spell, and read 'big' words. *Reading and Writing Quarterly* 14:189–219.

Cunningham, P. M. 2000. *Phonics They Use: Words for Reading and Writing.* 3rd. ed. New York: Longman.

Durgunoglu, A., W. Nagy, and B. J. Hacin-Bhatt. 1993. Cross-language transfer of phonemic awareness. *Journal of Educational Psychology* 85:453–65.

Eldredge, J. L. 1999. *Phonics for Teachers: Self-Instruction, Methods and Activities.* Columbus: Merrill.

Fry, E. 1998. The most common phonograms. *The Reading Teacher* 51:620–2.

Heilman, A. W. 2002. *Phonics in Proper Perspective.* 9th ed. Columbus: Merrill.

Jiminez, R. T. 2002. Fostering the literacy development of Latino students. *Focus on Exceptional Children* 6:1–10.

Johnson, F. R. 1999. The timing and teaching of word families. *The Reading Teacher* 53:64–75.

——— 2001. The utility of phonic generalizations: Let's take another look at Clymer's conclusions. *The Reading Teacher* 55:132–43.

Ladefoged, P. 1982. *A Course in Phonetics.* 2d ed. New York: Harcourt Brace Jovanovich.

McCardle, P., H. S. Scarborough, and H. W. Catts. 2001. Predicting, explaining, and preventing reading difficulties. *Learning Disabilities Research and Practice* 16:230–9.

Moats, L. C. 1994. The missing foundation in teacher education: Knowledge of the structure of spoken and written language. *Annals of Dyslexia* 44:81–102.

——— 1998. Teaching decoding. *American Educator* 22:42–9, 95–6.

Moustafa, M. 1997. *Beyond Traditional Phonics: Research Discoveries and Reading Instruction.* Portsmouth, NH: Heinemann.

National Reading Panel. 2000. *Teaching Children to Read: An Evidence-Based Assessment of the Scientific Research Literature on Reading and its Implications for Reading Instruction.* Washington, DC: National Institute of Child Health and Human Development.

Stahl, S. A., A. M. Duffy-Hester, and K. A. D. Stahl. 1998. Everything you wanted to know about phonics (but were afraid to ask). *Reading Research Quarterly* 33:338–55.

Templeton, S., and D. Morris. 1999. Questions teachers ask about spelling. *Reading Research Quarterly* 34:102–12.

Troia, G. A., F. P. Roth, and S. Graham. 1998. An Educator's Guide to Phonological Awareness: Assessment Measures and Intervention Activities for Children. *Focus on Exceptional Children* 31:1–12.

Wilson, R. M., and M. A. Hall. 1997. *Programmed Word Attach for Teachers.* 6th ed. Columbus: Merrill.

Children's Trade Books Cited in This Chapter

Ada, A. F. 1995. *Medio Pollito/Half-Chicken*. Illustrated by K. Howard. New York: Doubleday.

Dahl, R. 1982. *The BFG*. Illustrated by Q. Blake. New York: Putnam.

Dorros, A. 1991. *Abeula*. Illustrated by I. Klevin. New York: Dutton.

Griego, M. 1981. *Tortillas Para Mama and Other Spanish Nursery Rhymes*. Illustrated by B. Cooney. New York: Holt.

Miranda, A. 1997. *Al Supermercado* (translation of *To Market, To Market*). Illustrated by J. Stevens. Orlando: Harcourt Brace.

Soto, G. 1993. *Too Many Tamales*. Illustrated by E. Martinez. New York: Putnam.

Surat, M. 1983. *Angel Child, Dragon Child*. Illustrated by V-D. Mai. Austin, TX: Raintree.

Approaches to Teaching Phonics: Embedded and Direct Instruction

4

In many classrooms, phonics is embedded or integrated into ongoing reading and writing activities. Instead of beginning with a focus on sound-symbol relationships, phonics is included as part of children's regular encounters with print. In other instructional settings, children learn phonics through direct, systematic, explicit instruction on the orthographic features of their language system. This chapter

▼ examines ways in which decoding instruction and practice are woven into reading activities in which children's literature is used as the primary vehicle for helping children learn to read

▼ describes direct, systematic instructional programs designed to help children master phonics in classroom and clinical settings.

Part of the "great debate" about phonics centers on which approach teachers should take in helping children learn sound-symbol relationships that they can use in becoming fluent readers and confident writers.

On the one hand, some teachers and program designers recommend an analytic approach, which is defined as "a whole-to-part approach to word study in which the student is first taught a number of sight words and then relevant phonic generalizations, which are subsequently applied to other words" (Harris and Hodges 1995, 9). In an analytic approach, teaching starts with a focus on text rather than on specific sound-symbol relationships. Children acquire phonics knowledge by analyzing words and larger language units. Phonics is embedded into regular daily classroom language arts activities. This approach has also been described as a deductive approach or "whole word phonics."

On the other hand, other teachers and program designers use a synthetic approach, "a part-to-whole approach . . . in which the student learns the sounds represented by letters and letter combinations, blends these sounds to pronounce words, and finally identifies which phonic generalizations apply" (Harris and Hodges 1995, 250). This approach features an early direct and explicit emphasis on learning letter-sound relationships and blending or synthesizing these elements into whole words. The approach has also been described as an inductive or "code-emphasis phonics."

Experts continue to argue about the merits of these two approaches. Summarizing the report of the National Reading Panel, Armbruster, Lehr, and Osborn (2001) unequivocally state, "Systematic and explicit phonics instruction is more effective than non-systematic or no phonics instruction" (13). On the other side of the coin, Moustafa and Maldonado-Colon (1999) defend the whole-to-parts approach. "It starts with what emergent readers know and uses what they know to help them know more. It first capitalizes on children's knowledge of language and children's ability to recognize words holistically and then explicitly and systematically teaches them letter-sound correspondences using sounds they already know in print words that they have learned to recognize" (450).

While there are both philosophical and practical differences between synthetic and analytic phonics teaching, the content of what children learn remains the same in both approaches. In other words, whether one starts with "This is the letter **b** and it says /b/ as in *ball*."* or with "Here's a list of **b**-words; see if you can tell me what sound the letter **b** makes," the sound represented by the letter **b** doesn't change. The approach to learning the **b**-/b/ relationship is what changes.

In the practical world of schools, rarely does a particular program fit absolutely into one category or another. Some maintain that both approaches are incompatible and ought not be used together. Teachers are told, "Balance, but don't mix" (Lyon 1997, 15). Many programs and most teachers, however, use a combination of techniques in which direct instruction and deductive application interact.

Embedded Phonics

The ultimate purpose of phonics instruction is to help children acquire the ability to read and write. It's not surprising, then, to see phonics incorporated as an integral part of shared reading lessons, guided reading practice, and authentic reading experiences in the classroom. Embedded phonics involves instruction in letter-sound relationships as part of larger, authentic reading experiences. Authentic reading experiences are those that are carried on primarily for the purpose of information or pleasure, rather than for the explicit purpose of skill development.

Shared Reading

Shared reading involves teachers and children reading a book together. The story is read several times so that children can become directly involved in the reading experience. Shared reading involves three steps:

1. Using a big book or chart-sized version of a story, the teacher introduces the book and reads the story with fluency and expression. The children listen to absorb the mood and content of the story. The focus is on meaning and enjoyment.

*Technically, a letter doesn't "say" or "make" a sound; letters represent phonemes. The common classroom parlance of "B says /b/," however, is used here.

2. The teacher reads the story again, often several times, inviting the children to join in. During rereadings, the teacher points to the text of the story or the poem, calling children's attention to familiar words, demonstrating decoding strategies ("What do you think this word might be? How do you know? What letter does it begin with?"), modeling meaning-making strategies, and using comments and questions that invite children to act like skilled readers. The children participate by repeating familiar elements in text, by locating words that they can recognize, by commenting about what is going on in the story and predicting what will happen next, and by becoming involved in other ways in the experience of sharing the book.

3. As a follow-up, children do activities based on their shared reading— discussing alternative endings to the story, dramatizing story scenes, drawing pictures based on the story, and the like. Sometimes, follow-up involves reading the regular small book version of the story independently or with a partner.

Shared reading has a number of purposes. It serves as an induction of children into the literacy community by involving them directly in the act of reading. It creates an awareness of print conventions such as the left-to-right orientation of English writing. It provides a vehicle for phonemic awareness by suggesting opportunities to focus on specific sound elements. It provides for language development and promotes the love of literature. And it helps children become familiar with basic phonetic elements and decoding techniques.

Teaching Suggestions ▼

Phonics in a Shared Reading Lesson: *Rosie's Walk*

For a shared reading activity, the teacher selects *Rosie's Walk* by Pat Hutchins, the popular, simple story about Rosie the hen who takes a stroll around the barnyard and is followed by a hapless fox who encounters one hazard after another.

    The teacher introduces the story by calling attention to the book's title and author's name, by discussing the colorful illustration on the cover, and by inviting children to predict what the story is about. As part of the introduction, the teacher calls attention to Rosie's name and asks, "*Who else in the class has a name that begins like Rosie? That's right, Raymond and Rehema!*" Children can also suggest other names for the hen and the fox noting the phonetic elements in the names they create.

    In rereadings, children can find familiar words like *hen* and *yard*, and think of rhyming words that conform to these patterns:

        hen — *Ben, ten, den, pen, when*
        yard — *card, hard, lard*

As children use phrase cards to create their own "circle story" based on *Rosie's Walk,* as they compose their own original version of the story that they dictate to the teacher, and as they expand the word lists that they generate from the story, children continue to use phonetic elements found in the text.

In addition to the focus on phonics, a shared reading lesson on *Rosie's Walk* might also include the following:

- partner reading, where children sit side-by-side and read to one another;
- the recognition of function words found in the story (*over, under, around, through,* and so on);
- phrase reading (*across the yard, past the mill,* and so on);
- comprehension activities (*"What do you think will happen to Rosie next?"*);
- critical thinking (*"Do you think Rosie knows that the fox is following her? Why?"*);
- creative dramatics or art activities related to the story.

In short, the teacher can take the lesson well beyond phonics.

Predictable books such as the following lend themselves especially well to shared reading lessons:

- Wanda Gag's classic *Millions of Cats,* as the rhythmic sounds in the delightful refrain "hundreds of cats, and thousands of cats, and millions and billions and trillions of cats" rolls off the children's tongues as they become involved in the story;
- Pat Hutchins' *Good-Night, Owl,* as children repeat the sounds made by the animals and focus on the regular phonetic elements in the sounds that they make;
- Bill Martin, Jr.'s, well-known *Brown Bear, Brown Bear, What Do You See?,* as children take turns creating their own rhyming couplets using the "long **e**" sound and other vowel elements in a book full of language sounds that delight the ear and the imagination;
- Maurice Sendak's enormously popular *Chicken Soup with Rice,* as children engage the "long **i**" words as they repeat the last four lines of each stanza.

Predictable books like these contain repeated phrases and sentences that children can easily and quickly join in reading, and they generally contain phonetic elements that teachers can use in building phonemic awareness and phonics practice.

Although phonics is not the main point of shared reading activities, shared reading is an effective way to introduce young children to phonetic elements, while at the same time helping them enjoy literature. "Shared reading is an important part of whole-to-part phonics instruction. It both demonstrates the reading process to children and establishes a basis for the phonics lessons to come, making the phonics lessons more memorable, and hence, more effective" (Moustafa and Maldonado-Colon 1999, 415). Phonics is learned, reinforced, and applied as the teacher reads stories, poems, rhymes, songs, and other reading material and plans activities that focus on phonetic elements that the story suggests.

Teaching Suggestion ▼

Phonics in a Shared Reading Lesson: *Moveable Word Wall*
Moustafa and Maldonado-Colon (1999) suggest a "Movable Word Wall" as a follow-up phonics activity to a shared reading lesson. After a shared reading of a familiar piece of text such as "Eeensy-Weensy Spider" or "If You're Happy and You Know It," children identify familiar words from the piece, while the teacher writes these words on cards highlighting phonemic elements (the /sp/ in *spider* and *spout* or the initial /h/ in *happy* and *hands*.) The teacher pins these cards to a word wall for reading practice. The list grows as children add more familiar words that they encounter in their literacy activities. Thus, children learn phonemic elements using words with which they feel "ownership."

Guided Reading

Guided reading is a practice used with young children to help them, with teacher support, develop and apply effective reading strategies early in their school lives so that they can use these strategies to become independent and successful readers. "Guided reading is a context in which a teacher supports each reader's development of effective strategies for processing novel texts at increasingly challenging levels of difficulty" (Fountas and Pinnell 1996, 2). Phonics is one component of guided reading activities that helps children unlock the pronunciation and meaning of unknown words.

In guided reading, children of similar reading ability meet in small groups. The teacher selects the text based on children's interests, reading levels, and reading behaviors. The teacher introduces the book and previews the story by talking about the illustrations and by asking children to suggest what the story might be about. The teacher uses the language of the story so that children will be familiar with the words and sentence patterns that they will encounter on the page as they read. Each child independently reads the book aloud in a very soft voice, audible to the teacher but not so loud as to disturb other children in the group. As children encounter problems, the teacher helps them over rough spots with support and guidance. After reading, the teacher focuses the group's attention on the meaning of the text and discusses the story, inviting children's personal responses and returning to the text to locate evidence to support responses. Once they are familiar with the story, children often return to reread the book for practice or enjoyment, either independently or with a partner.

Phonics is an integral part of guided reading activities. Guided reading experiences provide multiple teachable moments for phonics, opportunities to apply knowledge of sound-symbol relationships in the context of real reading. Here is where the teacher models decoding strategies and where children apply their knowledge of phonics. The teacher guides the children in using sound-symbol relationships to figure out unfamiliar words that they encounter.

Teaching Suggestions ▼

Phonics in a Guided Reading Lesson: *Buzzz Said the Bee*

As part of guided reading, the teacher uses *Buzzz Said the Bee* by Wendy Cheyette Lewison, a delightfully funny story with predictable language and repeated word patterns about farm animals. On the second page of the story, Cassandra encounters the following passage:

> *"QUACK," said the duck.*
> *"There's a bee on me."*
> *And the duck said, "Scat,"*
> *but the bee just sat.*

Cassandra reads the first two lines with fluency, but she hesitates before the last word in the third line (*Scat*). The teacher covers the first two letters of the word with her finger:

Teacher:
What are the two final letters in this word?
Cassandra: *a* and *t*
T: *What does a-t say?*
C: *at*
T. *Good!* The teacher slides her finger, uncovering the **c.**
T: *Here's a word we've had before. Can you remember what it is?*
C: *cat*
T: *Good for you! Now, put the /s/ sound in front of the word and what does the word say?*
C: *Scat*
T: *Terrific! What does "scat" mean?*
C: *It means, "Get outta here!"*
T: *Right. That's what I'd say if a bee landed on me. Now, read the whole line again. And remember that word because you'll meet it again at other times in this story.*

Throughout the activity, children's knowledge of sound-symbol relationships is used to help them decode unfamiliar words. Lessons on word patterns and other elements of phonics are often follow-up activities to guided reading practice.

By using decoding skills as part of guided reading, children apply phonics knowledge as part of interacting with text and constructing meaning from print. Very early in their reading lives, with teacher guidance, they learn strategies that will continue to serve them well in their independent authentic reading experiences in which children read books for purposes other than skill development.

Authentic Reading Experiences

In children's authentic reading experiences inside and outside the classroom, phonics is purposefully applied. As they read for information and pleasure, children use decoding skills and develop independent strategies for attacking unfamiliar words in print. Children learn to sound out words by analogy and to look for little words within larger words.

In their independent reading, children decode by analogy when they recognize familiar patterns in unfamiliar words. In decoding the new word *hamper*, for example, the child might recognize the familiar word pattern *amp*, add an initial **h** to sound *hamp*, and recognize the familiar word ending *er* to determine the pronunciation of the word; or the child might recognize the two CVC syllables *ham* and *per* as a means of decoding the word. Whatever decoding strategies are employed, the child then draws on his/her language background to determine whether the word means "a place to put dirty laundry" or "to impede or interfere with somebody" in the context of the sentence.

Children also look for little words within larger unfamiliar words that they encounter as part of their independent reading experiences. Locating pronounceable word parts is an effective decoding strategy in independent reading. In approaching larger words that they don't recognize, children learn to ask the question, "Is there any part of the word that I already know?" In decoding *hippopotamus*, for example, children who recognize *hip*, *pot*, and *us* will be well on their way to figuring out how to pronounce the word. The same strategy for decoding *hippopotamus* cannot be used for decoding *elephant*, however, so the child has to look for patterns (such as *ant*) and other elements (**ph** = /f/) in decoding that word. And sometimes little words within big words can be misleading, as the *have* in *shave* or the *ash* in *squash*.

Decoding by analogy and finding known word parts in larger words are useful decoding techniques that children use in approaching words that they don't recognize in print.

Integrating Phonics and Encounters with Literature

Teachers have long selected works of quality children's literature for instructional and independent use in the classroom. All of the classroom encounters with books described earlier involve the use of trade books containing literature for children. Literature provides children with enriched language, exciting plots, imaginative materials, and stories that they love. Teachers often take advantage of the enormous values inherent in children's literature and use trade books as springboards for phonics lessons.

Teaching Suggestions ▼

*This lesson is adapted from one that was presented in the 1997 edition of *The English Language Arts Curriculum Frameworks for Massachusetts.* (Malden, MA: Mass. Department of Education).

Some books lend themselves especially well to teaching particular phonetic elements. Dr. Seuss's classic *Cat in the Hat,* for example, has examples of words featuring the short-**a** sound used in meaningful context in a way that has tickled children's funny bones for decades. As one of many follow-up activities to sharing and enjoying this story, children can compile lists of rhyming words in creating their own stories. Other books from which phonics lessons can be "teased" are

- *Is Your Mama a Llama?* by Deborah Guarino, with a focus on rhyming words and the short and long sounds of **a,** from which children can brainstorm other rhyming words and create their own riddles;
- *In the Small, Small Pond* by Denise Fleming, a beautifully illustrated story that can be used to help children generate lists of consonant blends;

- *A House Is a House for Me* by Mary Ann Hoberman, a delightful story with a variety of rhyming patterns that children can use as they compose and dictate their own original stories.

Nancy Shaw's trade books—*Sheep on a Ship, Sheep in a Jeep, Sheep Out to Eat,* and others—are wonderful stories that children enjoy and that teachers can use for teaching basic phonics elements.

Teaching Suggestions ▼

Phonics in a Literature-Based Lesson: *Sheep on a Ship*

Sheep on a Ship by Nancy Shaw begins with the following lines:

> *Sheep sail a ship on a deep-sea trip.*
> *Waves lap. Sails flap.*
> *Sheep read a map but begin to nap.*
> *Dark clouds form a sudden storm.*

The text continues with similar language, as the hapless sheep are forced to abandon their ship in the storm, but ultimately survive by drifting to land on a homemade raft. After the story has been shared and enjoyed, the teacher can distribute cards with words from the story to the class, and children can

- match word cards to the words in the text;
- identify rhyming words used in the story (for example, *ship, trip, slip, tip, whip, drip*) and add to this list other words with the *ip* rime;
- play games with word cards from the story—"When I say a word, I want everyone with a word card that rhymes with the word I say to stand" or "Find other children with a word that rhymes with the word on your card";
- think of other words beginning with consonant digraphs and blends found in the story;
- paste word cards to a large drawing of the ship (*sail, mast, waves,* and so on);
- use word cards to create sentences that the teacher dictates from the story or rearrange scrambled cards to correspond to sentences used in the story.

Creative teachers can think of many more activities with stories like Shaw's *Sheep on a Ship* and her other books, *Sheep in a Jeep, Sheep in a Shop, Sheep Out to Eat,* and *Sheep Trick or Treat.*

Not all trade books lend themselves to direct phonics instruction as readily as some stories do. By starting with a story, many children's trade books offer ample opportunities for children to learn certain phonics elements in a meaningful and enjoyable way.

Trachtenburg (1990), Blevens (1998), and others have published lists of children's trade books that repeat phonics elements in text. In using trade books as vehicles to help children learn phonics, however, it's imperative to remember that meaning, story, and love of literature are primary considerations.

The title of Esphyr Slobodkina's classic *Caps for Sale* has both a short-**a** word and a long-**a** word in the title. But to use this book for the purpose of teaching vowel sounds alone is unconscionable. This traditional tale of a peddler who sold hats is a story that generations of children have loved. While the title of the story can certainly be a jumping-off point for making children aware of these vowel elements by building word families based on *caps* and *sale* (words with which children will be familiar after sharing the story), the instructional focus should remain on children's enjoyment and appreciation of this delightful tale.

An embedded phonics program does not mean that phonics is neglected, as some critics have implied. Embedded phonics approaches are usually less explicit, although phonics content to be learned can still be presented systematically. Teachers who integrate phonics instruction into their regular reading and writing activities recognize the importance of phonics and make it an integral part of their teaching. Although word lists are often appropriately used as the focus of instruction on discrete phonics elements, instruction in sound-symbol relationships is focused largely on children's encounters with connected text. Phonics is presented as an essential part of the reading act itself, not separated from authentic reading and writing activities.

Direct, Systematic Phonics/Language Instruction

At the other end of the theoretical spectrum from embedded phonics is direct, systematic, explicit phonics instruction, a synthetic approach that focuses directly on sound-symbol correspondences. In this approach, letter-sound relationships are made explicit from the beginning. The teacher points to an alphabet symbol and tells children the sound: "This is **m** and it says /m/; this is **s** and it says /s/"; and so on. The phoneme-grapheme relationships that children learn are practiced every day, either in isolation or in the context of words. Children learn the double sounds of **c** and **g,** the phoneme-grapheme relationships in digraphs, the regular sounds of short vowels, the variant sound-symbol relationships of long and other vowel sounds. In short, direct phonics instruction involves children in learning explicitly the sound-symbol relationships that constitute our orthographic system.

"The hallmark of a systematic phonics approach or program is that a sequenced set of phonics elements is delineated and these elements are taught along a dimension of explicitness" (National Reading Panel 2000a, 8). Phonics elements to be learned are precisely identified and sequenced, and then these elements are taught directly and explicitly. The exact sequence of elements may differ from one program to another, but all programs have a carefully delineated order of items to be taught. Vowel patterns are presented one or two at a time rather than having several written representations presented at once. In theory and in design, systematic and explicit instruction leaves little to chance.

Blending is a basic phonics strategy that is essential to a synthetic approach to teaching phonics. Children practice blending isolated sounds to form words. The teacher points to the symbols in order as children say the sound that the symbols represent and blend these sounds into words—"/s/ . . . /sa/ . . . /sat/ *sat*." Drill and practice in sound-symbol connections and blending are essential to making decoding skills automatic. On a sound-by-sound basis, they build up to decoding longer and longer words.

Teaching Suggestions ▼

Direct, Systematic Phonics Instruction

Random Vowels

The five vowel letters are written on the board or arranged on cards:

a   e   i

o   u

As the teacher points to each letter in random order, children say the sound that the letter represents.

Sound Circles

Rimes or phonograms are arranged in a circle:

uke   uke

oke   oke

ike   ike

eke   eke

ake   ake

Children go "around the circle" by placing common consonant blends or phonograms in front of each rime as they say the words, for example "blake, bleke, blike, bloke, bluke" or "shake, sheke, shike, shoke, shuke." These combinations frequently create nonsense words, but nonsense words are often used in direct, systematic phonics instruction, since the primary emphasis is on the sound-symbol relationships and not on the meaning.

Blending

Blending sounds into words is an important part of direct phonics instruction. The teacher writes three separate letters of which children know the corresponding sounds on the chalkboard:

b a n   *p e n*

Placing her hand under the initial letter, the teacher asks the child to make the corresponding letter sound. The teacher sweeps her hand left-to-right under the first two letters and the child blends the first two sounds. Finally, the teacher moves her hand under all three letters and the child blends the three discrete sounds and says the word that the letters spell.

Also, many of the instructional activities suggested for teaching discrete phonics elements (see chapter 3) can be used directly in direct and explicit phonics instruction.

A synthetic approach typically uses nonsense words or pseudowords for decoding practice. These are words that can be pronounced (or "read") but which have no meaning, words like *bram, clard,* and *infractaneous*. Nonsense words provide a "pure" application of decoding skills. They provide a vehicle for having children directly apply their knowledge of sound-symbol relationships in saying the words. "Several authorities assert that pseudowords are the best item available for testing phonics skills" (Groff 2001, 299).

While nonsense words can be useful in teaching and practicing decoding skills, caution should be exercised when these words are used for assessment purposes (and many tests use pseudowords to diagnose and measure children's phonics knowledge and decoding ability). Some children, when presented with a pseudoword like *leck*, may be able to decode it accurately but know that the word does not make sense. So they pronounce the word as one they know is real (like *lick*), getting the response "wrong." Thus, these words can give a distorted view of the child's knowledge of phonics and ability to decode.

Phonics Readers

In a direct, systematic approach, children practice and apply decoding skills with "phonics readers," books containing stories with decodable text that focus directly on a particular phonetic element. "Decodable text refers to those beginning reading books and stories in which there is an attempt to write prose

Phonics readers have simple text with tightly controlled vocabulary focused on particular sounds. Right: This example is a simple story focusing on short vowel sounds. Next page: This phonics reader is aimed at the second grade level and focuses on the -eer and -ear phonograms.

From **Mac Camps** *by Eric Coates, Illustrated by John Magine. Lippincott Phonics Easy Readers, Level A. New York: Macmillan/McGraw-Hill, 1998. Reproduced with permission of the McGraw-Hill Companies.*

The cat tugs on the tent.
Mac trips.
The tent rips!

using the specific sound-symbol correspondences that the children have been taught" (Cassidy and Cassidy 2002/3, 18). As children read sentences like *The hen sat on a keg.* or *The goat rolls over the road.*, they apply and practice decoding with connected (if contrived) text rather than with lists of isolated words. Usually, these phonics readers focus on a single, specific vowel sound per book. Sight words are introduced as necessary. Stories get longer and additional elements are included as students' reading ability increases. These phonics readers are usually not the only reading books with which children interact; rather, they are generally used as a supplement to the regular program to strengthen children's phonics knowledge and decoding ability. Their purpose is to give beginning readers opportunities to read independently using the phonics elements they have been taught.

As with other reading materials, phonics readers have been praised and condemned. On the one hand, these supplementary series hardly constitute "real reading" in that the language is so controlled and contrived. Some critics say that the child is not really reading but rather merely "practicing phonics." On the other hand, these materials do give children a chance to hold books, to enjoy success, and to get a sense of personal achievement in reading while they rely heavily on sound-symbol correspondences in decoding what they read. "Adult distaste for decodable books fails to respect the child's need to exercise a skill. Children want to be self-reliant readers and are delighted when they can apply what they learn" (Moats 1998, 47).

Rocky, Rocky, the mountaineer
Wanted to be a pioneer.
He packed his food,
He packed his gear,
And he traveled alone
For more than a year.

From **Rocky the Mountaineer** *by Cass Hollander, Illustrated by Steve Haefele. Spotlight Phonics Books. New York: Macmillan/McGraw-Hill, 1997. Reproduced with permission of the McGraw-Hill Companies.*

Evidence on the effectiveness of a direct, systematic approach to explicit phonics has been cited by researchers (Adams 1990; Chall 1996; Lyon 1997; National Reading Panel 2000) and by practitioners who have witnessed the success of this approach, particularly with individuals who have learning disabilities and related problems that interfere with learning how to read.

Structured Language Programs

Entire programs have been developed to provide direct, explicit, systematic instruction in sound-symbol relationships to help children learn to read, especially those children who experience early difficulty in dealing with print. These programs, which typically combine both synthetic and analytic approaches, begin by directly teaching children the most basic elements of our orthographic system (sound-symbol correspondences) and by systematically helping children learn to blend these elements into syllables and words.

McIntyre and Pickering (1995) describe both the content and principles of instruction underlying multisensory structured language programs, programs that use more than one learning modality in acquiring sound-symbol knowledge. The content of these programs includes a strong emphasis on phonemic awareness; it deals extensively with sound-symbol associations through extensive practice in segmentation and blending; it focuses heavily on syllables; it includes instruction in structural elements (root words and affixes), syntax, and semantics. Teaching is done using multisensory techniques following a strict sequential order. The emphasis is on direct instruction, with careful diagnosis and the use of analytical as well as synthetic techniques.

The Orton-Gillingham Method

While sounding and blending of individual language elements have been used to teach reading since the days of the ancient Greeks, the pioneer in the modern age of structured language instruction based on sound-symbol relationships is Dr. Samuel Orton, a neurologist who believed that incorporating visual, auditory, and kinesthetic language stimuli would help children with reading problems. Orton reasoned that since poor readers had inadequate visual processing skills, they should learn to use other pathways to the brain and associate the form of letters (visual) with the sound of the letters (auditory) and how it feels to write or trace the letters (kinesthetic/tactile). Anna Gillingham, a teacher and research associate of Orton, teamed up with a remedial reading teacher, Bessie Stillman, and wrote a manual based on Orton's principles. Their techniques, which became known as the Orton-Gillingham (O-G) method, used a direct and structured process of presenting basic units of written language to children.

The Orton-Gillingham method is a multisensory approach that integrates visual, auditory, kinesthetic, and tactile (VAKT) modalities in the learning process. Children are introduced to alphabetic symbols and sounds in a systematic fashion. As the teacher pronounces a sound, the child repeats it and writes or traces the letter that represents that sound. The method emphasizes drill and repetition to increase automaticity of skills. The student overlearns basic concepts to the point of mastery. Students are taught spelling rules after they have mastered letter sounds, but students always say the name rather than the sound of the letter as they write it in a technique called Simultaneous Oral Spelling (SOS).

For More Information: The International Dyslexia Society, 8600 LaSalle Road, Baltimore, MD 21204.

A number of structured language programs involving direct, systematic phonics instruction evolved along the lines of Orton's theories and practices. In general, these programs have been designed for children who have extreme difficulty deciphering the code of written language, children with learning and language problems that interfere with success in beginning reading. Some programs have been extended for use with older children, and many have been adapted for use in whole class settings. While these structured language programs built around our orthographic alphabetic language system are most often recommended for children with learning disabilities and related problems that impact learning how to read (Clark and Uhry 1995), more and more school systems are looking toward these programs to address reading problems system-wide.

A sampling of structured language programs that are used in schools and clinics includes the following:

The Spalding Method

Romalda Spalding, a disciple of Samuel Orton, was a classroom teacher who adapted Orton's techniques to whole class instruction. While Spalding uses many multisensory strategies employed by other Orton-based programs, the Spalding-invented marking system makes her method unique. After learning the sounds of the letters along with the formation of the symbols they represent, children use the marking system to connect speech sounds to printed words. This is the bridge connecting spelling to reading. Children write, then read, high frequency words; hence, the title of her book *The Writing Road to Reading* (5th edition published by HarperCollins, 2003). The title is not just a play on words; writing and the phonograms create a wide-open road to knowing and using the written language. From the onset of instruction, children listen to and then read trade books rather than basal readers because the emphasis is on quality literature, with a strong focus on comprehension. The book includes a chapter on lesson planning with detailed spelling, writing, and reading procedures and example dialogues; a grade-level scope and sequence; updated and expanded children's literature recommendations, and an updated and expanded list of Ayres words.

For More Information: Spalding Education International, 2814 W. Bell Road, Suite 1405, Phoenix, AZ 85053-7531 (602) 866-7801. (*www.spalding.org*)

The Slingerland Approach

Beth Slingerland was another disciple of Samuel Orton who adapted the O-G techniques to whole class use. Slingerland's program features screening procedures for identifying children with reading disabilities. The method involves three sequential components: writing, auditory, and visual phases. Instruction begins with handwriting. Teachers give letter sounds and children name the letter that makes the sound while they trace the form of the letter in the air. In the auditory phase, children blend phonemes using letter cards, and then they write the letters. The visual phase involves decoding or "unlocking" printed words on the basis of phoneme-grapheme relationships. The program closely follows the O-G principles of multisensory instruction and strict structure.

For More Information: Educators Publishing Service, 31 Smith Place, Cambridge, MA 02138 (*www.epsbooks.com*)

Wilson Reading System® and Wilson Reading Fundations™

Barbara Wilson is another educator trained in Orton-Gillingham procedures, but Wilson saw the need to adapt these techniques for adolescents and older readers who had difficulty in learning to read. The Wilson Reading System is appropriate for students in upper elementary grades through adult. Wilson Reading Fundations™ for K-3 is a phonology/phonics/spelling program for the general education classroom. Fundations is complementary to most language arts programs and includes the basic components of the Wilson Reading System.® Teachers incorporate a 20–25 minute Fundations lesson into their language arts classroom instruction. Targeted small group intervention is available in phonology/phonics, fluency, and/or vocabulary as needed. The Wilson Reading System® follows a specified sequence of structured lessons in helping students master the coding system for reading and spelling beginning with phonemic awareness. The teacher introduces letters, sounds, and key words, and students learn to blend sounds into syllables and word patterns, using a system of finger tapping as they sound out words. Students move from one-syllable words to multisyllable words, then to structural elements of prefixes and suffixes. From the beginning, students apply skills with extensive controlled text (words, sentences, and stories) with a focus on both accuracy and fluency. Although the emphasis is on decoding and encoding, vocabulary and comprehension are emphasized throughout.

For More Information: Wilson Language Program, 175 W. Main Street, Millbury, MA 01527 (*www.WilsonLanguage.com*)

Project Read®/Language Circle®

Developed in the Bloomington (MN) public schools, Project Read®/Language Circle® is a mainstream language arts program for students who need a systematic learning experience with direct teaching of concepts and skills through multisensory techniques. Project Read® has five curriculum strands: phonology, linguistics, reading comprehension report form (expository), reading comprehension story form (narrative), and written expression. The strands are integrated at all grade levels, but specific strands are emphasized at certain grade levels. Project Read®/Language Circle® is designed to be delivered in regular classroom or by special education, Title I, and reading teachers who work with children or adolescents with language learning problems. Project Read® is recommended as an early intervention program for grades one through six but is equally effective with adolescents and adults. The program's principles of systematic learning, direct concept teaching, and multisensory strategies reach the alternative instructional needs of students, thereby reducing the number of students referred for special services.

For More Information: The Learning Circle, P.O. Box 20631, Bloomington, MN 55420 (*www.projectread@mn.uswest.net*)

Bradley Reading and Language Arts

Originally known as *The Won Way: A Winning Way to Teach Reading and Language Arts,* the Bradley Program is a whole class approach to providing systematic, direct instruction in phonics and language skills for kindergarten and primary grade youngsters. The teacher uses cards to introduce seventy-four individual alphabet symbols and letter combinations to the class. Children learn the multiple sounds of these letter combinations and practice by writing words and sentences in response to teacher dictation. Children apply their decoding skills in regular reading material rather than with controlled text tied directly to the sounds being taught. The program not only integrates multisensory modalities but also involves all aspects of the language arts.

For More Information: The Bradley Institute, P.O. Box 37, Upton, MA 01568

Wisnia-Kapp Reading Programs ("WKRP")

WKRP was originally designed for students with extreme difficulty in encoding and decoding written language. It is also used for in-class multisensory systematic phonics instruction in grades K–2. Students first identify letter names and engage in sound segmentation exercises. Sounds are introduced with stories, and drawings provide visual mnemonic cues to help children remember the sound-symbol correspondences they are expected to learn. Children progress through carefully organized sequenced steps from letters to words to text, always linking new information to what they already know.

For More Information: Wisnia-Kapp Reading Programs, 111 South Bedford Street, Burlington, MA 01803

The Lindamood™ Phoneme Sequencing (LiPS™) Program for Reading, Spelling and Speech

The Lindamood Program is another intensive phonics program in that it works with phoneme-grapheme relationships for reading and spelling. It differs from previously described programs, however, in that it is more deeply rooted in phonemic awareness. As a speech pathologist, Patricia Lindamood researched and recognized the importance of phonemic awareness and its predictive relationship to literacy development. The program develops phonemic awareness through articulatory feedback, with an emphasis on the physical aspects of sound formation. For example, /p/ and /b/ are categorized as "lip poppers" because the lips "pop" as the sounds are made. A unique Tracking step provides concrete experiences in coding sounds in syllables and words, first with mouth pictures and then with colored blocks. Rather than rote memorizing, the emphasis is on integrating intersensory information for thinking, reasoning, and independent self-correction in oral language, reading, and spelling.

For More Information: Lindamood-Bell Learning Processes, 416 Higuera, San Luis Obispo, CA 93401 (800) 233-1819

The preceding programs represent only a sample of the direct, explicit, systematic language/phonics programs available for use in school today. Other similar programs exist—the *Stevenson Language Program,* for example, or *Alphabetic Phonics*—and more are appearing on the educational horizon all the time. Programs develop and change so rapidly that it would be impractical to attempt to identify and describe all of them here.

What do these programs have in common? While they obviously differ from each other in some important details, in general all of them:

- begin with a strong emphasis on learning letters and sounds. They all build upon the alphabetic principle of English orthography and begin by introducing sound-symbol correspondences in a direct and systematic way.
- follow a specific sequence of instruction that is carefully scripted. Lessons begin with single phoneme-grapheme relationships and proceed in a strictly prescribed instructional sequence to larger language units.
- feature a multisensory approach to instruction. Visual, auditory, and kinesthetic/tactile modalities are closely integrated to reinforce learning.
- utilize cards for letters and words. Manipulating cards or tiles, which are frequently color coded, is part of the multisensory aspect of the program.
- color coding is often used as a visual clue. In Project Read, for example, "green words" are regular for both decoding and encoding, and "red words" are phonetically irregular. The Wilson Program uses different colored cards for consonants, vowels, syllables, and structural units (prefixes and suffixes).
- use nonsense words or pseudowords as part of instruction. These are words that can be pronounced but that have no meaning. While conventional phonics instruction usually eschews the use of nonsense words, synthetic programs use these elements to focus

directly on decoding rather than relying on context, pictures, or other clues.

- require considerable preparation in the content and procedures to be followed. It's not unusual for teachers to attend workshops for as long as a year before they are deemed qualified to teach the program.

Of course, there are differences among these structured phonics/language programs as well. While most begin with short vowel sounds, others teach long vowels first. Some programs insist that only controlled program-related reading materials be used for practice; others encourage the use of trade books or basal readers. Some make extensive use of diacritical marking systems; others don't. Programs vary from pull-out models for individual tutoring or small group work to procedures designed for large group or whole class teaching. Differences notwithstanding, these programs all focus on learning the structure and system of English orthography as a means of helping all children—but especially those who struggle with reading and writing—learn to succeed.

Other Programs That Include Phonics

One need not rely entirely on an embedded phonics approach or on a structured schoolwide phonics program in order to make phonics part of comprehensive instruction in reading and writing. Because of the alphabetic nature of our writing system, phonics is a direct dimension of instructional models that are not "phonics first" (such as Reading Recovery), basal reading programs, supplementary workbook programs, and computer-based programs designed to help children learn the alphabetic code of their language.

Models of Instruction

A number of programs or models of teaching reading have been designed to meet the needs of at-risk (as well as other) learners, and these typically include decoding practice as an essential element of instruction.

Reading Recovery is a widely used program based on the work of New Zealand literacy educator Marie Clay (1993). The program is designed to meet the needs of young children who are experiencing reading difficulty in the belief that early intervention will enable them to succeed before they fall into a pattern of failure. Tutoring sessions include reading familiar books, assessing the child's reading (including decoding) strategies, composing written messages with the help of the teacher as needed, and reading new books. Lessons include letter identification exercises for children who need it, hearing sounds in words, and focusing on sound-symbol relationships as essential elements in reading. While orthography is only one source of information that children use when learning as part of Reading Recovery, it is an important source of information in reading and writing.

Success for All is another intervention program that involves one-to-one tutoring with first graders in an attempt to head off reading problems before they start to interfere with a child's school success. Designed by Slavin and his colleagues (1996), the program is a school restructuring plan that involves a heavy emphasis on cooperative learning, homogeneous grouping for reading instruction, family support teams to get parents involved, and a heavy emphasis on the systematic presentation of phonics and on decoding practice. While instructional sessions involve comprehension exercises, oral reading for fluency, and writing activities, they also emphasize intensive drill on phonics.

Benchmark Word Identification Program is a program that was developed at the Benchmark School for delayed readers and is used in conjunction with literature-based reading and writing instruction. The program emphasizes the analogy approach to decoding. Children learn a set of 120 key high-frequency words that have common spelling patterns associated with vowel sounds, and they are taught to use these words to help them decode unknown words that they encounter in reading. Students read widely in basal texts and a variety of trade books. While there is a strong emphasis on decoding by analogy, phonics rules are not explicitly taught. Students are encouraged to generate their own rules as they interact with print (Gaskins et al. 1997).

Book Buddies is a supplementary intervention program carried on with community volunteers working one-on-one with children who need help (Invernizzi et al. 1997). The program involves repeated reading of familiar text to promote reading fluency, along with a heavy emphasis on word study that includes explicit instruction in sound-symbol relationships and manipulating onsets and rimes. Phonetic elements are emphasized in writing instruction as well.

Other instructional models for early intervention are used in schools nationwide, all with the intention of helping children avoid the risk of reading failure early in their school lives, and all with varying degrees of phonics instruction and decoding practice as a way of learning to read.

Basal Reading Programs

Over the years, basal reading programs—commercially published instructional materials packages designed to provide the basis and core of classroom reading instruction—have had enormous influence on the way in which reading was taught in most schools. The basal continues to be the primary tool used to teach reading in well over 80 percent of the classrooms in the United States, and many teachers and administrators view these programs "as embodying scientific truth" when it comes to teaching reading (Shannon 1983). Basal materials have remained among the most widely used instructional tools on the educational landscape.

To some degree, phonics has always been included as part of basal instruction. Phonics is included in basal programs in different components:

- the scope and sequence chart, which constitutes the overall plan or blueprint of the program, usually lists phonics elements, sometimes indicating where each element is introduced, reinforced, and mastered;

- the reading books, with stories that feature content constitutes the focus of instruction;
- the workbooks, which contain exercises and activities specifically designed to enable children to practice and apply decoding strategies based on specific phonics components;
- the teacher's editions, with detailed suggestions on how to introduce and teach particular phonetic elements;
- the assessment component, with tests and other devices designed to measure pupils' knowledge of the phonics elements being taught.

The degree of emphasis that basals placed on phonics has reflected the ebb and flow of phonics in schools. Throughout the era of look-say instruction, the emphasis was typically informal and incidental. There was often a phonics strand, "sometimes related to the reading materials, but more often unrelated, attached as an ongoing component to the day-to-day lesson plans" that was introduced after children had learned to recognize a large number of sight words (Aukerman 1984, 319). There was no control over vocabulary on the basis of sound-symbol correspondence at the beginning stages of reading instruction.

As the pendulum swung toward a decoding emphasis in the 1960s and '70s, phonics became much more prominent in basal reading instruction. Series such as Lippincott's *Basic Reading* and the Economy Company's *Phonetic Keys to Reading* strictly controlled vocabulary from the beginning stages on the basis of sound-symbol relationships. Stories were structured around specific phonological relationships; for example, a story about thunder and lightning emphasized "the loud pounding sound of thunder in the clouds" to teach the **ou**-/ou/ symbol-sound correspondence. Lessons included lots of phonics drill and practice.

When the whole language movement took root, authentic reading experiences with real books by real authors became the common practice in teaching reading. Basal readers became heavily literature-based. Programs were infused with quality children's stories written by recognized children's authors like Chris Van Allsburg and Julius Lester, poems by Nikki Giovanni and Myra Cohn Livingston, informational pieces by Seymour Simon and Gail Gibbons, folk literature from different cultures, and complete stories from award-winning books.

How does phonics fit into today's basal readers? Phonics remains an integral part of most basal programs, with phonics lessons derived from stories contained in the readers. Instead of starting with skills—for example, writing a story about "Grandmother's Grape Jelly" to teach the **gr** blend—stories come first and phonics lessons are teased out of these stories. For example, from a basal story about *Henry and Mudge* by Cynthia Rylant, the words *brother, friend, drooled,* and *dreamed* are selected to teach the **br, fr,** and **dr** consonant clusters. The story's themes of family life and wanting a dog are emphasized along with the decoding elements involved.

Not all contemporary basal reading programs are the same, of course, and some emphasize phonics more than others do. The Open Court basal series, for example, which has maintained a strong phonics emphasis since its original publication in the early 1960s, continues to include an explicit, systematic phonics component as part of its program. From the earliest levels, instruction focuses on phonemic awareness and involves structured activities that systematically introduce the spelling of sounds with sound/spelling cards, blending exercises, and decodable books for practice. Literature is not ignored in Open Court, however, as books also contain stories and poems by authors such as Lois Lowry, John Steptoe, and Patricia MacLachlan.

In sum, phonics remains part of basal reading instruction. Vowels and consonants are still listed in scope and sequence charts. Attention to phonemic awareness is prominently built into suggestions in the teacher's edition for early literacy experiences. In workbooks that are generally far more attractive than they used to be, children still circle pictures for words "that begin with the letter **b**" and fill in words that "have the same vowel sound as *tag*." Basals emphasize the centrality of decoding and phonics as a way of achieving fluency and independence in reading. But phonics is not an end in itself; it is strategically incorporated into a balanced program that emphasizes meaning as children use basal materials in learning how to read.

Supplementary Phonics Workbook Programs. One way to inject phonics directly into a reading program is to use a workbook series focusing exclusively on practice in the application of decoding skills and strategies. These programs contain a series of five or six books of increasing difficulty, which focus largely on pencil-and-paper exercises designed to teach and reinforce all components of phonics. Some of the more widely used supplementary phonics programs include:

- *Modern Curriculum Press Phonics* (Modern Curriculum Press, 299 Jefferson Road, Parsippany, NJ 07054 *www.pearsonlearning.com*);
- *Sadlier Phonics* (William Sadlier Co., 9 Pine St., New York, NY 10005);
- *Primary Phonics* (Educators Publisher Service, 625 Mount Auburn St., Cambridge, MA 02139 *www.epsbooks.com*);
- *Steck-Vaughn Phonics* (P.O. Box 26015, Austin, TX 78755);
- *SRA/Open Court Phonics* (SRA/Open Court, 8787 Orion Place, Columbus, OH 43240);
- *Explode the Code* (Educators Publisher Service, 625 Mount Auburn St., Cambridge, MA 02139 *www.epsbooks.com*).

Supplementary workbook programs have been extensively used for a long time as part of phonics instruction across the land. Examples of workbook exercises from some of these programs were provided in the previous chapter.

Phonics workbooks have practical appeal to teachers. They are a means of providing for direct phonics instruction in the classroom. They provide hands-on material that focuses very specifically on the discrete phonics elements that children are expected to learn in order to decode words. Children can complete activity sheets independently, and the completed exercises provide a convenient diagnostic measure of their mastery of sound-symbol relationships. Over the years, these workbook series have been popular teaching tools, indeed.

These programs have also received their share of criticism. Critics claim that the use of worksheets distorts the child's sense of what reading is all about, reduces reading instruction to a tedious chore, and deprives children of precious classroom time available for interacting with books. Johnson and Louis (1987) decry exercises that involve children in "huffing and puffing at letters, marking whether vowels are glided or unglided, deciding whether **b** or **d** goes at the beginning or ending of the tattered remnant of a mutilated word rendered meaningless by its isolation" (3). The act of completing a phonics worksheet is not the same as practicing reading in a more functional context.

Some worry about the excessive use of workbooks in schools. In their survey of reading practices in classrooms nationwide, Anderson and his colleagues (1985) reported that children spend as much as 70 percent of their reading instructional time doing "seatwork" involving workbooks and skills sheets, and there is little evidence that this amount of time has decreased. The demand for seatwork materials has been described as insatiable. Concern has been expressed that time spent working exclusively on workbook exercises deprives children of more meaningful interaction with books, which is so essential to developing the ability and the inclination to read.

Another concern is the level that workbooks typically demand of children. Many of these exercises require only a perfunctory level of reading that requires passive responses to low-level demands. Children rarely engage in higher-level thinking, use constructive or strategic reading, or do extended writing as they draw lines or fill in the blanks that are typical of workbook exercises. Besides, these exercises are often time-consuming and can be exceedingly tedious.

These supplementary programs are not, of course, the be-all and end-all of phonics instruction. Rather, they need to be part of a comprehensive program of direct phonics instruction. "When teachers assign a worksheet that requires children to fill in the missing words, only children who already know the correct response can successfully do the task. And *they* don't need the practice. Children who do not know what vowel to put in the blank space cannot acquire that knowledge from the worksheet" (Allington 2002, 744).

A key consideration in choosing and using phonics worksheets is to determine how they fit a child's needs. On the one hand, hop-scotching over blocks of initial consonant blends like **cr, bl,** and **fl** as they hear words read can be an efficient and worthwhile way to provide practice for children who need reinforcement on these elements. On the other hand, having children divide a list of unusually long words into syllables and mark their accents is unconscionable.

Although they have been blessed and cursed over the years, phonics workbook programs have been part of classroom reading instruction for a very long time, and there seems to be little evidence that the use of these programs is diminishing. In fact, with the new emphasis on phonics in schools, their use seems to be increasing.

Multisensory materials are also available for teaching phonics in the classroom. Programs such as *Touchphonics* (Cambridge, MA: Educators Publishing Service) contains color-coded, three dimensional letters that children can manipulate. The textured surface of these alphabet symbols adds a tactile dimension to learning. Larger magnetic tiles can be used for large group lessons. Commercial programs like these add a multisensory dimension to phonics learning.

"Worksheets are great for independent practices. When concepts have been well-taught, they are not categorically despicable, just often misused as a substitute for teaching" (Moats 1998, 48).

Computer-Based Phonics Programs

Given the impact of technology in today's world, it's not surprising that a plethora of computerized phonics programs continues to appear for home and school use. Computerized games and instructional programs for teaching all aspects of phonics are widely available, and Internet sites provide all kinds of information on the topic. Over half our homes have personal computers, and a growing number of teachers in our schools use computers as instructional tools. Beginning in the prekindergarten years, children use computers as learning tools in all areas of the curriculum. The computer has become "the ubiquitous icon of the digital age" (Walter 1998).

A number of CD-ROMs are available to help children learn the sound-symbol relationships of their language. Some incorporate decoding skills into a more comprehensive reading program that includes instruction on sight words, comprehension activities, story reading, writing practice, and other activities designed to help children become literate. Others are little more than "electronic workbooks" in which children point and click on words on the screen rather than circling letters or writing words on the page. Programs are available from the very beginning stages of learning to read (with alphabet and phonemic awareness activities) through elements taught in the upper primary grades.

Programs deal extensively with phonics by focusing specifically on learning letter names, connecting sounds to letters and letters to sounds, distinguishing between long and short vowels, blending letter clusters into words, identifying syllables, constructing simple sentences using phonetically regular words, and other aspects that are part of the regular regimen of phonics instruction. Many programs feature colorful graphics and lively animation. Digitized speech adds sound elements. Some programs feature songs and arcade-style games that illustrate sound-symbol relationships. Others include videoclips. Children get feedback on their responses—correct responses produce the sounds of cheering crowds or brass bands; incorrect responses generate sighs of disappointment with the encouraging words, "Try again." All offer interactive features that enliven and enrich the learning environment to get children actively involved in learning phonics.

A small sample of programs available includes the following:

- *'Tronic Phonics* (Macmillan/McGraw-Hill, New York, NY 10121 *www.mhschool.com*) With lively graphics and tools for drawing, writing, and painting, this program builds around reading selections targeted at specific phonics elements. In a series of lessons, children can create their own rhyme or sentence, which they can then record.

- *Lexia* (Lexia Learning Systems, Lincoln, MA 01773 *www.lexialearning.com*) This is an interactive skill development program with engaging but relatively unsophisticated graphics. It provides both assessment and instructional tools at two levels (for younger children and for older children and adults) on phonemic awareness, sound-symbol correspondence, decoding skills, and early comprehension.

- *Working Phonics* (Curriculum Associates, No. Billerica, MA 01862 *www.curriculumassociates.com*) This program of skill-building activities includes drill and practice for basic decoding elements with word building, cloze, and matching exercises. It also has a management system to record pupil progress.

- *Word Muncher* (Softkey International, Cambridge, MA) This CD-ROM uses a game format, as children send a "Word Muncher" to gobble up words that have particular vowel sounds.

- *Reader Rabbit Learns to Read With Phonics* (The Learning Company, Redwood, CA 94947 *www.learningcompanyschool.com*) This is a basic phonics/early reading program that also includes storybooks, flashcards, and print materials.

- *Disney's Phonics Quest* (Dorling Kindersley Multimedia Global Software, New York, NY 10001 *www.dk.com*) Mickey Mouse and company help children learn phonics with an engaging story line about a sorcerer and his apprentice.

- *Let's Go Read! 1 An Island Adventure: Let's Go Read! 1 An Ocean Adventure;* and *Let's Go Read! 2 An Ocean Adventure* (EDMARK Corp., Cambridge, MA 02140 *www.riverdeep.net/edmark*) These colorful and lively programs focus on a range of phonics skills, from alphabet training in the early stages to phoneme identification, onsets and rimes, word-building, and working with phonics elements that build phonics into reading practice with attention to comprehension.

- *Leap Into Phonics* (Leap Into Learning, Inc., Omaha, NE 68154 *www.LeapIntoLearning.com*) *Leap Into Phonics* is a software program that helps pre-readers master phonemic awareness and beginning phonics skills. Focus areas include rhyming words, hearing syllables and sounds, identifying sounds in words, blending, phoneme substitution, and more. The program also provides student progress reports.

Some computerized phonics programs spin directly from children's literature, for example:

- *Dr. Seuss Kindergarten Deluxe* (Broderbund Software, Novato, CA 94947 *www.broderbund.com*) Dr. Seuss's characters come to life in helping kindergarten-aged children learn multiple phonics components.
- *Curious George Learns Phonics* (Houghton Mifflin Interactive, Somerville, MA *www.hmco.com*) This program teaches phonics with the help of H. A. and Margaret Rey's engaging character.

This list represents only a tiny sample of programs that are available for use in teaching and practicing phonics in school and at home.

More and more computerized programs for helping children learn letter-sound relationships and practice decoding skills are appearing in the educational marketplace all the time. Formats differ from one program to another. And while programs differ in details, content and quality, all bring phonics instruction into the technological age of the twenty-first century and provide a particularly valuable means for helping children learn to read.

Too often, technology is used for its own sake. Parents and teachers are challenged to separate the entertainment elements from the instructional factors so that phonics instructional programs don't become merely substitutes for Saturday morning cartoon shows. In many programs, children need to get through a lot of "stuff" before they get to the substance of the program! The goal is to help children learn the sound-symbol system of their language.

The Internet is a valuable source of ideas and information about phonics. When one begins to surf or mine the Net for material related to phonics, one finds advertisements describing and extolling the virtues of the many commercial programs and products for home and school. Beyond the commercial dimensions, one finds ideas that directly apply to teaching phonics in the classroom.

As a technological tool, the Internet provides a wealth of classroom-tested suggestions for activities and lesson plans related to decoding skills. The websites of some government agencies, publishing companies, commercial enterprises, and individual home pages provide ideas for teaching all aspects of phonics. Using website links, one can find teaching suggestions (many of which are linked to children's trade books), lesson plans, curriculum units, projects, games, activity sheets, and other ideas for practical application in the classroom. Visit the McGraw-Hill Higher Education website at *www.mhhe.com/ education* for a list of useful phonics links.

The multiple interconnections that exist on the Internet allow the teacher to explore virtually every dimension on phonics instruction. Sharing ideas electronically provides opportunities for teachers to work collegially.

The Internet also provides online resources for research about phonics. One can find articles, papers, citations, bibliographies, and related reference tools that allow teachers to explore scholarly and professional aspects of decoding practices. Professional agencies and organizations also provide material that promote or explain their particular perspective or position on teaching phonics.

Given the impact of the Internet on our daily lives, it's hardly surprising to find phonics all over the World Wide Web. As with any source of information, however, teachers need to approach information on the Internet with a critical eye to judge the validity, veracity, and usefulness of what is presented there.

Phonics Materials for Home Use

With the current public attention focused on phonics, it's not surprising to find a plethora of materials designed for parents to use at home with their children. In addition to interactive programs that can be used on home computers, there is a bull market in phonics workbooks, games, charts, videotapes, and other materials designed for parents. These materials include whole programs designed for phonics instruction at the kitchen table as a supplement to classroom instruction or for use in home schooling.

When one visits a school supply store or major bookseller, one finds shelves and racks bulging with activity books to teach phonics. While some of these books are designed for school use (parents generally have no occasion to use a book of black-lined masters), most are aimed at parents anxious to anticipate or to supplement any phonics instruction that their child might (or might not) be receiving in the classroom. Most have "Dear Parent" messages at the beginning, with general suggestions on how to use the activities in the book. These books cover the full range of phonics information and skills found in any reading curriculum—alphabet exercises and phonemic awareness activities for young children; exercises on tracing and copying letters; games and puzzles for teaching letter names and sounds; activities and skills sheets focusing on words with long, short, and other vowel sounds; games and activities involving blends and digraphs at the beginning and end of words; skills sheets on syllables and silent letters—in short, all the elements of a comprehensive school-based phonics program "that you and your child can do at home." For the most part, these programs consist of extensions of school-based phonics activities and include exercises exactly like those that children would do in the classroom.

Phonics books for parents come in all shapes and sizes and for children of all ages. There are workbooks for preschoolers (some with suggestions for test-taking strategies) to "help your child get a head start on being smart." Other books reflect the curriculum content of the primary and intermediate grades. There are even workbooks designed to be completed over the summer months to help get the child ready for the next grade. Many are colorfully illustrated. Some feature Big Bird and his Muppet friends, cartoon characters like Bugs Bunny and Daffy Duck, and Star War characters teaching the sounds of letters. Some books have stickers and other gimmicks, and some have audiotapes with songs and rhymes designed to develop phonemic awareness and

Figure 4.1 *Guidelines for evaluating phonics packages.*

The International Reading Association has developed guidelines on what teachers and parents should look for in a phonics package (Osborn, Stahl, and Stein 1997). These guidelines suggest the following questions to ask in selecting phonics programs to use with children:

- In addition to letter-sound instruction, does the package provide or recommend including other types of reading and writing activities?
- Does the package include rhyming activities?
- Does the package include other activities that will provide children with practice in distinguishing sounds in spoken words?
- Does the package provide for the teaching of letter names?
- Does the instruction help children understand the relationship between letters and the sounds they stand for?
- Are the instructions clear? Are the activities instructive?
- Does the package provide interesting and high-quality stories and other materials for children to read?
- Do the materials include many words that children can figure out by using the letter and sound relationships they are being taught?
- Does the package provide opportunities for children to apply what they are learning by writing? If not, is the package flexible enough to allow you to include spelling and writing opportunities along with the instruction?

Additional questions relate to practical issues of time demands, ease of use, cost, and other factors.

Obviously, some programs won't meet all criteria. There is a difference between a forty-eight-page alphabet puzzle book designed for home use and a comprehensive set of workbooks designed for use on a schoolwide basis. Nevertheless, these questions do give potential users a lens through which to examine phonics programs.

Source: Osborn, J., Stahl, S. A., and Stein, M. (1997) Teacher's guidelines for evaluating commercial phonics packages. *Newark, DE: International Reading Association. Reprinted with permission.*

sound-symbol knowledge. Many have videotapes, and there are also multi-part video programs that are highly entertaining while they attempt to teach children the sound-symbol system of their language.

Nor is the merchandise available for home use limited to workbooks. Jigsaw puzzles with letters, illustrated alphabets, phonics flashcards, board games, and other materials are available for parent purchase, with names like *Quizmo Phonetic Bingo Games* and *Prof. Wacky's Wahoo's Wordlab*. Through these and other materials, phonics is stretched beyond the classroom walls and into children's homes.

In addition to workbooks and games for toddlers and older children that parents can use to teach phonics at home, there are nationally advertised programs "guaranteed to help your child learn to read or your money back." Programs like the *Hooked on Phonics* (Gateway Educational Products, Orange, CA), *The Phonics Game* (A Better Way of Learning, Costa Mesa, CA), and *Frontline Phonics* (Frontline Phonics, Orem, UT) claim to address reading problems through phonics. These materials include sets of flash cads, audio tapes, and practice books with word lists and sentences designed to provide a complete phonics program for individuals (children and adults) learning to read. They claim to use a game format "for homeplay that makes learning fun" with card games, audio and videotapes, reading selections for practice, and other materials (word charts, stickers, and so on). A CD-ROM is also available. While developed primarily as home reading products, these programs have also been used in school resource rooms, Title I classes, remedial reading settings, and even in some classrooms.

Priced anywhere from $200 to $400 (depending on which components one purchases) "plus shipping and handling," these products generate huge revenues. They are advertised in media blitzes on radio, on television, and in popular publications. For the most part, they rely on testimonials and sales figures rather than any hard research as evidence of their effectiveness. In fact, some have been taken to court for making false and unsubstantiated claims about how well they work.

While most popularly advertised home reading products are designed for parents who want to extend or supplement phonics instruction that their children are receiving at school, other programs have been designed for parents who engage in home schooling of their children; that is, those who opt not to send their children to public schools but rather to educate them exclusively at home. Home study programs for teaching phonics, such as the *Saxon Phonics Program* (Saxon Publishers, Inc., Norman, OK) tend to be more comprehensive than parent-oriented materials often found in school supply stores. They contain a sequenced multilevel phonics curriculum with teachers' guides (sometimes with videotape backup), practice books for children, alphabet cards for word-building activities, booklets with simple stories with tightly controlled vocabulary, and other teaching tools for a home instructional program that covers the full range of fundamental phonics concepts and skills.

Conclusion

What's good phonics instruction? The answer will vary depending on one's view of language and how it ought best be taught. Some would say the answer involves a systematic, direct approach that includes plenty of sounding and blending based on explicit knowledge of sound-symbol relationships. Others would say that good instruction involves incidental teaching of phonics content as children need it. Some would say that good phonics instruction is embedded in children's purposeful encounters with authentic reading materials. Others would include systematic drill and practice in orthographic elements. Some would include practice in decoding nonsense words; others would eschew nonsense words. Some would include mastery of rules and patterns; others would not.

While one's view of "good" phonics instruction may differ, few would argue that the ultimate purpose of phonics is learning to read and write more effectively and efficiently, and that phonics instruction that produces the ability and the inclination to read and write must indeed be judged as "good."

Stahl, Duffy-Hester, and Stahl (1998) suggest seven principles of good phonics instruction that research and common sense suggest:

- *good phonics instruction should develop the alphabetic principle,* the notion that letters represent specific sounds;
- *good phonics instruction should develop phonological awareness,* including phonemic awareness;
- *good phonics instruction should provide a thorough grounding in the letters* so that children will recognize letters automatically and effortlessly;
- *good phonics instruction should not teach rules, need not use worksheets, should not dominate instruction, and does not have to be boring,* since rules often don't work and worksheet exercises may take time away from other worthwhile and interesting reading activities;
- *good phonics instruction provides sufficient practice in reading words,* since the purpose of phonics is to help children learn to recognize and read the words they encounter in print;
- *good phonics instruction leads to automatic word recognition,* since phonics is not an end in itself but a means of helping children read with ease and efficiency;
- *good phonics instruction is one part of reading instruction,* and children will hardly come to enjoy reading if all they do in reading class is sound out words and complete phonics worksheets.

Source: From Stahl, S.A., Duffy-Hester, A.M., and Stahl, K.A.D. (1998)
Everything you wanted to know about phonics (but were afraid to ask).
Reading Research Quarterly *33:338-355. Reprinted with permission*
of Stephen A. Stahl and the International Reading Association. All
rights reserved.

In the final analysis, good phonics instruction is teaching that enables children to learn the components of their orthographic system in a way that they can apply in decoding and encoding words in independent reading and writing activities.

In looking at programs designed to provide intensive phonics instruction—complete programs, kits and games, computer disks and audio tapes, workbooks, or total packages designed for home or classroom use—it's important to remember that reading involves the construction of meaning from print. The print may be as simple as the movie schedule at the local theatre, as functional as the directions on the back of a frozen pizza box, as personal as a letter from a loved one, or as spiritual as an inspirational poem or scripture passage.

Intensive phonics programs focus almost exclusively on helping children develop mastery of sound-symbol relationships. This awareness of sound-symbol relationships is important to getting meaning from print, because without being able to decode the movie schedule, directions, letter or poem, the meaning of the message remains inaccessible. The aim of systematic phonics is ultimately to provide children with the tools they need to become fluent and confident independent readers and writers. The ability to apply this knowledge, however, in interacting with stories and poems is important, too. That's what reading is all about.

Intensive phonics instruction is important, but it's only one part of learning how to read. Within the child's classroom, resource room, or living room, programs that focus on sound-symbol relationships should be used in conjunction with other language activities—reading aloud, verbal interaction that stimulates language and vocabulary growth, writing letters and words, and other activities that will build a solid foundation for reading success.

References

Adams, M. J. 1990. *Beginning to Read: Thinking and Learning About Print.* Cambridge, MA: MIT Press.

Allington, R. L. 2002. What I've learned about effective reading instruction. *Phi Delta Kappan* 83:740–7.

Anderson, R. C., E. H. Hiebert, J. A. Scott, and I. A. G. Wilkinson. 1985. *Becoming A Nation of Readers: The Report of the Commission on Reading.* Washington, DC: National Institute of Education, U.S. Department of Education.

Armbruster, B., F. Lehr, and J. Osborn. 2001. *Put Reading First: The Research Building Blocks for Teaching Children to Read.* Jessup, MD: National Institute for Literacy.

Aukerman, R. 1984. *Approaches to Beginning Reading.* 2d ed. New York: John Wiley and Sons.

Blevins, W. 1998. *Phonics from A to Z.* New York: Scholastic.

Cassidy, J., and D. Cassidy. 2002/3. What's hot, what's not for 2003. *Reading Today.* December 2002/January 2003.

Chall, J. S. 1996. *Learning to Read: The Great Debate.* 3d ed. Fort Worth: Harcourt Brace.

Clark, D. B., and J. K. Uhry. 1995. *Dyslexia: Theory and Practice of Remedial Instruction.* 2d ed. Baltimore: York Press.

Clay, M. 1993. *Reading Recovery: A Guidebook for Teachers in Training.* Portsmouth, NH: Heinemann.

Gaskins, I. W., L. C. Ehri, C. Cress, C. O'Hara, and K. Donnelly. 1997. Procedures for word learning: Making discoveries about words. *The Reading Teacher* 50:312–27.

Groff, P. 2001. Teaching phonics: Letter-to-phoneme, phone-to-letter, or both? *Reading and Writing Quarterly* 17:291–306.

Harris, T. L., and R. E. Hodges. 1995. *The Literacy Dictionary.* Newark, DE: International Reading Association.

Invernizzi, M., C. Juel, and C. A. Rosemary. 1997. A community volunteer tutorial that works. *The Reading Teacher* 50:304–11.

Johnson, T. D., and D. R. Louis. 1987. *Literacy through Literature.* Portsmouth, NH: Heinemann.

Lyon, R. 1997. *30 Years of NICHD Research: What We Now Know About How Children Learn to Read.* Washington, DC: National Institute of Child Health and Human Development (NICHD).

Massachusetts Department of Education. 1997. *English Language Arts Curriculum Framework.* Malden, MA: Mass. Dept. of Education.

McIntyre, C. W., and J. S. Pickering, eds. 1995. *Clinical Studies of Multisensory Structured Language Education for Students with Dyslexia and Related Disorders.* Salem, OR: International Multisensory Structured Language Education Council.

Moats, L. C. 1998. Teaching decoding. *American Educator* 22:42–9, 95–6.

Moustafa, M., and E. Maldonado-Colon. 1999. Whole-to-part phonics: Building on what children know to help them know more. *The Reading Teacher* 52:448–58.

National Reading Panel (2000) *Teaching Children to Read: An Evidence-Based Assessment of the Scientific Research Literature on Reading and its Implications for Reading Instruction.* Washington, DC: National Institute of Child Health and Human Development.

National Reading Panel. (2000a). *Teaching Children to Read: An Evidence-Based Assessment of the Scientific Research Literature on Reading and its Implications for Reading Instruction: Reports of the Subgroups.* Washington, DC: National Institute of Child Health and Human Development.

Osborn, J., S. Stahl, and M. Stein. 1997. *Teachers' Guidelines for Evaluating Commercial Phonics Packages.* Newark, DE: International Reading Association.

Shannon, P. 1983. The use of commercial reading materials in American elementary schools. *Reading Research Quarterly* 19:68–85.

Slavin, R. E., N. A. Madden, N. Darwest, C. J. Dolan, and B. A. West. 1996. *Every Child, Every School; Success for All.* Newbury Park, CA: Corwin.

Stahl, S. A., A. M. Duffy-Hester, and K. A. D. Stahl. 1998. Everything you wanted to know about phonics (but were afraid to ask). *Reading Research Quarterly* 33:338–55.

Trachtenburg, P. 1990. Using children's literature to enhance phonics instruction. *The Reading Teacher* 43:648–52.

Walter, V. A. 1998. Girl power: Multimedia and more. *Book Links* 7:37–41.

Children's Trade Books Cited in This Chapter

Fleming, D. 1998. *In the Small, Small Pond.* New York: Henry Holt.

Gag, W. 1928. *Millions of Cats.* New York: Putnam.

Geisel, T. (Dr. Seuss). 1957. *Cat in the Hat.* New York: Random House.

Guarino, D. 1991. *Is Your Mama a Llama?* New York: Scholastic.

Hoberman, M. 1993. *A House is a House for Me.* New York: Penguin Putnam.

Hutchins, P. 1972. *Good Night, Owl!* New York: Macmillan.

———. 1968. *Rosie's Walk.* New York: Macmillan.

Lewison, W. C. 1992. *Buzzz Said the Bee.* Illustrated by H. Wilhelm. New York: Scholastic.

Martin, B., Jr. 1989. *Brown Bear, Brown Bear, What do You See?* Illustrated by E. Carle, New York: Henry Holt.

Sendak, M. 1986. *Chicken Soup with Rice.* New York: Scholastic.

Shaw, N. 1986. *Sheep on a Ship.* Illustrated by M. Apple. Boston: Houghton Mifflin.

———. 1986. *Sheep in a Jeep.* Illustrated by M. Apple. Boston: Houghton Mifflin.

———. 1992. *Sheep out to Eat.* Illustrated by M. Apple. Boston: Houghton Mifflin.

Slobodkina, E. 1947. *Caps for Sale.* New York: Harper and Row.

Steig, W. 1992. *Amos and Boris.* New York: Farrar Straus & Giroux.

Phonics and Learning to Spell

5

Phonics is as important to encoding as it is to decoding. In order to spell words correctly, writers need to apply their knowledge of sound-symbol relationships in some sophisticated ways. While the alphabetic principle is applied in learning to spell, other factors impact the choice of correct orthographic options in writing. This chapter

▼ examines spelling within the context of the writing process

▼ presents the stages of invented spelling as part of children's language development

▼ describes phonological processing, visual processing, and word knowledge as three dimensions of what it takes to be a good speller.

Over seventy years ago, L. S. Tierman (1930) summed up the secret of successful spelling. "The essential fact of spelling," Tierman wrote, "is to write all the letters and have them in the right order." Easier said than done!

Spelling has long been a concern of school and society. Spelling is both a school subject and a functional writing skill. Over the years, children have used tons of graphite and barrels of ink taking spelling tests, and then copying the words they got wrong over and over. Teachers have spent countless hours teaching children how to spell, and then spent many more hours correcting the spelling in their pupils' written work. For many adults, until the advent of spellcheckers, poor spelling was seen as something of a genetic burden that they carried through their lives.

Spelling and reading have much in common. "A general consensus in the research community (is) that the process of *writing* words and the process of *reading* words draw upon the same underlying base of word knowledge. . . . Orthographic or spelling knowledge is the engine that drives efficient reading as well as efficient writing" (Templeton and Morris 1999, 103). Both depend on the alphabetic principle and deal with the code of written language. Reading involves decoding; spelling involves encoding. Both rely on a solid knowledge of sound-symbol relationships. Ehri and Wilce (1987) have demonstrated the value of linking spelling instruction to reading instruction when children first begin learning to read.

While both are closely related, reading and spelling are different in significant ways. Reading requires the rapid recognition of groups of written symbols; spelling involves the production of these symbols one at a time. Readers have the context of a total passage to help arrive at the pronunciation and meaning of words; writers must put the words into context. And although there is a positive correlation between scores on reading and spelling tests, reading ability does not guarantee spelling proficiency. (Poor readers, however, are likely to be poor spellers as well.)

Spelling as Part of Writing

Spelling is a written language skill. Despite the popularity of spelling bees—including the annual National Spelling Bee, which may be described as an orthographic beauty pageant—spelling is unique to written language. Spelling involves the visual representation of spoken sounds by written symbols, and is part of learning to write. "It is only in the social and functional context of writing that children make sense of spelling; separated from writing, spelling serves no purpose" (Heald-Taylor 1998, 409).

For many years, spelling was treated as a separate subject within the school curriculum. It had its own scheduled time slot within the school day, a separate curriculum guide specifying what should be taught, a separate textbook series to be used for instruction and practice, and its own place on the report card. Children were presented with a discrete list of weekly words to be mastered by rote memory, and they were tested on these words on Friday.

With the advent of process writing, spelling was more closely integrated into written language instruction. "The idea of writing as a process arrived on the educational scene in the mid-1960s. Its swift and almost universal acceptance marked it as a 'paradigm shift,' a new way of understanding, which at once rendered traditional 'product-centered composition teaching' as obsolete" (Walshe 1988, 212). People like Donald Murray (1968), Donald Graves (1983, 1994), Lucy Calkins (1994), and others changed the primary instructional focus from the stories, poems, reports, and other written materials that writers produce to the process that they follow in producing these products.

In a nutshell, the model of process writing suggests that composing written language—whether it's done by a professional novelist working on a best seller or by a group of first graders putting together an experience story—involves three steps or stages:

- *prewriting*, during which the author decides on a topic, brainstorms ideas about the topic, narrows the focus, decides on audience and form, does research as appropriate, and otherwise organizes ideas related to the writing. Pupils often discuss ideas with teachers and peers as part of writing workshop.
- *writing*, the time when children commit their ideas to paper in first draft form. Ideas take form, details are reduced to words, thoughts are forged into sentences and sentences gathered into paragraphs.

The work is done as a first draft, because rare indeed is the writer who can produce a polished product the first time around.

- *postwriting*, which involves editing, revising, and publishing the child's written work. Editing involves proofreading to check that the writing is mechanically sound: that all sentences are complete and begin with capital letters, that proper punctuation marks are used, and that words are spelled correctly. Revising focuses on meaning and effective communication, with an eye to interesting word choice, sentence variety, and clarity of ideas. Publishing, the culmination of the writing process, occurs when pupils post their writing on the bulletin board, send their stories home to be read by parents and others, or gather their writing into class books.

Where does spelling fit in as part of the writing process? At the writing stage, the time when pupils are working on first drafts, spelling is not a primary concern. Writers should feel free to use words without regard to exact orthographic accuracy. With an overemphasis on spelling in the first draft stage, a child who is drafting a story about a *gigantic* monster and doesn't know how to spell "gigantic" will stick with the orthographically safe *b-i-g.* Young writers need to be told, "Get your ideas down on paper so that you can read it to an audience. If you don't know how to spell a word, write it the way it sounds and we can get it right later on."

The "later on" occurs during the postwriting stage, as children edit their work prior to publication. Spelling is in part a social skill; that is, writing is judged as effective by others in part on the basis of its mechanical accuracy. Poor spelling gets in the way of effective communication. Poor spelling detracts from the effectiveness in a piece of writing, no matter how creative the writing is and no matter how skilled are aspects such as word choice, sentence structure, or organization of ideas. (Conversely, a piece of poor writing with all the words spelled correctly is still a piece of poor writing.)

This is a very important point. Spelling impacts the effectiveness of writing to the extent that the writing is shared. If I'm making a grocery list and I'm the one doing the shopping, it makes little difference how I spell the word for the dressing I use on my sandwiches, as long as I know what I have to buy. If my wife is doing the shopping, I need to make it orthographically clear enough that she won't forget to pick up *maynese* (sic). But if I'm writing a recipe to a local newspaper, I had better be sure to spell *mayonnaise* correctly because my writing is going to a wider audience. Invented spelling is a legitimate part of first draft writing, but standard spelling is a courtesy to readers and a mark of effective written communication.

While spelling instruction is effectively integrated into process writing, there is a place in the language arts program for direct instruction in helping children learn to spell correctly. As children examine word patterns, as they learn to add prefixes and suffixes to form new words, as they explore the etymology and development of words that are new to them, as they focus on orthographic patterns such as the multiple spellings of long vowel sounds, as they complete lists of high frequency words, as they enjoy multiple encounters with written words as part of their classroom language experiences—all offer opportunities for explicit instruction in spelling. "Knowledge about the English spelling system will enable them to get in the right ball park (in getting the correct spelling of individual words). . . . Only specific knowledge will allow students to remember correct spelling. The relationship between specific knowledge and knowledge of the system is reciprocal. Each supports the other" (Bear et al. 2000, 4). And that specific knowledge about spelling is developed through direct instruction.

With the focus on direct instruction and spelling as a distinct part of the language arts curriculum, teachers often ask about the role of published spelling programs and weekly spelling lists. Traditionally, a weekly list of words was prescribed by a spelling basal and pupils were expected to learn these words by rote memorization. Lists are still appropriate, but words should be selected according to the developmental spelling levels of the children and organized according to spelling patterns. Templeton and Morris (1999) suggest that at the primary grade levels, words should be known automatically as sight words in reading; at the intermediate levels, new words may be included that are related in spelling and meaning to known words. Templeton and Morris also suggest that, as a source of word lists, teachers should examine published spelling programs with an eye to determining the appropriateness of the words.

With regard to the number of words that should be included in the weekly lists, "enough words to allow students the opportunity to discern one or more patterns has been suggested" (Templeton and Morris 1999, 107). Again depending on children's developmental stage(s) of spelling, fewer than 10 a week seems appropriate for first graders, 10 to 12 a week for second and third graders, and 20-plus words for those above this level.

Spelling fits into the picture in a comprehensive phonics program. Through direct, explicit instruction with formal word lists, children learn to apply the alphabetic principle as they engage in writing activities from the very early grades. At the same time, spelling is integrated into writing instruction as a functional language skill. Spelling receives its share of attention in writers workshops, as children engage in authentic writing activities that are part of a comprehensive literacy program.

Invented Spelling

Invented or "temporary" spelling has become one of the most widely discussed and controversial topics in education today. In invented spelling, children create their written versions of words based on the letter-sound relationships that they know. Invented spelling reflects children's attempts to spell a word according to the way it sounds. It is a normal part of a child's development as a writer and a powerful indicator of the child's literacy awareness. Through invented spelling, children demonstrate their developing understanding of how written language works. Children's attempts to "spell words like they sound" builds on their knowledge of sound-symbol relationships, which is the essence of phonics.

Since Charles Read (1971) published his pioneer research on invented spelling, the idea has been applauded and widely used in classrooms, but it has also been met with vehement opposition by critics who fear that the use of invented spelling will lead children away from ultimate spelling correctness. Critics ascribe all types of writing problems to invented spelling, equate invented spelling with misspelling, and claim that invented spelling involves the "dumbing down" of the educational process. They fail to recognize, however, that children's mistakes are not random errors rooted in ignorance, but rather are genuine attempts to apply the alphabetic principle to written English. Children use their knowledge of phonics to support their attempts at spelling. Ideas and language in writing are restricted if children are afraid to make educated guesses based on their developing understanding of the sound-symbol correspondences in their language. This is what invented spelling is all about.

Ironically, many critics of invented spelling see phonics as a way to help children overcome the "errors" they perceive in children's writing. Invented spelling reflects an authentic involvement in phonics, since the practice is rooted in phonetic logic. It's a way of discovering how the alphabetic principle works and gets children involved in meaningful writing from the start. Invented spelling is not a failure to achieve correctness; it's a step on the road to mastering the system that leads to spelling accuracy.

Invented spelling is supported by research and best practice. Based on her review of research, Adams (1990) concluded, "Classroom encouragement of invented spelling and independent writing from the start seem a promising approach toward the development of literacy skills" (386). The Committee on the Prevention Difficulties in Young Children recommends, "Instruction should be designed with the understanding that the use of invented spelling is not in conflict with teaching correct spelling. Beginning writing with invented spelling can be helpful for developing understanding of the identification and segmentation of speech sounds and sound-spelling relationships" (Snow, Burns, and Griffin 1998, 7–8). In one study, first graders who used invented spelling got off to an early start in independent writing and (ironically, perhaps) at the end of a year, these children had significantly greater skill in spelling than did children who were urged to use traditional spelling (Clarke 1988). "In a sense, invented spelling continues throughout our lives. We engage in it whenever we take a risk or have a go at a word about which we are uncertain" (Templeton and Morris 1999, 108).

Learning to spell, like learning to speak, is a developmental process. Children go through stages on their way to competency as mature spellers. Each stage indicates a different level of sophistication and a different level of cognitive awareness about how spelling works. The stages proceed from simple to complex. "Though inventive spellers tend to move in the direction of conventional spelling, the end of this progression is not so much the acquisition of expert spelling ability as a setting for the foundation from which expert spelling might be constructed" (Gentry and Gillet 1993, 21).

Although different experts define and describe the stages of invented spelling in slightly different terms (Weaver 1988; Henderson 1990; Gentry and Gillet 1993; Bear and Templeton 1998; Fresch 2001), the five stages generally identified include scribbling or precommunication, random or prephonetic spelling, phonetic spelling, transitional spelling, and finally, conventional spelling. Traill (1993) combines descriptions of spelling stages with corresponding writing stages.

Scribbling

In literate cultures, when children learn to hold a writing implement—pencil, pen, marker, crayon—they soon begin to imitate adults in writing notes, grocery lists, telephone messages, and other day-to-day writing activities. With encouragement from caregivers, they begin "playing at writing." At about the age of three, as children develop a basic awareness of the form and function of print, they learn to differentiate between drawing and writing. They progress from drawing pictures to producing scribbles—usually repetitive angular marks—that are arranged horizontally on the page. "The scribbles may be looping or wavy, pointed or curved, but are almost always made of continuous horizontal lines" (Gentry and Gillet 1993, 23).

At this preliterate stage, children draw pictures, imitate writing, and begin to learn some letter names and forms. Scribbling is part of the child's emergent literacy development; parents and other caregivers need to encourage young children as they indicate their interest and awareness of using writing as a tool of communication.

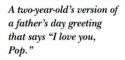

A two-year-old's version of a father's day greeting that says "I love you, Pop."

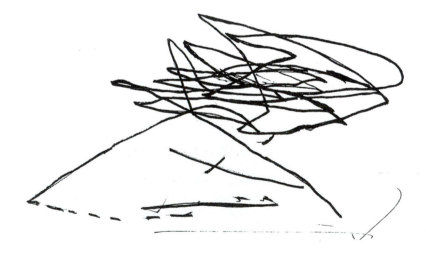

Random Spelling

(Birds are in the sky.)

Random Spelling

As their exposure to print increases, children enter a prephonetic spelling stage in which they begin to randomly use some letter forms but with no reference to sound correspondences. Children begin to develop the awareness that writing is somehow related to what people have to say. At this stage, many children are learning letters, particularly the letters in their own names. Aware of the function of writing but not yet aware of the alphabetic principle, children make marks that approximate the shape of letters as a means of putting their thoughts on paper. As a rule, letters they make bear no relationships to corresponding sounds, although some random letter-sound matches may be evident. This prephonetic writing is often accompanied by pictures, and the writing may reflect divisions between words.

The more opportunities the child has to interact with language—hearing stories and nursery rhymes, engaging in conversation and word play with adults, being encouraged to draw and tell their own stories, singing the alphabet song, dictating stories that are transcribed by adults, and learning how to recognize and write letters—the greater will be the chances of moving more quickly toward the next stages of invented spelling.

At the prephonetic stage, children themselves are usually the only ones who can read what they have written. They do, however, eventually progress to producing messages that adults can actually read.

Phonetic Spelling

As they begin to become more aware of sounds and letters, letter-sound correspondences begin to appear. Spelling begins to be guided by a phonetic strategy as children demonstrate their initial recognition that letters have some relationship to sounds. This usually corresponds to the beginning stages of reading as well.

This stage typically begins with *semiphonetic* attempts at spelling. Often, the initial or first couple of letters are included, followed by series of random letters. Consonants typically appear first; vowels, a little later. Vowel sounds are

(Our new car.)

often omitted (*bed* is written BD, *game* is GM) or substituted (*pet* is spelled PAT, *hot* is spelled HIT). Breaks between words begin to appear. Children typically use a combination of upper case and lower case letters.

Part of early phonetic spelling is a "letter name stage" where children use letter names to represent words—GRL for girl, SAVNRG for Save Energy. "Armed with knowledge of the alphabet and an awareness that letters can be used to represent sounds, children apply the names of the letters quite literally to the sounds they are trying to write (GROM/drum, PEK/pink)" (Invernizzi, Abouzeid, and Gill, 1994, 157). Bissex's account of her child's learning to spell in *GYNS AT WRK* (Genius at Work) demonstrates and documents this stage (1980).

Phonetic spelling reflects a growing awareness of how words in speech match words in print. As children progress through the latter phases of this stage of spelling development and begin to develop initial reading skills, more and more written words begin to approach conventional spelling. Vowels begin to appear and syllables become apparent in words like *tishyou* (tissue). Children learn to spell high frequency function words that so often appear in print—*the, is, was, of,* and so on—and which are often phonetically irregular. As they approach the end of the phonetic stage, their spelling moves closer to standard form.

Transitional Spelling

At the transitional stage, spelling extends beyond the one-to-one correspondences that characterize earlier stages and begins to demonstrate children's increasing awareness of the more complex nature of our orthographic system. Children experience concomitant growth in reading ability. As they start to achieve independence and fluency in reading, they start to grow in independence and fluency in writing.

At the transitional stage, children start to use consonants and vowels fairly consistently in spelling words. "Children conceptualize word structures in relational terms rather than in strictly linear, left-to-right fashion" (Templeton 1991, 187). They get beyond the one-to-one relationships found in early attempts at spelling and learn to group letters into patterns.

Henderson (1990) calls this stage *within-word pattern* of spelling development. The stage is marked by the consistently correct use of short vowels, greater accuracy in the spelling of blends, and the use of silent letters in words like *climb*. As children learn discrete phonics elements by working with word families and in word sorting activities, they become aware of spelling patterns as well. Children may spell *boat* as *bote* according to the "silent e" pattern and *wire* as *whire* in response to learning the initial /wh/ phoneme. The invented spellings that children use are generally recognizable, since they use consistent patterns in expressions like *clouning around*.

Throughout this stage of children's development as writers, spelling is an integral component of word study in the classroom. Children expand their vocabularies enormously, acquire a considerable store of sight words, learn to use prefixes and suffixes, and learn to deal with homophones. All of these activities influence their ability to spell as well. Explicit instruction in examining words helps them learn the common conventions that govern spelling. Writing becomes a functional tool, and children learn to attend to conventional spelling in proofreading at the postwriting stage of the writing process.

Conventional Spelling

Conventional spelling occurs when the child approaches the consistent application of standard rules of orthography. At the conventional stage, children's awareness of consistencies and variations in sound-symbol correspondences is largely established. Two phases of the conventional spelling with implications for classroom instruction involve *syllable juncture* and *derivational constancy*. Both aspects of spelling development are closely related to one another (Bear et al. 1996).

In the syllable juncture phase, children begin to understand how single syllables are combined into polysyllabic words. They learn that when syllables are joined, letters may be added or dropped. For example, the final **g** in *dig* is doubled when adding *-ing* (because the word has a short vowel pattern) while the final **e** in *make* is dropped in adding *-ing* (because the word has a long vowel pattern). Children come to learn these spelling "rules" by examining word patterns as part of explicit spelling instruction.

Knowledge of polysyllabic words is extended as children use words with prefixes and suffixes in their writing. They recognize, for example, the proper spelling of *misspell* (and not *mispell*) because the word is formed by adding the prefix *mis-*. Knowledge of roots, prefixes, and suffixes is part of the word meaning dimension that promotes spelling ability.

Derivational constancy refers to the relationships that are preserved in the spelling of words that are derived from other words. For example, children will learn to use the letter **e** to spell the vowel in the second syllable of *competition* if they understand that the word derives from *compete*, and they will use the letter **i** to represent a similar sound in *confidence* when they are aware that the word derives from *confide*. Meaning and spelling relationships can often be traced through roots and affixes. "Spelling preserves meaning linkages across words" (Cunningham 1998, 132). The final **b** in *bomb*, which is "silent," is pronounced in *bombardment;* the "silent **g**" in *sign* is pronounced in *signature*. Despite changes in sound, words that are related in meaning are typically related in spelling as well.

How words are derived is integral to vocabulary study that is part of language arts instruction in the classroom. The focus on the orthographic features of words extends vocabulary study and leads to a deeper knowledge and appreciation of how language works. Children also learn the conventional spelling of words as they expand their vocabulary through wide reading and other engagements in print.

The developmental stages of invented spelling are not static or fixed, and there is considerable overlap between stages. Children's movement from one stage to another is typically gradual. Children will often show some characteristics from different stages at the same time, and some children may miss a stage altogether. There are wide variations in individual differences at any age; while one six-year-old is still struggling with early phonetic spelling, his agemate may be entering the transitional stage. Nevertheless, being aware of the stages of invented spelling helps explain children's development as writers and suggests leads for spelling instruction.

In the final analysis, only a very few fortunate humans achieve the total mastery of conventional spelling. The state of formal spelling mastery is like reaching ultimate goodness or absolute happiness—it is a goal to strive for, yet one that is reached by only rare individuals. The rest of us have to depend on the dictionary and spellchecker.

Learning to Speak; Learning to Spell

In dealing with invented spelling, it's important for educators and parents to recognize the developmental aspects of learning to spell. As they learn to speak, children pass through stages of language acquisition. They begin by experimenting with sounds through cooing and babbling, progress to single-word sentences and holophrastic speech, learn to put two and three words together in approximate grammatical patterns, and finally reach a stage in which they can use language as a tool of communication. No one gets upset with the child who says, "Doggie go bye-bye" or "He runned and catched the ball." Such expressions are part of the normal development of speech in the language acquisition process.

Yet many people do get upset when children spell *cautious* as KASHUS in a story about "a cautious kitten" or when they spell *gigantic* as JIGANTIK in their Halloween story about a large monster. People fail to realize that these versions are as acceptable as "Doggie go bye-bye" as children are mastering the orthographic system that leads to conventional spelling. When spelling is overemphasized in the first draft stage of the writing process, children are driven from using interesting words like *gigantic* to more orthographically safe, but less interesting and less colorful, alternatives. As they pass through stages of invented spelling, children are focusing on different types of information about language as they attempt to spell words.

Of course, no one would expect the child in third grade to speak in sentences like "Doggie go bye-bye," especially in a formal language situation. Nor should *kashus kittens* and *jigantik monsters* characterize the final drafts of children's writing as children progress through the grades. The effectiveness of final published written products is judged in part by accurate spelling.

Correct spelling is a courtesy that authors owe their readers. Nevertheless, invented spelling should be recognized as an important phase that children go through as they learn to write. It is part of a developmental process, a way of helping young children become effective writers. Rather than something to be avoided, as some critics suggest, invented spelling should be encouraged. It requires a knowledge of letter-sound relationships and reflects an attempt to apply logic and strategies to producing written communication. Besides, invented or temporary spelling represents a useful vehicle for teaching phonics as part of learning to write.

Spelling: How to Teach It

Children do not learn to spell by osmosis; from the early years, they need a program of direct, explicit instruction involving "teacher-directed as well as student-directed examination of words . . . in such a way as to guide students to an understanding of how particular spelling features and patterns operate" (Templeton and Morris 1999, 108–9).

Heald-Taylor (1998) presents three paradigms or models of the way spelling has been taught over the years. Traditionally, spelling was taught with an emphasis on drill and rote memorization, with an emphasis on correctness. Then, a transitional model emerged based on the notion that spelling strategies were closely linked to reading and involved the integration of numerous language qualities that extended well beyond merely memorizing words. Spelling is learned largely in conjunction with word study activities. In a student-oriented paradigm, spelling is seen as a developmental process that is taught as a functional component of writing. Heald-Taylor explains traditions, theories, research, and instructional implications of these models more fully.

Bear and Templeton (1998) suggest research-based instructional practices related to teaching spelling. Based on the careful assessment of their developmental stages of spelling, children should be grouped appropriately and given different words to study. They should be given opportunities to examine known words with an eye to exploring and discovering spelling patterns and generalizations that relate to many words.

In most contemporary classrooms, spelling is closely tied to reading. "A spelling or word study program should reflect the following organizational and instructional principles: (1) at all levels, a common core of words should be examined; (2) in accordance with students' development, a variety of strategies and activities should be offered in which words are productively examined; and (3) the philosophy that spelling is logical should be reflected" (Templeton 1991, 190).

Spelling instruction involves a closely integrated combination of phonics, visual processing, and word meaning. The ability to spell is rooted in a solid knowledge of sound-symbol relationships that is at the core of phonics instruction. But phonics alone is not enough. Spellers also need visual processing to produce and recognize the appropriate orthographic options as they write words; in other words, they need to know that the word "looks right." Finally, correct spelling is enhanced enormously by word knowledge. Here is where spelling is integrated into a classroom program that emphasizes vocabulary development.

Phonetic Processing

Knowledge of the orthographic system is a cornerstone of successful spelling, just as it is essential to successful reading. Phonics is one of the links in the reading-writing connection. The starting point with spelling, as with reading, is phonemic awareness. "There is a direct relationship between phonemic awareness and spelling in that each enhances the other" (Orton 2000, 17). Classroom materials designed to teach spelling in the early grades are virtually indistinguishable from similar materials designed to teach phonics. The relationship between spelling and phonics is reciprocal. On the one hand, a knowledge of sound-symbol relationships is essential in learning how to spell. On the other hand, research and best practice indicate that "learning to spell words facilitates the acquisition of phonics rules" (Groff 2001, 299).

Spelling involves a series of phonics-related processes. "To spell a word, a student must be able to orally segment the word into individual phonemes (a phonological awareness skill), map each sound to its corresponding letter (alphabetic understanding and knowledge of letter-sound correspondences), write the letters in correct order, and read back the word to see if it is spelled correctly (a decoding strategy)" (Coyne, Kame'enui, and Simmons 2001, 68).

The ability to spell is built in part on a knowledge of sound-symbol relationships. To spell the word /s/ /t/ /o/ /p/, we need four written symbols corresponding to the four sounds **stop.** Teaching spelling is a way of teaching phonics. Whether trying to sound out *balloon* or attempting to spell *baboon,* the child needs to know that "**b** says /b/." Children's early attempts at spelling require a basic knowledge of sound-symbol relationships, and writing activities offer opportunities for teachers to help children learn these relationships.

Teaching Suggestions ▼

Phonetic Processing

Word Building

Using individual letters to build words is a spelling activity in itself. Children use letter cards or letter tiles to spell words that the teacher dictates. Seeing how many words they can spell from the letters in longer words is another form of word building for spelling purposes.

Word Families

Word families use phonograms or rimes that are orthographically similar. "Learning to spell is a process of making associations between the spelling patterns of words and their pronunciations" (Invernizzi, Abouzeid, and Gill 1994, 161). In working with word families, children use patterned combinations rather than individual letters in encoding words. In practice with onsets and rimes, children's attention is focused specifically on the spelling of these phonetic elements.

Word patterns such as the following are written on the board and children add onsets to make lists of words:

-ock   *rock, block, clock,* and so on. Here children learn the **ck** correspondence at the end of words.

-ade   *made, trade, shade,* and so on. Here the "silent **e**" spelling pattern is reinforced

-and   *hand, band, grand,* and so on. As children learn to spell words like *hand,* they learn to apply the pattern in words like *handkerchief.*

Word Walls

Areas of the classroom where words are displayed have proven to be effective for both reading and spelling. The focus of words can extend from variant orthographic patterns of long vowel sounds to silent letters. Phonetically irregular function words frequently used in writing and words centered around curriculum topics can also be posted for children's reference as they write stories about Thanksgiving or reports on the Westward Movement. Word walls with a phonics focus provide convenient reference points for children learning how to spell.

Word Sorts

Sorting words that involve the examination, comparison, and classification of words based on specific phonetic elements are essential to direct spelling instruction in the classroom. Word sorts focus children's attention directly on orthographic patterns such as *able/ible* and *tion/sion* by having children sort words that end in *-able* in one column and those that end in *-ible* in the other column:

dependable	*possible*	*predictable*	*breakable*	*terrible*
horrible	*agreeable*	*acceptable*	*remarkable*	*visible*

Sort words that end in *-tion* in one column and those that end in *-sion* in the other column:

information	*extension*	*discussion*	*prevention*	*invention*
confusion	*television*	*question*	*conclusion*	*intention*

> ## Phonetic Processing, continued
>
> Often, there is no easy rule of thumb in deciding which orthographic option to use. Through word sorts, children begin to discover that variations in the ways sounds are spelled are not entirely haphazard, however. A careful analysis of English orthography indicates that the spelling of a particular sound is often determined on the basis of where the sound occurs in words (Hanna, Hodges, and Hanna 1971). The long **a** sound is generally not spelled **ay** or **ey** in the middle of a word, for example, nor is it normally spelled **ai** at the end of a word (except in a word like *lanai,* which is borrowed from Polynesian). Word sorts involve the systematic examination of words and how they are spelled, which is essential to direct spelling instruction in the classroom.
>
> ### *Sort, Search, and Discover*
>
> Fresch and Wheaton (1997) describe a strategy called "Sort, Search, and Discover," a classroom spelling program that relies extensively on word sorts to help children develop generalizations about regularities and exceptions in the spelling of English words. Children use open sorts (with words grouped by self-designated categories) and closed sorts (with key words to guide the categorization of items). Based on their work, children make tentative hypotheses about principles governing the spelling of the words and apply their discoveries in their written work.
>
> It should be noted that all of these suggested activities add an element of visual processing as well.

Direct instruction in spelling also involves dictation. "For spelling instruction, words can be dictated that use the letter-sound correspondences previously taught to make students more conscious of the separate letters and of the fact that just one different letter (or sound) at the beginning, middle, or end of a word makes a different word. It is also useful to dictate words that are not known but whose spelling can be reasoned by analogy" (Chall and Popp 1996, 38). As children hear words, either in isolation or in sentence context, they become adept at matching the symbols and symbol patterns that correspond to the sounds in the words. Dictation is an important part of some of the structured, systematic phonics programs described in the previous chapter (pp. 119–124). "While there is a place for spelling dictations, we need to keep in mind that the spelling children do while the teacher dictates sentences to them is not the same as the spelling they do while composing. Dictation scores may be higher because the child is highly focused on spelling correctly. That is, she does not have to create meaningful content while spelling (Routman 2000, 412).

A popular competitive spelling activity that has been used for a long time is the good old spelling bee. Although spelling bees remain part of the fabric of our culture, their value as an instructional activity for developing spelling strategies is suspect. Spelling is a written language activity, and spelling bees are distinctly oral. Perhaps we could have children write the words rather than spell them o-n-e l-e-t-t-e-r a-t a t-i-m-e.

Phonics is important in learning how to spell, but there's more to achieving orthographic accuracy than the knowledge of letter-sound correspondences. Correct spelling depends on visual processing as well.

Visual Processing

Although phonics is essential to spelling, it is not enough to achieve consistent accuracy. In fact, it has been said that the worst spellers are the ones who spell phonetically (Smith 1999). As Henderson (1990) wrote, "Those who try to spell by sound alone will be defeated" (67). Visual recognition of how words are represented in writing also needs to be part of direct spelling instruction in schools.

Let's go back to the spelling of our old friend **ukulele** from chapter 2. Phonetically, we know that the initial sound of this word is "long **u**," but there are different ways to represent this sound—**u, eu, yu, you.** Similarly, the vowel sound in the second syllable is "short **a**," but it is represented in this word by the letter **u.** Recognizing visual structures enables spellers to exercise these orthographic options.

Spelling instruction based on phonetic processing necessarily involves a visual dimension. As children engage in word building, word sorts, and similar activities, they necessarily have to deal with visual forms, as well as the phonetic structures, of the words.

Teaching Suggestions ▼

Visual Processing

Recognising Wurds Spelt Rong

Good spellers are aware of when a word "looks right" and when it doesn't. Instruction in proofreading and editing that is part of the postwriting phase of the writing process, word searches for items spelled incorrectly, and minilessons on spotting the correct spelling of words all require children to use their visual processing abilities in becoming good spellers. Standardized tests often use this method of measurement in assessing children's spelling abilities. The technique can also be used informally in classroom assessment. Instead of the conventional dictation of words for spelling tests, children can be given versions of target words spelled incorrectly either as a multiple choice item or in context, and then asked to correct the word. Some, however, believe that showing incorrectly spelled words to struggling readers and writers is not a good idea.

Color Coding Trouble Spots

Color is a visual element that can help children remember how words look. When children misspell a word, they often vary on only a single letter or syllable. In spelling *ukalele* (sic), for example, only the vowel in the second syllable is misspelled. As children practice copying misspelled words, they can write the letter or syllable that they got wrong in a different color, focusing their attention on the "demonic" part of the word:

ukulele   **ukulele**   **ukulele**

Copying trouble spots in different colors calls pupils' attention to the specific parts of the words they need to remember.

Personal Lists

In the children's trade book *Donovan's Word Jar* by Monalisa DeGross (HarperCollins 1994), Donovan Allen, like most third graders, collects things. But instead of collecting coins or baseball cards like his classmates, Donovan collects words and keeps them in his special word jar. As part of vocabulary study, children can make collections of their own special words, ones that they want to learn to spell such as words related to dinosaurs or other topics of interest. The words can be recorded on index cards, in notebooks, on a rolodex, or in any special place that appeals to children. Children will likely be familiar with the meaning of the words they choose to include in their personal collections, but as they copy words onto their lists, they need to focus specifically on the visual form, that is, the proper spelling of each word.

Spelling is a process of exercising orthographic options. There are multiple ways in which sounds may be represented in writing, and awareness of the visual elements of written language helps reinforce what is correct and contributes to one's ability in learning to spell. Correct spelling is also buttressed significantly by knowledge of word meaning.

Word Knowledge

Vocabulary development is an essential component of any classroom language arts program. Vocabulary knowledge is closely related to reading comprehension (as it is to intelligence), and vocabulary instruction supports pupil achievement in reading and writing (Stahl 1999). Children's word recognition ability, vocabulary growth, and reading comprehensions are all interrelated as essential components of a balanced reading program (Rupley, Logan, and Nichols 1998/99).

Instruction in vocabulary spills directly over into spelling as well. The more a child knows about a word, the greater will be the child's chances of spelling the word correctly. Henderson (1990) speaks to the importance of linking spelling instruction to word meaning as part of instruction in the classroom. "Children and young adults who learn to look for meaning relations among words and to observe their common spellings learn two things. First, they learn the various patterns by which roots and affixes are combined; they learn the sound logic, or phonology, of English words. Second, they learn to look for these root forms in each new word they meet and from that they learn not one but many new words at one reading. Formal instruction prepares young adults to master a rich vocabulary of English on their own" (77).

Vocabulary activities that focus on expanding children's store of words are part of the language arts program in any classroom, of course, and spelling is closely tied to the many dimensions of word study in the classroom. Children's vocabularies grow through:

- *Word alerts,* as children examine where words come from and explore the meanings of new words they encounter;
- *Exercises with synonyms and antonyms,* as children find words to use instead of "boring" or words to replace the overused items like "said" and "nice" in their writing;
- *Webbing,* as children create semantic webs, Venn diagrams, branching tree diagrams, semantic feature analysis, and other visual devices that connect the meaning of new words to familiar concepts and experiences;
- *Cross-curriculum word study,* as children focus on technical and specific vocabulary from science, social studies, and other school subjects;
- *Games,* as children engage in word play and engage in games such as "The Minister's Cat" and "Hink-Pink" that bring out the fun of language;
- *Encounters with books,* since the amount of free reading that pupils do has been shown to be the best predictor of vocabulary growth in the elementary grades (Fielding, Wilson, and Anderson 1988). Books such as *Frindle* by Andrew Clements, which put the spotlight directly on word meaning, add depth to vocabulary study.

As children engage in these vocabulary-building exercises and activities, they learn to spell the new words that become part of their vocabularies. Here's where spelling instruction becomes an integral part of the language arts.

Areas of word meaning instruction with direct spelling implications include specific attention to homophones, roots and affixes, and word derivation. Spelling ability is also linked closely to wide reading. Through reading, children discover new and intriguing words that become part of their writing repertoire.

Homophones

As the structure of the word suggests, homophones are words that sound the same but are spelled differently (such as *no/know, sail/sale, their/there*). Making the right choice of homophones is a function of meaning and linguistic context. These words are often confused in writing, and even though the orthographic representation of the word *your* may be correct, its use is not correct in the sentence, "I hope *your* going to the party." The incorrect choice of homophones represents one of the most common errors in written language.

Although focused and isolated exercises calling children's attention to the proper choice of homophones may be important, the ultimate pay-off comes as children exercise the proper choices in their writing experiences in and out of school. Children can also be put on the alert for spotting the incorrect choice of homophones in environmental print. A national advertising campaign for a well-known automobile, for example, recently described the car as "the best in it's [sic] class" in its television ads.

Teaching Suggestions ▼

Homophones

Word Wall

Here are sets of homophones that young children often confuse in their writing:

ant/aunt	*ate/eight*	*bare/bear*	*be/bee*
blue/blew	*buy/by*	*cell/sell*	*cent/sent*
flour/flower	*for/four*	*knew/new*	*know/no*
hole/whole	*hour/our*	*its/it's*	*made/maid*
mail/male	*pail/pale*	*meat/meet*	*one/won*
peace/piece	*right/write*	*road/rode*	*principle/principal*
see/sea	*son/sun*	*there/their*	*to/too/two*
where/wear	*which/witch*	*your/you're*	*weather/whether*

Children can expand the word wall as they encounter examples of other homophones in their writing.

Homophones in Context

Context determines which homophone is appropriate in a sentence, so children should have plenty of practice with sentences such as the following:

The children placed _____ books over _____. (their/there)

The team _____ only _____ game all season. (one/won)

_____ you know that ice cubes melt _____ to heat? (do/due)

Do you _____ why there are _____ cookies left? (no/know)

My brother _____ all _____ cookies. (ate/eight)

Children's Literature

Children enjoy books that play with language in different ways, including the use of homophones. Books by Fred Gwynne—*A Chocolate Moose for Dinner, The King who Rained,* and *A Little Pigeon Toad*—involve the use of words that are pronounced the same but have different meanings. For older children, the *Phantom Tollbooth* by Norman Juster can be the focus on language and use of homophones as well.

Roots and Affixes

Words are created in many different ways. Shorter words are made from longer ones: *dormitory* becomes *dorm; examination* becomes *exam.* But many more words are built from smaller word parts, mostly the roots (or stems), prefixes, and suffixes, many of which have been borrowed from Greek and Latin. These morphemic elements are the building blocks of words, and knowing their meaning and orthographic form enhances vocabulary and spelling ability.

The root, stem, or base of a word determines its meaning; affixes (prefixes and suffixes) change the form and often the meaning of the word. Understanding the meaning of word parts is closely linked to the ability to spell words. The Latin root **duc(t)** meaning "to lead" can be found in *conduct, deduce, educate, introduce, produce, aqueduct,* and several other English words. Adams (1990) speaks to the importance of instruction that shapes the connection between meaning elements and orthographic elements in words: ". . . such instruction might be expected to improve both spelling and visual word perception. Conversely . . . such instruction should strengthen students' vocabularies and refine their comprehension abilities" (151).

Teaching Suggestions ▼

Roots and Affixes

Building Blocks

Children should understand that morphemes (roots and affixes) are the building blocks for words. A common base word can be written on the chalkboard: for example,

　　　like

and groups of children can see how many new words they can build by adding prefixes and suffixes to the base (*alike, unlike, dislike, likely, unlikely, likable, unlikable,* and so on).

Here are lists of ten prefixes and suffixes that children may encounter in their early experiences with reading and spelling:

Prefixes			Suffixes		
anti-	against	*antisocial, antipollutant*	-able	capable of	*pleasurable, usable*
auto-	self	*automobile, automatic*	-ance	state or quality	*appearance, avoidance*
bi-	two	*bicycle, binary*	-ant	one who does	*servant, assistant*
cent-	hundred	*centimeter, century*	-ary	relating	*military, literary*
inter-	among or between		-ette	small	*dinette, majorette*
		international, intermission			
micro-	small	*microscope, microphone*	-ful	full	*careful, fearful*
re-	again	*revise, rework*	-ist	one who does	*biologist, socialist*
tele-	distant	*telephone, television*	-less	without	*careless, fearless*
tri-	three	*triangle, tricycle*	-ly	in the manner of	*quickly, slowly*
un-	not	*unhappy, unaware*	-ship	ability or skill	*showmanship*

Syllables

Attention to meaning-based word parts begins as part of instruction related to syllables. As pupils examine morphemes that make common syllables—such as the *un-* in *unkind* and the *-ness* in *kindness*—they become aware of the nature of these word elements and the effect they have on word meaning.

Roots and Affixes, continued

Word Sorts

Children classify words according to the Greek or Latin roots from which they originate, with guide words like *transport* (port/ "to carry"), *symphony* (phone/ "sound"), and *rupture* (rupt/ "to break").

Word Walls

Teachers can create word walls with different structural elements. For example, using the prefix *in-* meaning not, and its variants *im-/-ir/il-,* they can generate lists such as:

incomplete	*improper*	*irregular*	*illegal*
inactive	*impatient*	*irrelevant*	*illegible*
inconvenient	*immature*	*irresistible*	*illogical*
etc.	etc.	etc.	etc.

Children can add to these lists with words they encounter in word study activities and in independent reading. They can also note spelling patterns in the lists and can identify words that begin with the same syllable but don't have meaning links to *in-* (for example: *incense, impetus, irrigate, illustrate*).

Content Areas

Many of the technical and specific vocabulary items used in math, science, social studies, and other parts of the curriculum contain morphemes that lend themselves to word study and spelling activities. In science, as children learn words like *thermal, thermostat,* and *thermometer,* they can focus on the meaning of *therm-. Thermometer* leads to *barometer,* which leads to looking at *-meter.* In social studies, words like *import, export* and *transport* can extend word knowledge of *-port,* meaning to carry. Word study and spelling extends across the entire curriculum.

Twenty Questions

Children ask each other questions about word meanings based on the origins of words: "I'm thinking of a word that means to carry things from one place to another" (**transport**). "I'm thinking of a word for the biggest word book in the language" (**dictionary**).

Children can discover much about roots and affixes by exploring language meaning as part of vocabulary development activities in the classroom. In exploring the function of the suffix *-or/er* as "one who does something," the group was talking about *teacher* (one who teaches) and *sailor* (one who sails) when someone suggested *tailor* as "one who tails." In exploring the meaning of the root word *tail,* children discovered that the word comes from an Old French verb meaning "to cut," and they were on their way to a better understanding of the meaning of *retail, curtail, detail,* and other words that derive from that root. Here's where spelling becomes part of the larger picture of word study.

Examining how we use word parts to shape or mask meaning is an interesting study in semantics. In a recent merger of two large companies, a number of jobs were cut and employees were offered severance packages. Those who were so designated were "deselected"; the prefix *de-* means *from* or *down* and *selected* means *chosen,* so those whose employment was terminated were *deselected.* Being "deselected" sounds better than being fired!

In decoding unfamiliar words they encounter in reading, children apply their knowledge of basic word parts in figuring out the pronunciation and meaning of words. In writing, they apply this knowledge in encoding print to achieve orthographic correctness.

Derivations

The meaning-spelling connection is also established in working with derivations, words that are derived from other words. For example, the adjective *democratic* and the verb *democratize* are both derived from the noun *democracy.* A huge number of words in our lexicon are linked in this fashion.

Spelling clues are often found as children work with derivatives as part of vocabulary development activities. Children learn to distinguish between *compliment* (an expression of praise) and *complement* (the full amount) when they know that the latter derives from *complete.* Knowing the derivation of a word can be helpful in knowing the correct letters to use in representing sounds; the **e** in *comedy* represents a schwa sound that can be represented by any vowel letter, but children who link *comedy* with *comedian* have a clue as to which letter to use. Tracing and linking words like this promote a conceptual and linguistic awareness that serves children well in their reading and writing development.

Teaching Suggestions ▼

Derivations

Creating Word Charts

Using a common word with which they are familiar, groups of children can develop charts converting derived words to different parts of speech, with a specific focus on spelling shifts:

Noun	Verb	Adjective	Adverb
writer	write	written	
democracy	democratize	democratic	democratically
prosperity	prosper	prosperous	prosperously
resident	reside	residential	
pleasure	please	pleasurable	pleasingly

Here's where spelling overlaps with vocabulary development as well as with grammar.

At times, sound shifts occur in derivatives. The long **i** in *divine* shifts to a short sound in *divinity* because of the addition of the suffix/syllable *-ity*. Also, letters may be pronounced that were not sounded in the original word; the final **b** in *bomb* is silent, but it's pronounced in *bombardment*. These are qualities that children begin to discover as they explore words.

Dictionary Work

The dictionary is an important and reliable aid to spelling, the ultimate authority when it comes to determining the correct orthographic form of a word. Before the first English dictionaries were written in the seventeenth century, words were spelled in any way that allowed writers to convey meaning to their audiences. But once the dictionary was introduced as a means of regulating a language that was perceived as being "copious without order and energetic without rules," spelling became more strictly governed. Once the dictionary designated one spelling as being "correct," all others became "incorrect."

While spellcheckers have taken much of the pressure off the directive to "look it up," dictionary usage remains part of direct spelling instruction in the classroom. As children learn to use the dictionary as a spelling tool, they acquire the concomitant skills needed to use this book as a reference tool—awareness of alphabetical order, the use of guide words, the meaning of symbols used as part of the pronunciation key, the use of multiple meanings, and the like. The aim of dictionary work is to help children learn to use this tool quickly and efficiently in determining the spelling of unfamiliar words.

Mnemonic Devices

No discussion of learning to spell would be complete without some attention to mnemonic devices; memory tricks can be useful in spelling certain words. Most of us remember "**i** before **e** except after **c**." As youngsters, we learned little memory tricks to help us remember how to spell particular words. We learned to differentiate between *principle* and *principal* because the latter has *pal* at the end and the principal (or chief) of the school is our pal. We learned that *dessert* has two *s*'s because we want a second helping. We learned to spell *separate* because it has *a rat* in it. We deliberately pronounced words (*to-get-her*), made up mnemonic sentences, put letters to music, or devised other idiosyncratic procedures to help us get the correct spelling of certain words. Although most of the mnemonic devices that we learned as children were corny, we still rely on some of them as adults.

Memory devices can be useful but only for a limited number of words. Can you imagine inventing a trick to help children remember to spell each and every word they need in writing? Learning to spell well involves a lot more than memory tricks to get children over the rough spots. It involves a solid grasp of sound-symbol relationships, skill in recalling the visual form of words, and a background of word knowledge on which to build the power to communicate.

Direct and explicit spelling instruction takes many forms as children progress through the grades. It involves the study of basic word patterns as children initially learn to put their thoughts on paper in a way that others can read them. It involves minilessons on the difference between *there* and *their* and on when to double the final consonant before adding *-ing*. It involves proofreading and editing in the postwriting stage of the writing process, as teachers conference with pupils in preparing them to publish their work. It involves calling attention to the orthographic features of new words that children learn as part of their expanding vocabularies. It involves direct instruction in how to check a word in the dictionary. It involves instilling an attitude of pride in making one's work as good as it can be. And it involves teacher guidance and modeling, along with direct instructional strategies for accurately processing the spelling of words on a regular and consistent basis.

Assessing Children's Spelling Ability

In the traditional paradigm of spelling instruction, pupils' spelling ability was assessed with a Friday test on the list of weekly words that children were required to memorize. With attention to direct and explicit spelling instructions, tests to measure pupils' orthographic understandings remain part of the classroom landscape. The ability to spell a finite list of words can provide a general measure of a child's spelling ability and can provide the basis of a grade for a report card; however, it gives a very narrow picture of children's overall ability to handle the orthographic system of our language. As instruction focuses on particular features of written language—the variant spellings of a particular vowel sound, a generalization regarding adding suffixes, certain word derivatives, for example—spelling tests remain effective classroom assessment devices.

Spelling tests are not enough, however, to get a full picture of a child's ability to spell. Spelling is a functional writing skill, and the ultimate pay-off is children's ability to spell words correctly in their regular writing activities. Routman (2000) suggests students' writing, spelling inventories, spelling tests, and dictation exercises as sources of information for spelling assessment.

Formal, standardized measures are also available (Murphy, Conoley, and Impara 1994). These include subtests on group-administered norm-referenced achievement tests such as the *California Achievement Test* (CTB Macmillan/McGraw-Hill 1992) and the *Stanford Achievement Test* (Psychological Corporation 1993). Others focus more specifically on spelling, such as the *Test of Written Spelling* by Stephen C. Larson and Donald D. Hammill (PRO-ED 1994). Some of these tests are designed for the general population; others are intended primarily for children with written language processing problems and related learning disorders. Some cover a K–12 grade range, while some are aimed at a more narrow grade range. Some have children write words from dictation; others use a multiple choice mode that requires children to identify words that are spelled correctly from a list of four or five foils. All are aimed to give teachers and others a measure of children's ability to spell.

The ultimate test of children's ability to spell rests in the application of spelling in their authentic writing experiences. Spelling is a mark of effective writing. No matter how well a child performs on the weekly spelling test or what level he/she achieves on a standardized achievement battery, spelling must be judged within the broader context of writing. Phonics, visual processing, and word meaning come together in the stories, poems, letters, reports, and other forms of written discourse that children produce. That's the fundamental assessment measure of children's ability to spell.

Conclusion

For most children (and many adults), spelling is not an easy task. Learning to spell is a complex and intricate process requiring cognitive and linguistic awareness rather than rote memorization. Children need to be immersed in writing and receive direct instruction aimed at their developmental level and their awareness of the orthographic structure of our language.

Although it needs to receive its own direct and explicit focus, spelling instruction is part of the overall area of word study. It requires knowledge of the orthographic system inherent in phonics; it involves visual processing ability to recognize and exercise the correct orthographic options; and it is supported by word meaning that expands vocabulary.

Learning to spell is closely related to learning to read. Children's spelling often reflects their ideas about how language works. Children's spelling indicates their grasp of phonics and reflects a great deal about how they read.

When all is said and done, however, spelling remains part of the broader picture of written communication. Spelling is only one dimension of effectiveness in writing, but is often the part that gets the lion's share of the public's attention. There's a certain social uneasiness about the inability to spell well and even open hostility when misspellings are encountered in a piece of written communication. Spelling remains an essential element in children's literacy development.

References

Adams, M. J. 1990. *Beginning to Read: Thinking and Learning About Print.* Cambridge, MA: MIT Press.

Bear, D. R., and S. Templeton. 1998. Explorations in developmental spelling: Foundations for learning and teaching phonics, spelling, and vocabulary. *The Reading Teacher* 52:222–42.

Bear, D. R., M. Invernizzi, S. Templeton, and F. Johnson. 1996. *Words Their Way: Word Study for Phonics, Vocabulary and Spelling.* Columbus: Merrill.

Bear, D. R., M. Invernizzi, S. Templeton, and F. Johnson. 2000. *Words Their Way: Word Study for Phonics, Vocabulary, and Spelling Instruction.* Upper Saddle River, NJ: Merrill.

Bissex, G. 1980. *GYNS AT WRK: A Child Learns to Write and Read.* Cambridge, MA: Harvard University Press.

Calkins, L. M. 1994. *The Art of Teaching Writing.* Portsmouth, NH: Heinemann.

Chall, J. S., and H. M. Popp. 1996. *Teaching and Assessing Phonics: Why, What, When, and How.* Cambridge, MA: Educators Publishing Service.

Clarke, L. K. 1988. Invented versus traditional spelling in first graders' writing: Effects on learning to spell and read. *Research in the Teaching of English* 22:281–309.

Coyne, M. D., E. J. Kame'enui, and D. C. Simmons. 2001. Prevention and intervention in beginning reading: Two complex systems. *Learning Disabilities Research and Practice* 16:63–73.

Cunningham, P. M. 1998. The multisyllabic word dilemma: Helping students build meaning, spell, and read 'big' words. *Reading and Writing Quarterly* 14:189–219.

———. 2000. *Phonics They Use.* 3d ed. New York: Longman.

Ehri, L. C., and L. S. Wilce. 1987. Does learning to spell help beginners learn to read words? *Reading Research Quarterly* 22:47–65.

Fielding, L. G., P. T. Wilson, and R. C. Anderson. 1988. A new focus on free reading: The role of trade books in reading instruction. In T. Raphael, ed., *The Contexts of School-Based Literacy.* New York: Random House.

Fresch, M. J. 2001. Journal entries as a window on spelling knowledge. *The Reading Teacher* 54:500–13.

Fresch, M. J., and A. Wheaton. 1997. Sort, search, and discover: Spelling in the child-centered classroom. *The Reading Teacher* 51:20–31.

Gentry, J. R., and J. W. Gillet. 1993. *Teaching Kids to Spell.* Portsmouth, NH: Heinemann.

Graves, D. H. 1983. *Writing: Teachers and Children at Work.* Portsmouth, NH: Heinemann.

———. 1994. *A Fresh Look at Writing.* Portsmouth, NH: Heinemann.

Groff, P. 2001. Teaching phonics: letter-to-phoneme, phoneme-to-letter, or both? *Reading and Writing Quarterly* 17:291–306.

Hanna, P. R., R. E. Hodges, and J. S. Hanna. 1971. *Spelling: Structure and Strategies.* Boston: Houghton Mifflin.

Heald-Taylor, G. 1998. Three paradigms of spelling instruction in grades 3 to 6. *The Reading Teacher* 51:404–13.

Henderson, E. H. 1990. *Teaching Spelling.* 2d ed. Boston: Houghton Mifflin.

Invernizzi, M., M. Abouzeid, and J. T. Gill. 1994. Using students' invented spellings as a guide for spelling instruction that emphasizes word study. *The Elementary School Journal* 95:155–67.

———. 1994. *A Fresh Look at Writing.* Portsmouth, NH: Heinemann.

Moats, L. C. 1998. Teaching decoding. *American Educator* 22:42–9, 95–6.

Murphy, L. L., J. C. Conoley, and J. C. Impara, eds. 1994. *Tests In Print: An Index to Tests, Test Reviews, and the Literature of Specific Tests.* Lincoln, NE: The Buros Institute of Mental Measurements, University of Nebraska.

Murray, D. 1968. *A Writer Teaches Writing: A Practical Method of Teaching Composition.* Boston: Houghton Mifflin.

Orton, J. G. 2000. Phonemic awareness and inventive writing. *The New England Reading Association Journal* 36: 17–21.

Read, C. 1971. Preschool children's knowledge of English orthography. *Harvard Educational Review* 41:1–34.

Routman, Regie. 2000. *Conversations: Strategies for Teaching, Learning, and Evaluating Literacy Learning.* Portsmouth, NH: Heinemann.

Rupley, W. H., J. W. Logan, and W. D. Nichols. 1998/99. Vocabulary instruction in a balanced reading program. *The Reading Teacher* 52:336–46.

Scott, J. E. 1994. Spelling for readers and writers. *The Reading Teacher* 48:188–90.

Smith, F. 1999. Why systematic phonics and phonemic awareness instruction constitute an educational hazard. *Language Arts* 77:150–5.

Snow, C. E., M. S. Burns, and P. Griffin. 1998. *Preventing Reading Difficulties in Young Children.* Washington, DC: National Academy Press.

Stahl, S. A. 1999. *Vocabulary Development.* Cambridge, MA: Brookline Books.

Templeton, S. 1991. Teaching and learning the English spelling system: Reconceptualizing method and purpose. *The Elementary School Journal* 92:185–201.

Templeton, S., and D. Morris. 1999. Questions teachers ask about spelling. *Reading Research Quarterly* 34:102–12.

Tierman, L. S. 1930. The value of marking hard spots in spelling. *University of Iowa Studies in Education* 5:8.

Traill, L. 1993. *Highlights My Strengths: Assessment and Evaluation of Literacy Learning.* Crystal Lake, IL: Rigby.

Walshe, R. D. 1988. Questions teachers ask about teaching writing K–12. In *Teaching Writing K–12,* edited by R. D. Walshe and P. March. Melbourne, Australia: Dellastar.

Weaver, C. 1988. *Reading Process and Practice: From Socio-psycholinguistics to Whole Language.* Portsmouth, NH: Heinemann.

Children's Trade Books Cited in This Chapter

Clements, A. 1996. *Frindle*. New York: Simon and Schuster.

DeGross, M. 1994. *Donovan's Word Jar*. New York: HarperCollins.

Gwynne, F. 1988. *A Chocolate Moose for Dinner*. New York: Simon and Schuster.

———. 1988. *The King Who Rained*. New York: Simon and Schuster.

———. 1988. *A Little Pigeon Toad*. New York: Simon and Schuster.

Juster, N. 1961. *The Phantom Tollbooth*. Illustrated by J. Feiffer. New York: Random House.

Phonics in a Comprehensive Reading Program

Phonics remains an essential part of the educational lives of children who are learning to read and write. It is an important element in a comprehensive classroom literacy program. This chapter

▼ examines phonics in relation to other elements in a comprehensive reading program

▼ describes comprehensive literacy instruction.

Phonics and Other Reading Components

In a literate society, reading has always been essential to young children's education. More public attention is centered on reading than on any other school subject. More research is conducted, more money is spent on curriculum materials, and more support services are provided for reading than any other aspect of the curriculum. School effectiveness is often judged on the basis of the scores that pupils achieve on reading tests. Teaching children to read remains the central educational priority of the day.

English has an alphabetic writing system. Individual spoken sounds (phonemes) are represented by individual written symbols (graphemes). Knowledge of this sound-symbol (phoneme-grapheme) relationship is essential to becoming literate. Therefore, phonics will always remain an essential part of the mix in beginning reading instruction. With the recognized role of phonemic awareness in beginning reading success and the importance of decoding in early reading experiences, phonics will continue to be a vital element in reading and writing instruction. For some children, especially those who experience unusual problems in learning to read due to dyslexia or a related learning disorder, a structured program of systematic phonics will remain the key to success in opening the door to decoding print.

Phonics is a crucial part of learning to read and write. But in addition to applying their knowledge of sound-symbol relationships in decoding words, readers use a combination of skills and strategies in figuring out the pronunciation and meaning of words they encounter in print. The multiple types of word identification strategies that are part of reading instruction include the recognition of sight words, application of skills of structural analysis, and the use of context clues. Readers use all of these in combination to arrive at meaning, which is the ultimate goal of reading.

Sight Words

Sight words are words that readers recognize instantaneously in print. From labeling objects with cards in the early childhood learning environment to practice in the repeated recognition of common words, learning to automatically recognize words by sight is an important part of learning to read. The aim of developing a large store of sight words is the rapid and accurate recognition of words that children encounter in print.

Building a large store of sight words is important for a number of reasons. While our writing system is alphabetic in nature, it isn't perfect. Many words that children encounter in their early reading and writing experiences do not have a consistent one-to-one sound-symbol relationship that make them easy to sound out. Familiar and frequently used words like *is, was, has, said,* and others are not easily decodable on a sound-symbol basis. Children need to quickly recognize these words as whole units.

Recognizing words instantly promotes ease and fluency in reading. Given the alphabetic nature of our writing system and the number of words in our language (approximately 750,000), however, it's impractical to think about learning to recognize each word by sight as an individual entity. For words that are essential to the meaning of a piece of written material, for words that occur frequently in a written passage, and for words that are not phonetically regular, an instructional focus on word recognition integrated with phonics makes sense.

Structural Analysis

Structural analysis is closely related to phonetic analysis in the process of learning to read and write. Just as phonics involves attention to the phonetic elements in words (phonemes), structural analysis involves attention to the structural elements in words (morphemes), which are roots and affixes. These structural units are the building blocks of words, and learning about them constitutes an important part of word study in the classroom.

Learning about roots, prefixes, and suffixes begins early when children use compound words as part of phonemic awareness activities. It continues with practice in syllabication, since most structural units constitute separate syllables in words. It extends throughout word study as children explore the meaning of Greek and Latin roots and trace word meaning through etymological connections in conjunction with explicit instruction in spelling and vocabulary. Children use word knowledge along with phonetic elements in structural analysis as a word recognition skill.

Context Clues

Context clues consist of information in the surrounding passage that helps readers determine the meaning (and sometimes the pronunciation) of unknown words. Emergent readers often use pictures as clues to identify words and to derive meaning. Using context clues in conjunction with phonics is another strategy that readers rely on as they interact with print.

In order to see how readers use a combination of phonics and context in learning to read, consider the following sentence:

Crazy Horse was a great Indian chief who fought at the Battle of Little Big Horn.

Billy reads the sentence, stopping at the word *chief* and tells the teacher, "I don't know that word."

The teacher tells him to "sound it out." Billy recognizes the /ch/ sound of the initial digraph and the final /f/, and he remembers the generalization, "When two vowels go walking, the first one does the talking." So he pronounces the word "chiyf," rhyming it with *knife*. A knowledge of phonics has enabled Billy to decode the word, but not correctly. Phonics enables readers to make educated guesses at words; context and language background provide readers with flexible strategies they can use to get the information they need to "get it right."

Word meaning frequently depends on the context in which a word is used. Apart from using context clues as a word recognition strategy, learning from context in independent reading is a major means of vocabulary acquisition throughout children's entire school careers.

Comprehension

The ultimate aim of reading and writing is comprehension, the ability to build meaning from (or *with,* in the case of writing) print. Even the most ardent or zealous phonics advocates acknowledge that meaning is the ultimate goal of reading and that phonics is merely a step in the process of achieving that goal.

Comprehension is a complex process that depends on a constellation of text-based and meaning-based factors. It is related to the level, structure, and content of text. It is also related to factors "behind the reader's eye"—language background, cognitive processing, schemata, metacognitive awareness, motivation, and other factors. As teachers help children build meaning in what they read, they take these factors into account as part of the instructional process.

Phonics is closely related to comprehension in a number of ways. Comprehension is dependent upon language processing; phonics deals with processing language at a micro level. The ability to recognize words is crucial to understanding written language, and phonics is often an essential ingredient of that word recognition process. Phonics supports automaticity in word recognition which leads to fluency that is highly related to comprehension. The relationship between vocabulary and comprehension is strong and direct; word knowledge is a fundamental factor in understanding what one reads. When children can easily decode words, their attention can be devoted to understanding and response. For those who struggle with decoding, reading can be a frustrating and unpleasant experience. In short, phonics is an essential step on the way to building meaning in print.

Poor readers struggle at the decoding level. In order to get easy access to comprehension, words must be decoded easily. Children who have problems figuring out what the words are will be handicapped in building meaning from print.

Phonics, then, is one dimension in the constellation of skills important in learning to read. How important is phonics in relation to these other components? The way in which one answers questions about phonics will depend in large part on one's beliefs about reading and how it ought to be taught. Testifying before Congress, Reid Lyon (1997) called phonics "nonnegotiable beginning reading skills that *all* children must master" (5). At the other end of the ideological spectrum, Frank Smith (1999) wrote that phonics "can only confuse and interfere with anyone learning to read" (152).

Routman (1996) suggests the following commonsense perspective about phonics:

- phonics is a tool in the reading process and not an end in itself;
- phonics knowledge is necessary to be a competent reader and writer/speller;
- it is easier to decode a word that you have heard before and know the meaning of;
- phonics can be taught and reinforced during shared reading and shared writing;
- phonics can be assessed and taught during writing time;
- most of the time set aside for reading in school should be spent reading meaningful texts (93–5).

In other words, phonics is important to reading and spelling, but it's not the only thing that children need to become literate.

In 1964, Arthur Heilman wrote a book called *Phonics in Proper Perspective*. The book has been revised several times over the years and has remained popular. Heilman's "proper perspective" on phonics is this: "the optimum amount of phonics a child should be exposed to is the minimum the child needs to become an independent reader" (Heilman 2002, 3). While he provides oodles of ideas and suggestions for helping children learn phonics, Heilman consistently cautions teachers to avoid overkill.

In the opening chapter, phonics was described as "an essential but not sufficient part of learning to read and write"; that is, children need to acquire and apply a knowledge of sound-symbol relationships in learning to decode and encode an alphabetic language, but just knowing these relationships is not enough to become a competent independent reader. Most teachers who face the daily practical task of helping children learn to read and write in a classroom setting strive to maintain the place of phonics in a comprehensive literacy program.

Comprehensive Literacy Instruction

In any classroom, teachers need to maintain a comprehensive approach to literacy instruction. Comprehensive instruction involves modeling and teaching a variety of skills and strategies that children can apply in their development as readers and writers. Along with direct and systematic instruction in decoding, it involves attention to teaching children to use sight words, context clues, and other word recognition strategies. It places a heavy emphasis on reading comprehension, the ultimate goal of reading. It saturates instruction with language and builds on the close connection that exists between reading and writing. It gives children many opportunities to apply what they have learned in reading and writing experiences. It includes the use of all kinds of print—basal readers, decodable text, trade books, newspapers, magazines, and the like—that can serve as vehicles for children to develop and practice the ability to read and write. In a nutshell, a comprehensive literacy program gives all children every opportunity to learn to read and write as members of a classroom literacy community.

A comprehensive literacy program involves a balanced approach to reading and writing. Although some people consider "balanced" a code word for "whole language," phonics plays a prominent role in comprehensive, balanced classroom programs. Balanced reading instruction remains a "hot topic" in literacy education (Fitzgerald 1999). Although it has been defined and described in a number of different ways, for most teachers a balanced program means using the best methods they can in helping each child become a better reader and writer. To many teachers, it means synthesizing parts of different models that can work together as part of reading and writing instruction that meets the needs of children. Strickland (1995) suggests that it involves a search for "bridges between the conventional wisdom of the past and the need to take advantage of new wisdom and research" (295). Pressley et al. (2002), Garan (2002), and others support a program that includes lots of skills instruction, including phonics.

The debate about how to teach reading has gone on for centuries. Proponents of one side or the other of the debate argue that different approaches can't be used together in the same classroom. Some advise, "Balance, but don't mix. . . . A common misconception regarding the balance that is called for by the research is that the teacher should teach sound-spelling relationships in the context of real stories. The mixture of decoding and comprehension instruction in the same instructional activity is clearly less effective" (Center for the Future of Teaching and Learning 1997, 16). Others compare combining approaches with "serving a slightly diluted poison with a heavily diluted antidote" (Smith 1999, 155). Views are polarized, with each side blaming the other for the perceived literacy crisis in schools.

Research, however, supports balanced instruction in a comprehensive literacy program. In studies comparing instructional programs for reading, "approaches in which systematic code instruction is included alongside meaning emphasis, language instruction, and connected reading are found to result in superior reading achievement overall" (Adams 1990, 49). In other words, neither an approach that uses phonics alone nor an approach that emphasizes meaning to the exclusion of phonics is as effective as an approach that combines the two.

In the practical reality of most classrooms, creative teachers skillfully synthesize various aspects of both approaches to create a reading and writing program that makes sense in what Duffy (1992) calls inspired teaching. "Inspired teaching does not originate in a particular philosophy, theory, approach, or program. It originates in the creativity of teachers." These teachers use a rich diet of literature, plenty of shared reading and writing experiences, and direct instruction in phonics as well.

The teacher remains the key to effective classroom reading instruction. "Time and time again, research has confirmed that regardless of the quality of a program, resource or strategy, it is the teacher and learning situation that make the difference" (International Reading Association, 2002). After extensively reviewing research and examining effective classroom practice, Allington (2002) concludes, "Good teachers, effective teachers, matter much more than particular curriculum materials, pedagogical approaches, or 'proven programs.' . . . Effective teachers manage to produce better achievement regardless of which curriculum materials, pedagogical approach, or reading program they use" (740, 742).

A comprehensive reading program involves "an interweaving of explicit strategies and skill instruction with rich reading and writing experiences" (McIntyre and Pressley 1996, xi). Although this model of reading and writing instruction is emerging and has a number of unresolved issues, research and descriptions of programs have been detailed (Baumann and Ivey 1997; Dudley-Marling 1996). As children are engaged in authentic literacy-related tasks, teachers provide direct instruction on skills and strategies that children need to succeed as readers and writers. Instruction involves the type of lessons suggested in chapter 4 of this book.

There is no single model of a comprehensive or balanced approach to reading and writing. Instructional routines will differ from teacher to teacher, from grade to grade, from classroom to classroom, and from child to child within a classroom. Teaching reading is more than a formula that suggests two pounds of children's literature, a cup of direct phonics instruction, a dash of motivation, and ten minutes of practice. "A comprehensive and balanced program is a philosophical perspective about what kinds of reading knowledge children should develop and how those kinds of knowledge can be attained" (Fitzgerald 1999, 100).

Phonics is an essential quality in learning to read. Phonemic awareness is a powerful predictor of reading achievement, and knowledge of letter names and sounds is highly related to success in beginning reading. Children who don't know how sounds and symbols relate to one another are at an enormous disadvantage in attacking unfamiliar words that they encounter while reading, and in spelling words that they want to use when writing. But phonics is not a stand-alone skill. It works in concert with all the other competencies that children can draw upon in constructing meaning from printed text.

Literacy is essential for citizens of our technological, contemporary, democratic society. But literacy is more than a means of meeting the functional needs of day-to-day living such as reading the newspaper, filling out job applications, understanding the directions on the back of a frozen pizza box, or correctly interpreting the schedule in *TV Guide*. Literacy is a self-actualizing process that defines, in part, who we are. Patricia Polacco summarizes the essence of literacy in her children's trade book *Pink and Say* (Philomel 1994).

Pink and Say is about two young Civil War soldiers, Pinkus Alley (Pink) who is black and Sheldon Curtis (Say) who is white. Wounded and separated from their units, Pink takes Say to his home and helps nurse him back to health. Pink, who has been taught to read by his former slave master, promises to teach his illiterate friend to read, and he speaks to the power of literacy: "To be born a slave is a heap o' trouble, Say. But after Aylee taught me to read, even though he owned my person, I knew that nobody, ever, could really own me."

To the extent that phonics contributes to helping children reach their full potential as human beings, it remains an important part of their educational lives.

References

Adams, M. J. 1990. *Beginning to Read: Thinking and Learning About Print.* Cambridge: MIT Press.

Allington, R. L. 2002. What I've learned about effective reading instruction. *Phi Delta Kappan* 83:740–7.

Baumann, J., and G. Ivey. 1997. Delicate balances: Striving for curricular and instructional equilibrium in a second-grade, literature/strategy-based classroom. *Reading Research Quarterly* 32:244–75.

Center for the Future of Teaching and Learning. 1997. *30 Years of NICHD Research: What We Now Know About How Children Learn to Read.* Washington, DC: Center for the Future of Teaching and Learning.

Dudley-Marling, C. 1996. Explicit instruction within a whole language framework: Teaching struggling readers and writers. In *Balanced Instruction: Strategies and Skills in Whole Language,* edited by E. McIntyre and M. Pressley. Norwood, MA: Christopher Gordon Publishers.

Duffy, G. G. 1992. Let's free teachers to be inspired. *Phi Delta Kappan* 72:442–7.

Fitzgerald, J. 1999. What is this thing called "balance?" *The Reading Teacher* 53:100–7.

Garan, E. M. 2002. *Resisting Reading Mandates: How to Triumph with the Truth.* Portsmouth, NH: Heinemann.

Heilman, A. W. 2002. *Phonics in Proper Perspective.* 9th ed. Columbus: Merrill. Original edition, 1964.

International Reading Association. 2002. *What Is Evidence-Based Reading Instruction: A Position Statement of the International Reading Association.* Newark, DE: International Reading Association.

Lyon, G. R. 1997. Statement of G. Reid Lyon, Ph.D., Chief, Child Development and Behavior Branch, National Institute of Child Health and Human Development, National Institutes of Health Before the Committee on Education and the Workforce, U.S. House of Representatives. Washington, DC: NICHD.

McIntyre, E., and M. Pressley. 1996. Preface. In *Balanced Instruction: Strategies and Skills in Whole Language,* edited by E. McIntyre and M. Pressley. Norwood, MA: Christopher Gordon Publishers.

Pressley, M., A. Roehrig, K. Bogner, L. M. Raphael, and S. Dolezal. 2002. Balanced literacy instruction. *Focus on Exceptional Children* 34:1–14.

Routman, R. 1996. *Literacy at the Crossroads: Crucial Talk About Reading, Writing, and Other Teaching Dilemmas.* Portsmouth, NH: Heinemann.

Smith, F. 1999. Why systematic phonics and phonemic awareness instruction constitute an educational hazard. *Language Arts* 77:150–5.

Strickland, D. S. 1995. Reinventing our literacy programs: Books, basics, and balance. *The Reading Teacher* 48:294–302.

Children's Trade Book Cited in This Chapter

Polacco, P. 1994. *Pink and Say.* New York: Philomel.

Posttest of Phonics Knowledge

You have (presumably) taken the **Pretest of Phonics Knowledge** as a self-check at the beginning of this book (p. 1–2). Now complete the Posttest and compare your results.

1. How many phonemes or basic sounds are in the general sound system of American English?

   ____ a. about 10
   ____ b. approximately 19
   ____ c. about 44
   ____ d. over 50
   ____ e. Nobody knows for sure.

2. Which pair(s) of words contains short vowel sounds?

   ____ a. lions and tigers
   ____ b. birds and bees
   ____ c. fleas and tics
   ____ d. cats and dogs
   ____ e. They all do.

3. Which pair(s) of words contains long vowel sounds?

   ____ a. plate and knife
   ____ b. knife and fork
   ____ c. table and chair
   ____ d. cup and saucer
   ____ e. They all do.

4. Which pair(s) of words contain vowel digraphs?

   ____ a. rain and pail
   ____ b. sail and boat
   ____ c. seat and steak
   ____ d. blue and shoe
   ____ e. They all do.

5. Which pair(s) of words contains consonant blends?

   ____ a. red and pink
   ____ b. blue and green
   ____ c. orange and purple
   ____ d. black and white
   ____ e. They all do.

6. Which pair(s) of words contains consonant digraphs?

   ____ a. pen and ink
   ____ b. dish and chair

_____ c. pencil and paper
_____ d. teacher and pupil
_____ e. They all do.

7. What's the *onset* in the word **house?**

_____ a. h
_____ b. ho
_____ c. hou
_____ d. hous
_____ e. It has no onset.

8. What's the *rime* in the word **house?**

_____ a. h
_____ b. ho
_____ c. ou
_____ d. ouse
_____ e. It has no rime.

9. How many phonemes are in the word **fish?**

_____ a. 1
_____ b. 2
_____ c. 3
_____ d. 4
_____ e. 5

10. How many phonemes are in the word **box?**

_____ a. 1
_____ b. 2
_____ c. 3
_____ d. 4
_____ e. 5

11. How many syllables are in the word **television?**

_____ a. 1
_____ b. 2
_____ c. 3
_____ d. 4
_____ e. 5

12. Which pair(s) of words has open syllables?

_____ a. hotel and motel
_____ b. song and dance
_____ c. trains and planes
_____ d. until and because
_____ e. They all do.

For the answers, see p. 187.

Appendix A

Phonemic Awareness and the Teaching of Reading:
A Position Statement from the Board of Directors
of the International Reading Association

Much has been written regarding phonemic awareness, phonics, and the failure of schools to teach the basic skills of reading. The Board of Directors offers this position paper in the hope of clarifying some of these issues as they relate to research, policy, and practice.

We view research and theory as a resource for educators to make informed instructional decisions. We must use research wisely and be mindful of its limitations and its potential to inform instruction.

What Is Phonemic Awareness?

There is no single definition of phonemic awareness. The term has gained popularity in the 1990s as researchers have attempted to study early-literacy development and reading disability. Phonemic awareness is typically described as an insight about oral language and in particular about the segmentation of sounds that are used in speech communication. Phonemic awareness is characterized in terms of the facility of the language learner to manipulate the sounds of oral speech. A child who possesses phonemic awareness can segment sounds in words (for example, pronounce just the first sound heard in the word *top*) and blend strings of isolated sounds together to form recognizable word forms. Often, the term *phonemic awareness* is used interchangeably with the term *phonological awareness*. To be precise, phonemic awareness refers to an understanding about the smallest units of sound that make up the speech stream: phonemes.

Phonological awareness encompasses larger units of sound as well, such as syllables, onsets, and rimes. We use the term phonemic awareness in this document because much of the theoretical and empirical literature focuses specifically on phonemes. We also choose to use this term because of its more common use in the professional literature and in professional discussions.

Why the Sudden Interest in Phonemic Awareness?

The findings regarding phonemic awareness are not as new to the field of literacy as some may think, although it is only in recent years that they have gained wide attention. For over 50 years discussions have continued regarding the relation between a child's awareness of the sounds of spoken words and his or her ability to read. In the 1940s some psychologists noted that children with reading disabilities were unable to differentiate the spoken word into its sounds and put together the sounds of a word. Psychological research intensified during the 1960s and 1970s. Within the reading educational community there was research (for example, the "First Grade Studies" in 1967) hinting at the important relation between sound awareness and learning to read.

Recent longitudinal studies of reading acquisition have demonstrated that the acquisition of phonemic awareness is highly predictive of success in learning to read—in particular in predicting success in learning to decode. In fact, phonemic awareness abilities in kindergarten (or in that age range) appear to be the best single predictor of successful reading acquisition. There is converging research evidence to document this relation, and few scholars would dispute this finding. However, there is considerable disagreement about what the relation means in terms of understanding reading acquisition and what the relation implies for reading instruction.

Isn't Phonemic Awareness Just a 1990s Word for Phonics?

Phonemic awareness is not phonics. Phonemic awareness is an understanding about spoken language. Children who are phonemically aware can tell the teacher that *bat* is the word the teacher is representing by saying the three separate sounds in the word. They can tell you all the sounds in the spoken word *dog.* They can tell you that, if you take the last sound off *cart,* you would have *car.* Phonics, on the other hand, is knowing the relation between specific, printed letters (including combinations of letters) and specific, spoken sounds. You are asking children to show their phonics knowledge when you ask them which letter makes the first sound in *bat* or *dog* or the last sounds in *car* or *cart.* The phonemic awareness tasks that have predicted successful reading are tasks that demand that children attend to spoken language, not tasks that simply ask students to name letters or tell which letters make which sounds. In fact, if phonemic awareness just meant knowledge of letter-sound relations, there would have been no need to coin a new term for it.

How Does Phonemic Awareness Work to Facilitate Reading Acquisition?

That phonemic awareness predicts reading success is a fact. We can only speculate on why the strong relations exist. One likely explanation is that phonemic awareness supports understanding of the alphabetic principle—an insight that is crucial in reading an alphabetic orthography. The logic of alphabetic print is apparent to learners if they know that speech is made up of a sequence of sounds (that is, if they are phonemically aware). In learning to read, they discover that it is those units of sound that are represented by the symbols on a page. Printed symbols may appear arbitrary to learners who lack phonemic awareness.

If Phonemic Awareness Is the Best Predictor of Success in Beginning Reading, Shouldn't We Put All Our Time and Effort in Kindergarten and Early Reading into Developing It?

Most researchers in this area advocate that we consciously and purposefully attend to the development of phonemic awareness as a part of a broad instructional program in reading and writing. Certainly, kindergarten children should have many opportunities to engage in activities that teach them about rhyme, beginning sounds, and syllables. How much time is needed for this kind of focused instruction is something only the teacher can determine based on a good understanding of the research on phonemic awareness and of his or her students' needs and abilities. Research suggests that different children may need different amounts and forms of phonemic awareness instruction and experiences. The research findings related to phonemic awareness suggest that although it might be necessary, it is certainly not sufficient for producing good readers. One thing is certain: We cannot give so much attention to phonemic-awareness instruction that other important aspects of a balanced literacy curriculum are left out or abandoned.

Is Phonemic Awareness a Single Momentary Insight? Or, Is It Best Described as a Skill That Develops Gradually over Time?

Phonemic awareness has been measured using a variety of tasks that appear to tap into an individual's ability to manipulate the sounds of oral language. However, some tasks may require a more sophisticated understanding of sound structures than others. For example, rhyming appears much earlier than segmentation abilities for most children. Also, it seems to matter that children can hear the sounds of a spoken work in order, but it is not clear how early or late this ability does or should develop. Researchers are still working to identify the kinds of tasks and what aspects of phonemic awareness they might tap. It appears from the research that the acquisition of phonemic awareness occurs over time and develops gradually into more and more sophisticated levels of control. Some research suggests that there is a diversity of developmental paths among children. How much control is necessary for the child to discover the alphabetic principle is still unclear. There is no research evidence to suggest that there is any exact sequence of acquisition of specific sounds in the development of phonemic awareness, only that there is increasing control over sounds in general.

It Has Been Stressed That Phonemic Awareness Is an Oral Skill and That It Has Nothing to Do with Print, Letters, or Phonics. Is This True?

It is true that phonemic awareness is an insight about oral language, and that you can assess phonemic awareness through tasks that offer no reference to print. However, to suggest that there is no relation between the development of phonemic awareness and print is misleading. There is evidence to suggest that the relation between phonemic awareness and learning to read is reciprocal:

phonemic awareness supports reading acquisition, and reading instruction and experiences with print facilitate phonemic awareness development. The question remains as to the amount and forms of phonemic awareness one must have in order to profit from reading instruction that is focused on decoding. For instance, some research suggests that the abilities to blend and isolate sounds in the speech stream support reading acquisition while the ability to decode sounds from spoken words is a consequence of learning to read. The precise relation between phonemic awareness abilities and reading acquisition remains under investigation.

How Can Phonemic Awareness Be Taught?

The answer to this question has both theoretical and practical implications. Theorists interested in determining the causal contribution of phonemic awareness to learning to read have conducted experimental studies in which some students are explicitly taught phonemic awareness and some are not. Many of the early studies in this genre focused on treatments that emphasize oral language work only. The findings from these studies suggest phonemic awareness can be taught successfully.

More recently, there have been studies of phonemic awareness training that combine and contrast purely oral language approaches to the nurturing of phonemic awareness abilities, with approaches that include interaction with print during the training. These studies suggest that programs that encourage high levels of student engagement and interaction with print (for example, through read-alouds, shared reading, and invented spelling) yield as much growth in phonemic awareness abilities as programs that offer only a focus on oral language teaching. These studies also suggest that the greatest impact on phonemic awareness is achieved when there is both interaction with print and explicit attention to phonemic awareness abilities. In other words, interaction with print combined with explicit attention to sound structure in spoken words is the best vehicle toward growth.

Some research suggests that student engagement in writing activities that encourage invented spelling of words can promote the development of phonemic awareness. These findings also are consistent with continuing research into the sources of influence on phonemic awareness abilities before students enter school. It is clear that high levels of phonemic awareness among very young children are related to home experiences that are filled with interactions with print (such as being read to at home, playing letter games and language play, and having early writing experiences).

Do All Children Eventually Develop Phonemic Awareness? Shouldn't We Just Let Them Develop This Understanding Naturally?

Naturally is a word that causes many people difficulty in describing language development and literacy acquisition. In so far as it is natural for parents to read to their children and engage them with print and language, then phonemic awareness may develop naturally in some children. But if we accept that these kinds of interactions are not the norm, then we have a great deal of work to do in encouraging parents to engage their young children with print. We need to provide the information, the tools, and the strategies that will help them ensure that their young children will be successful in learning to read.

In schooling, the same advice holds true. Most children—estimated at more than 80%—develop phonemic awareness by the middle of first grade. Is this natural? Yes, if the natural model of classroom life includes opportunities to engage with print in a variety of ways and to explore language. However, we know that there are many classrooms where such engagement and explicit attention to sounds and print are not natural. We must equip teachers with the information, tools, and strategies they need to provide these kinds of learning opportunities in their classrooms.

The problem is most severe in terms of consequences when the students from economically disadvantaged homes, where the resources and parent education levels are lowest, enter schools that have limited resources and experience in promoting engagement with print. The students who need the most attention may be those who receive the least. We have a responsibility in these situations to not rely on the "natural" and to promote action that is direct, explicit, and meaningful.

What Does This Mean for Classroom Practice?

First, it is critical that teachers are familiar with the concept of phonemic awareness and that they know that there is a body of evidence pointing to a significant relation between phonemic awareness and reading acquisition. This cannot be ignored.

Many researchers suggest that the logical translation of the research to practice is for teachers of young children to provide an environment that encourages play with spoken language as part of the broader literacy program. Nursery rhymes, riddles, songs, poems, and read-aloud books that manipulate sounds may be used purposefully to draw young learners' attention to the sounds of spoken language. Guessing games and riddles in which sounds are manipulated may help children become more sensitive to the sound structure of their language. Many activities already used by preschool and primary-grade teachers can be drawn from and will become particularly effective if teachers bring to them an understanding about the role these activities can play in stimulating phonemic awareness.

What About the 20% of Children Who Have Not Achieved Phonemic Awareness by the Middle of First Grade?

The research on this statistic is as clear as it is alarming. The likelihood of these students becoming successful readers is slim under current instructional plans.

We feel we can reduce this 20% figure by more systematic instruction and engagement with language early in students' home, preschool, and kindergarten classes.

We feel we can reduce this figure even further through early identification of students who are outside the norms of progress in phonemic awareness development, and through the offering of intensive programs of instruction.

Finally, there may be a small percentage of students who may have some underlying disability that inhibits the development of phonemic awareness. Several scholars speculate that this disability may be at the root of dyslexia. More research is needed in this area, however. There is some promise here in the sense that we may have located a causal factor toward which remedial assistance can be tailored.

Some people advocate that primary teachers allocate large amounts of time to teaching students how to perform better on phonemic awareness tasks. There are no longitudinal studies that support the effectiveness of this practice in increasing the reading achievement of the children when they reach the intermediate grades.

What Position Does the International Reading Association Take Regarding Phonemic Awareness and the Teaching of Reading?

The International Reading Association already has issued a position paper on the role of phonics in the teaching of reading. That paper stresses the importance of phonics in a comprehensive reading program.

In this position statement we have attempted to elaborate on the complex relation between phonemic awareness and reading. We do so without taking away from our commitment to balance in a comprehensive reading program.

On the positive side, research on phonemic awareness has caused us to reconceptualize some of our notions about reading development. Certainly, this research is helping us understand some of the underlying factors that are associated with some forms of reading disability. Through the research on phonemic awareness, we now have a clearer theoretical framework for understanding why some of the things we have been doing all along support development (for example, work with invented spelling). Additionally, the research has led us to new ideas that we should continue to study.

On the negative side, we are concerned that the research findings about phonemic awareness might be misused or overgeneralized. We are very concerned with policy initiatives that require teachers to dedicate specific amounts of time to phonemic awareness instruction for all students, or to policy initiatives that require the use of particular training programs for all students. Such initiatives interfere with the important instructional decisions that professional teachers must make regarding the needs of their students. We feel the following suggestion for good reading instruction will lead to the development of phonemic awareness and success in learning to read:

- Offer students a print-rich environment within which to interact;
- Engage students with surrounding print as both readers and writers;

- Engage children in language activities that focus on both the form and the content of spoken and written language;
- Provide explicit explanations in support of students' discovery of the alphabetic principle; and
- Provide opportunities for students to practice reading and writing for real reasons in a variety of contexts to promote fluency and independence.

We must keep in mind, though, that it is success in learning to read that is our goal. For students who require special assistance in developing phonemic awareness, we should be prepared to offer the best possible instruction and support.

Appendix B

The Role of Phonics in Reading Instruction: A Position Statement of the International Reading Association

The best approaches for how to teach children to read and write have been debated throughout much of the 20th century. Today, the role of phonics in reading and writing has become as much a political issue as it has an educational one. Teachers and schools have become the focus of unprecedented public scrutiny as the controversy over phonics is played out in the media, state legislatures, school districts, and the home. In response to the many requests that have been received, the International Reading Association offers the following position statement regarding the role of phonics in a total reading program.

We begin with three assertions regarding phonics and the teaching of reading. We conclude with an expression of concerns for the current state of affairs and a call for professionalism.

1. The Teaching of Phonics Is an Important Aspect of Beginning Reading Instruction.

This assertion represents a long-standing and widely shared view within the reading education community. The following statements from leaders in the field reveal the strength and history of this understanding.

> "When the child has reached the maturity level at which he can make the best use of formal instruction in phonics, certainly no time should be lost in launching an extensive and carefully organized program to promote the wide and independent use of phonics in attacking new words, regardless of the grade or the time in the school year when this occurs."
>
> *Nila Banton Smith*
> *IRA Founding Member*

> "Phonics instruction serves one purpose: to help readers figure out as quickly as possible the pronunciation of unknown words."
>
> *Dolores Durkin*
> *Reading Hall of Fame Member*

"Perhaps the most widely respected value of letter-sound instruction is that it provides students with a means of deciphering written words that are visually unfamiliar."

Marilyn Jager Adams
Author, Beginning to Read:
Thinking and Learning About Print

"Phonics is a tool needed by all readers and writers of alphabetically written languages such as English. While I am not a proponent of isolated drill, overreliance on worksheets, or rote memorization of phonic rules, I support the teaching of phonics that children actually need and use to identify words quickly and accurately. These strategies need to be taught systematically in well-planned lessons."

Richard T. Vacca
IRA President, 1996–1997

"Early, systematic, explicit phonics instruction is an essential part, but only part, of a balanced, comprehensive reading program. Phonics and other word-identification skills are tools that children need to read for information, for enjoyment, and for developing insights. The intensity and form of phonics instruction must be adjusted to the individual needs of children by a well-prepared teacher."

John J. Pikulski
IRA President, 1997–1998

We do not wish to suggest through these quotations that there is perfect harmony within the field regarding how phonics should be taught in a total reading program, rather that there is nearly unanimous regard for its importance.

2. Classroom Teachers in the Primary Grades Do Value and Do Teach Phonics as Part of Their Reading Programs.

A recent national study (Baumann, Hoffman, Moon, & Duffy, 1996) of reading instruction in American public schools found that 98% of primary-grade teachers regard phonics instruction as a very important part of their reading program. Further, the study found that primary-grade teachers engage their students in phonics lessons on a regular basis as part of instruction in reading and writing.

Although there are many different types of or approaches to phonics instruction (e.g., intensive, explicit, synthetic, analytic, embedded), all phonics instruction focuses the learner's attentions on the relationships between sounds and symbols as an important strategy for word recognition. Teaching phonics, like all teaching, involves making decisions about what is best for children. Rather than engage in debates about whether phonics should or should not be taught, effective teachers of reading and writing ask when, how, how much, and under what circumstances phonics should be taught. Programs that constrain teachers from using their professional judgment in making instructional decisions about what is best in phonics instruction for students simply get in the way of good teaching practices.

3. Phonics Instruction, to Be Effective in Promoting Independence in Reading, Must Be Embedded in the Context of a Total Reading/Language Arts Program.

Reading is the complex process of understanding written text. Children learn to read by using many sources of information such as their experiences, illustrations and print on the page, and knowledge of language—including their knowledge of sound-symbol correspondences. When teachers share interesting and informative books, nursery rhymes, songs, and poems with predictable language patterns, children develop and refine their use of these various information sources. Children become aware of and understand how print on a page relates to meaning. When children engage with texts themselves, as reader or writers, they begin to orchestrate this knowledge of how written language works to achieve success. It is within these kinds of contexts of language use that direct instruction in phonics takes on meaning for the learner. When phonics instruction is linked to children's genuine efforts to read and write, they are motivated to learn. When phonics instruction is linked to children's reading and writing, they are more likely to become strategic and independent in their use of phonics than when phonics instruction is drilled and practiced in isolation. Phonics knowledge is critical but not sufficient to support growing independence in reading.

A Professional Stance Toward Phonics

The International Reading Association supports:

- research into effective phonics instruction and how this instruction supports the development of reading and writing abilities;
- teacher education initiatives at the preservice and inservice levels that encourage broader use of best practices in the teaching of phonics;
- parent education that is informative regarding the place of phonics within the total view of reading development and what parents can do to be supportive;
- curriculum development that helps articulate the specific goals of phonics instruction within the context of a total reading program as well as suggestions for tools and strategies for effective teaching; and,
- authors and other artists who create the kind of engaging literature that provides the rich linguistic context for effective reading instruction.

The International Reading Association is concerned with:

- the exaggerated claims found in the press and other media regarding the inattention to phonics in beginning reading instruction;
- the growth in the number of curricular and legislative mandates that require teachers to blindly follow highly prescriptive plans for phonics instruction;
- the distortions in the professional literature surrounding the place of

phonics instruction in a well-rounded, comprehensive reading program;

- the pitting of phonics against literature, as if the two are incompatible or at odds with each other; and,
- the inaccurate claims in the public media regarding the failure rates of students in learning to read that are attributed to the lack of phonics instruction.

Teachers *are* being successful in helping children learn to read. Every U.S. study of reading achievement conducted over the past two decades has reported increasing numbers of primary-grade students performing successfully. A recent international comparison study (Binkley & Williams, 1996) has shown that in the area of reading, primary-aged students from the United States outperformed students from all other countries but one. Recognition for the tremendous advances that have been made by teachers in the teaching of reading is long overdue. We applaud teachers for the great strides they have made in improving the quality of reading instruction for all students.

We are not satisfied with the achievement levels reflected in the national assessments or the international comparisons. We will not be satisfied until we can claim success for all children. We have a long way to go and there is much to learn. However, exaggerated claims of the failure of students in learning to read serve only to divert our attention, energies, and resources from the important issues we must face. Explanations that focus on simple solutions like more phonics instruction are misguided. The problems we face are complex and require inquiring minds.

Toward this end, the International Reading Association will continue to promote research and professional development activities focused on literacy. Through our research we will continue to study more effective ways of teaching reading, including phonics instruction, to achieve our common goal of literacy for all.

References

Adams, M. J. 1990. *Beginning to Read: Thinking and Learning About Print.* Cambridge, MA: MIT Press.

Baumann, J., Hoffman, J., Moon, J., and Duffy, A. 1996, December. *The First "R" in 21st Century Classrooms.* Paper presented at the Annual Meeting of the National Reading Conference, Charleston, SC.

Binkley, M., and Williams, T. (1996). *Reading Literacy in the United States: Findings from the IEA Reading Literacy Study* (Report No. NCES 96-258). Washington, DC: U.S. Department of Education Office of Educational Research and Improvement.

Durkin, D. 1989. *Teaching Them to Read.* Needham Heights, MA: Allyn & Bacon, 218.

Pikulski, J. J. 1997, January. *Becoming a Nation of Readers: Pursuing the Dream.* Paper presented at the meeting of the Wisconsin State Reading Association, Milwaukee, WI.

Smith, N. B. 1963. *Reading Instruction for Today's Children.* Englewood Cliffs, NJ: Prentice-Hall, 213.

Vacca, R. T. 1996, October/November. The reading wars: Who will be the winners, who will be the losers? *Reading Today,* 14, p. 3.

Adopted by the Board of Directors, January 1997

A Mini-Glossary of Phonics Terms

Here's a basic list of terms that are frequently used in teaching phonics.

accent   The force or vocal emphasis applied to syllables in words and in longer segments of speech; in **phon-ics,** the first syllable is the accented syllable. (The term *accent* is also sometimes used to refer to the speech characteristics of a regional dialect, as in "He has a Boston accent.")

affix   Meaning units that are added to root words (or stems) to form new words; *prefixes* are added to the beginning of root words; *suffixes* are added to the end of root words.

alphabetic method   A method of teaching beginning reading that involves learning letter names and attaching sounds to these letters as a way of learning to read.

alphabetic principle   The principle that the written language system of English (and other languages) is based on the relationship between spoken sounds and written symbols and that each speech sound has its own graphic counterpart.

analytic phonics   An approach to phonics that involves learning letter-sound relationships in connection with previously learned words; also called whole-to-part or inductive approach.

automaticity   The rapid, effortless, accurate decoding of words.

basal reading program   An instructional materials package designed for teaching reading from kindergarten through sixth (and sometimes eighth) grade; consists of anthologies of reading selections, teachers' editions, skill development workbooks, assessment devices, and other ancillary support materials.

base   A word to which affixes are added to create new words.

blend   Two or three consonant letters with closely related but separate sounds, for example, **br**oom, **dr**op, **str**eam; sometimes called consonant *clusters*.

blending   The process putting discrete sounds together to form a word. (See *phonemic awareness*.)

closed syllable   Syllable that ends in a consonant sound, as the second syllable in **ho-tel.**

cluster   Another word for *blend*.

compound word   A word consisting of two free morphemes or meaning units that can stand alone, for example, **mailbox, hallway, jellybean.**

consonants   Sounds produced when there is maximum interference of air in the vocal tract; represented by letters other than **a, e, i, o,** and **u.**

context clues   Information found in the surrounding text that enables a reader to determine the meaning (and sometimes the pronunciation) of a word.

decoding   The process of deriving pronunciation or identifying words by attaching the appropriate sound or sound sequences to the corresponding letter or letter sequences.

deletion   The process of removing phonemic elements from spoken words. (See *phonemic awareness*.)

digraph   Two letters that together represent a single sound; for example, consonant digraphs are the **ch** in **chip** or the **sh** in **ship;** vowel digraphs are sounds like those represented by the **oa** in **boat** and the **ea** in **seat.**

diphthong Two letters that together represent a closely blended vowel sound, for example, the **oi** in boil or the **ou** in **sound.**

embedded phonics An approach that includes phonics instruction as part of text reading.

encoding The process of selecting the appropriate letter sequence for the sounds of written words.

explicit phonics A sequential set of phonics elements is clearly identified, and these elements are explicitly taught in a prescribed sequence.

fluency The ability to read connected text accurately, quickly, and with expression.

glide Sound made when tongue glides from one position to another rather than staying in stable position.

grapheme Basic, minimal unit of writing; usually, letters of the alphabet, but graphemes also include numerals, punctuation marks, and the like.

invented spelling A process by which writers create their own version of written words based on their knowledge of sound-symbol relationships.

isolation The process of identifying individual sounds within spoken words. (See *phonemic awareness.*)

juncture The transition that occurs between sounds in spoken words. (See *suprasegmental phoneme system.*)

onset The part of the syllable that precedes the vowel, for example, **str**um.

open syllable Syllable that ends in a vowel sound, as the first syllable in **ho-tel.**

orthography The written system of any language.

phoneme The basic, minimal, indivisible unit of sound; **pin** has three phonemes /p/ /i/ /n/.

phonemic Having to do with phonemes.

phonemic awareness A knowledge that spoken words are made up of sequences of discrete sounds and the ability to manipulate these sounds.

phonetic A general term that refers to aspects of sound related to language.

phonics The conscious, concentrated study of sound-symbol relationships for the purpose of learning to read and spell.

phonogram See *rime.*

pitch The level to which the voice rises and falls in the process of oral communication. (See *suprasegmental phoneme system.*)

psycholinguistics An interdisciplinary field that involves the study of the interaction of language and thinking.

rhyme Terminating sound elements in words that consist of the same sound combination of vowel and consonant; recognition and production of rhyme are part of *phonemic awareness.*

r-controlled vowel The vowel sound made when the vowel is followed by an **r,** as in words like **star, germ, bird, fort,** and **hurt.**

rime The vowel and any consonants that follow it in a syllable, for example, b**ook;** also called *phonogram* or *word pattern.*

schwa Vowel phoneme that is articulated with the tongue in a neutral position in the mouth; occurs only in unaccented syllables and represented by all five vowel letters as in **about, children, pencil, button,** and **circus;** represented by the symbol /ə/.

segmentation The process of breaking words into their component phonetic elements. (See *phonemic awareness.*)

short vowel   Vowel sounds that occur in the words **cat, hen, pig, dog, bug.**

sight words   Words that readers recognize instantaneously without needing to analyze them.

silent letters   Letters that have no corresponding sound elements in words, for example, **k**nee, lam**b**, **p**sychology.

stress   The relative force of articulation or emphasis placed on words or syllables in the stream of speech. (See *suprasegmental phoneme system.*)

structural analysis   The process of determining the pronunciation and meaning of words by analyzing the structural elements of roots and affixes.

suprasegmental phoneme system   The system of sound features that serves as an "overlay" that accounts for intonation in spoken language and expression in reading; consists of *pitch, stress,* and *juncture.*

syllable   Combinations of phonemes that constitute larger sound units within words, consisting of a single vowel sound or a combination of vowel and consonant sounds, for example, **syl.la.ble** or **com.bin.a.tion.**

synthetic phonics   An approach to phonics that involves learning letter-sound relationships and then blending or synthesizing these sounds into words; also called part-to-whole or deductive approach.

systematic phonics   See *explicit phonics.*

vowel   Sound made when there is minimum interference with the column of air in the vocal tract; most frequently represented in writing by the letters **a, e, i, o, u,** and sometimes **y** (and sometimes **w**) or a combination of these letters.

whole word method   An approach to teaching reading that involves having children memorize entire words.

Answers to Tests of Phonics Knowledge

Answers to Pretest

1. c. *approximately 19*. There are 5 vowel letters (**a, e, i, o, u**) but these letters represent approximately 19 vowel sounds.
2. b. *rat and rug*. At least one word in each of the other pairs has a long vowel sound.
3. c. *rail and rule* and d. *write and right*. *Rail* and *rule* have the long **a** long **u** vowel sounds, respectively; *write* and *right* both have long **i** sounds.
4. d. *oil and joy*. The **oi** (**oy**) combination blend together to form the vowel sound in these words.
5. a. *slow and fast*. The blends are **sl** at the beginning of *slow* and **st** at the end of *fast*.
6. c. *when and where* and e. *fish and chips*. *When* and *where* both have the **wh** digraph; **sh** is the digraph in *fish;* **ch** is the digraph in *chips*.
7. a. *b*. The onset is the part of the word that precedes the vowel.
8. d. *oat* The rime is the vowel and all the sounds/letters that follow it in a syllable.
9. b. *3*. The word *laugh* has 5 letters but three distinct sounds, /l/ /a/ /f/.
10. c. *4*. The word *fox* has only three letters but four sounds, /f/ /o/ /k/ /s/.
11. c. *6*. The syllables are en.cy.clo.pe.di.a.
12. c. *koala and kangaroo*. The final syllables in these words are open syllables because they end with vowel sounds.

Answers to Posttest

1. c. *about 44*. The 44 phonemes consist of 19 vowel sounds, and 25 are consonant phonemes.
2. d. *cats and dogs*. *Cats* has the short **a** sound; *dogs* has the short **o** sound.
3. a. *plate and knife*. *Plate* has a long **a** sound; *knife* has a long **i** sound.
4. e. *They all do*. Each pair of words contains a double vowel combination that represents a single vowel sound.
5. b. *blue and green*. *Blue* contains the initial blend **bl;** *green* contains the initial blend **gr**.
6. b. *dish and chair*. *Dish* has the final consonant digraph **sh;** *chair* has the initial digraph **ch**.
7. a. *h*. The onset is the part of the word that precedes the vowel.
8. d. *ouse*. The rime is the vowel and all the sounds that follow it in a word.

9. c. *3*. The word *fish* has four letters but only three sounds, /f/ /i/ and /sh/.

10. d. *4*. The word *box* has three letters but four sounds, /b/ /o/ /k/ and /s/.

11. d. *4*. The syllables are tel.e.vis.ion.

12. a. *hotel and motel*. The first syllables in these words end with the long o sound.

INDEX

A

accent, 184
affixes, 184. *See also* structural analysis
alphabet books, 49–51, 67
alphabet cards, 48–49
alphabet knowledge, 25, 48– 55
alphabetic method, 4, 184
alphabetic principle, 9– 10, 11, 59, 163, 184
analytic phonics, 97, 105, 184
articulatory phonetics, 62
assessment
   of phonemic awareness, 45–47
   of spelling, 159–160
authentic reading experiences, 98, 106, 111
automaticity, 104

B

basal readers, 6, 116, 124–126, 184
Benchmark Word Identification Program, 124
blending, 30, 42, 115, 124, 184
   teaching suggestions for, 42
blends. *See* consonant blends
book buddies, 126
Bradley Reading and Language Program, 121

C

children with learning problems, 94–96, 163
children's literature, 29, 33, 49–51, 98,108, 111–114, 154
   teaching suggestions for 107, 110, 112, 113
closed syllables, 90, 184
compound words, 34, 40, 184
comprehension, 118, 165–166
comprehensive reading instruction, 163–169
computer-based phonics, 128–131
consonant blends, 62, 72–75, 184
   teaching suggestions for, 73, 75
consonant clusters. *See* consonant blends
consonant digraphs, 62, 71–72, 75, 184
   teaching suggestions for, 71–72

consonants, 62, 65–67, 184. *See also* consonant blends, consonant digraphs
   teaching suggestions for, 67–68
context clues, 61, 66, 68, 70, 72, 74, 78, 88, 164–165, 184
conventional spelling, 145–146
cueing systems, 20–21, 97
curriculum standards, 15–16

D

decoding, 11, 185
decoding by analogy, 63, 111
decodable text. *See* phonics readers
deletion, 30, 39–40, 184
derivational constancy, 145
derivations, 157–158
   teaching suggestions for, 157
diacritical marking, 76
dialect, 89
dictation, 150
dictionary work, 158
digraphs. *See* consonant digraphs
diphthongs. *See* vowel diphthongs
direct, systematic phonics instruction 12, 114–123, 185
discrete phonics elements, 62–63
double vowels, 85–87
   teaching suggestions for, 86

E

Embedded phonics, 106–114, 185
Encoding, 11, 185
English Language Learners, 54, 96–98
ESL. *See* English Language Learners
explicit phonics instruction. *See* direct, systematic, phonics instruction

F

fluency, 98–102, 185

G

glides, 80–81, 185
guided reading, 109–111
   teaching suggestions for, 110

H

history of phonics instruction, 3–8
home schooling. *See* phonics materials for home use
homophones, 153–154
   teaching suggestions for, 154

I

International Reading Association Guidelines for Evaluating Phonics Materials, 132
International Reading Association Position Statement on Phonemic Awareness, 173–179
International Reading Association Position Statement on Phonics, 180–183
Internet, 130–131
invented spelling, 142–147, 185
isolation, 30, 37–39, 185
   teaching suggestions for 38–39

J

juncture, 100, 185

L

Lindamood Phoneme Sequencing Program for Reading, Spelling, and Speech, 62, 121–122
long vowels, 65, 81–83,
   teaching suggestions for, 81–83

M

McGuffey Readers, 5
medial vowels, 63, 84
   teaching suggestions for, 84–85
mnemonic devices, 158–159
Mother Goose, 29, 30, 33
multisensory instruction, 53, 118, 122

N

National Reading Panel, 8, 13–14, 98
New England Primer, 4